State, Society and Memories of the Uprising of
17 June 1953 in the GDR

State, Society and Memories of the Uprising of 17 June 1953 in the GDR

Richard Millington
Lecturer, University of Chester, UK

© Richard Millington 2014
Softcover reprint of the hardcover 1st edition 2014 978-1-137-40350-6

All rights reserved. No reproduction, copy or transmission of this publication may be made without written permission.

No portion of this publication may be reproduced, copied or transmitted save with written permission or in accordance with the provisions of the Copyright, Designs and Patents Act 1988, or under the terms of any licence permitting limited copying issued by the Copyright Licensing Agency, Saffron House, 6–10 Kirby Street, London EC1N 8TS.

Any person who does any unauthorized act in relation to this publication may be liable to criminal prosecution and civil claims for damages.

The author has asserted his right to be identified as the author of this work in accordance with the Copyright, Designs and Patents Act 1988.

First published 2014 by
PALGRAVE MACMILLAN

Palgrave Macmillan in the UK is an imprint of Macmillan Publishers Limited, registered in England, company number 785998, of Houndmills, Basingstoke, Hampshire RG21 6XS.

Palgrave Macmillan in the US is a division of St Martin's Press LLC, 175 Fifth Avenue, New York, NY 10010.

Palgrave Macmillan is the global academic imprint of the above companies and has companies and representatives throughout the world.

Palgrave® and Macmillan® are registered trademarks in the United States, the United Kingdom, Europe and other countries.

ISBN 978-1-349-48702-8   ISBN 978-1-137-40351-3 (eBook)
DOI 10.1057/9781137403513

A catalogue record for this book is available from the British Library.

A catalog record for this book is available from the Library of Congress.

Contents

Acknowledgements	vi
List of Abbreviations	viii
1 Introduction	1
2 Day X: Fascists, Spies and Thugs	27
3 Tales of That Day	47
4 Watching the West	75
5 Remembering and Discussing the Uprising of 17 June 1953	97
6 17 June 1953: A Symbolic Talisman of Opposition in the GDR?	128
7 Remembering 17 June 1953 in 1989	150
8 Conclusion	170
Appendix A: Interviewees	183
Appendix B: Publishing Figures of the Novels Featuring Scenes of 17 June 1953	185
Notes	187
Bibliography	193
Index	202

Acknowledgements

I would like to thank the Arts and Humanities Research Council; the School of Cultures, Languages and Area Studies at the University of Liverpool, UK; and the Access to Learning Fund at the University of Liverpool for the generous financial support that made this project possible. I am extremely grateful for the invaluable guidance and advice provided by Professor Eve Rosenhaft, Dr Frank Brunssen, Dr Lyn Marven and Dr Andrew Plowman at the University of Liverpool, and Professor Patrick Major at the University of Reading, UK. I am also grateful to the staff of the Bundesarchiv, the library of the Bundesstiftung zur Aufarbeitung der SED-Diktatur, the Deutsches Rundfunkarchiv, the Staatsbibliothek zu Berlin, the Behörde der Bundesbeauftragten für die Stasi-Unterlagen in Magdeburg, the Landeshauptarchiv Sachsen-Anhalt Abteilung Magdeburg, the Stadtarchiv in Magdeburg, the Magdeburger Volksstimme, the British Library and the Sydney Jones Library at the University of Liverpool for their help throughout my research. I owe particular thanks to the staff of the Gedenkstätte Moritzplatz in Magdeburg.

I am especially indebted to Dr Lutz Miehe and his wife Karola. Not only did they provide me with a place to live in Germany and ask for nothing in return, but they also helped me to find interviewees, establish contacts with archives and offered their own views on my findings, as well as answering any questions I had about life in East Germany. I will always be amazed by their generosity and kindness (*ohne euch hätte ich es nicht geschafft!*). I must also thank my interviewees. They were always ready to help in any way they could and always willing to share their often dark, sad and painful memories with me. I will never forget the hospitality they showed me, from a welcoming handshake to a cup of tea bought especially for the young man all the way from Liverpool.

Most of all, I would like to thank my friends and family, for it is to them that I dedicate this book. I deeply appreciate the support and understanding shown by my parents, Ron and Jean Millington. I also give special thanks to my brother, Dr Chris Millington. He was always willing to listen to my ideas, read my work and offer his advice, despite my jokes about French history. Thanks must also go to my friends Dr Fanie Tsiamita-Dobrat, Dr Katy Dale and Phil Prescott for listening to and joining in with my many complaints about the demands of academic life. And I thank Nadia Alsafaar for her emotional support during troubled times. Finally, I would like to thank Elizabeth Millington for bringing love and light into my life. She has managed to make a historian excited about the future.

Abbreviations

BArch	*Bundesarchiv* (Federal Archive)
BDVP	*Bezirksbehörde der Deutschen Volkspolizei* (Regional Authority of the German People's Police)
BGL	*Betriebsgewerkschaftsleitung* (Works Union Management)
BStU	*Bundesbeauftragte/r für die Unterlagen des Staatssicherheitsdienstes der ehemaligen DDR* (Federal Commissioner for the Documents of the State Security Service of the former GDR)
BV	*Bezirksverwaltung/Bezirksvorstand* (Regional Administration/Executive)
CDU	*Christlich Demokratische Union Deutschlands* (Christian Democratic Union of Germany)
CIA	Central Intelligence Agency
CSU	*Christlich Soziale Union* (Christian Social Union)
DDR	*Deutsche Demokratische Republik* (German Democratic Republic/East Germany)
DEFA	*Deutsche Film-Aktiengesellschaft* (German Film Company (state-owned film studio in the GDR))
DGB	*Deutscher Gewerkschaftsbund* (German Trade Union Federation)
DRA-F	*Deutsches Rundfunkarchiv Frankfurt am Main* (German Broadcasting Archive in Frankfurt am Main)
DSF	*Gesellschaft für Deutsch-Sowjetische Freundschaft* (Society for German–Soviet Friendship)
FDGB	*Freier Deutscher Gewerkschaftsbund* (Free German Trade Union Federation)
FDJ	*Freie Deutsche Jugend* (Free German Youth)
FDP	*Freie Demokratische Partei* (Free Democratic Party)
FRG	Federal Republic of Germany/West Germany
GDR	German Democratic Republic/East Germany
KFERF	*Komitee für Einigkeit und Recht und Freiheit* (Committee for Unity and Justice and Freedom)
KgU	*Kampfgruppe gegen Unmenschlichkeit* (Taskforce against Inhumanity)

KPD	*Kommunistiche Partei Deutschlands* (Communist Party of Germany)
KUD	*Kuratorium Unteilbares Deutschland* (Advisory Board of Indivisible Germany)
KVP	*Kasernierte Volkspolizei* (Garrisoned People's Police)
LDPD	*Liberal-Demokratische Partei Deutschlands* (Liberal Democratic Party of Germany)
LHSA-Ma	*Landeshauptarchiv Sachsen-Anhalt Abteilung Magdeburg* (Main State Archive of Sachsen-Anhalt Magdeburg Branch)
LPG	*Landwirtschaftliche Produktionsgenossenschaft* (Agricultural Co-operative)
MfS	*Ministerium für Staatssicherheit* (Ministry for State Security)
MTS	Maschinen-Traktoren-Station (Machine and Tractor Station)
MVS	*Magdeburger Volksstimme* (Magdeburger People's Voice)
ND	*Neues Deutschland* (New Germany)
NDPD	*National-Demokratische Partei Deutschlands* (National Democratic Party of [East] Germany)
NPD	*Nationaldemokratische Partei Deutschlands* (National Democratic Party of Germany)
NTS	*Narodnyi Trudovoy Soyuz* (National Labour Council)
NVA	*Nationale Volksarmee* (National People's Army)
RIAS	*Rundfunk im amerikanischen Sektor* (Radio in the American Sector)
SAM	*Stadtarchiv Magdeburg* (Magdeburg City Archive)
SAPMO	*Stiftung Archiv der Parteien und Massenorganisationen der DDR* (Archive Foundation of Parties and Mass Organisations of the GDR)
SBB	*Staatsbibliothek zu Berlin* (State Library of Berlin)
SED	*Sozialistische Einheitspartei Deutschlands* (Socialist Unity Party of Germany)
SKET	*Schwermaschinenbaukombinat 'Ernst Thälmann'* ('Ernst Thälmann' Heavy Machinery Combine)
SPD	*Sozialdemokratische Partei Deutschlands* (Social Democratic Party of Germany)
USSR	Union of Soviet Socialist Republics
VEB	*Volkseigener Betrieb* (People's Owned Factory)
VEG	*Volkseigenes Gut* (People's Owned Property)

1
Introduction

1.1 The Uprising of 17 June 1953 in the German Democratic Republic

On 17 June 1953 an uprising against the ruling Socialist Unity Party (SED) took place in the German Democratic Republic (GDR). Up to one million people took part in the unrest which spread to over 700 localities across East Germany, including major cities, towns and rural areas (Dale, 2005, p. 9). Demonstrators called for the resignation of SED leader Walter Ulbricht and his government, free elections, better living and working conditions and the reunification of Germany (Diedrich, 2003, p. 143). A combination of a lack of preparation, uncertainty and chaotic management, as well as the sheer number of demonstrators, contributed to the failure of the East German security forces to quell the unrest (Diedrich, 2003, pp. 173–80). Visible symbols of the regime, as well as buildings housing state authorities, were attacked and destroyed. Protesters also laid siege to prisons in the hope of freeing political prisoners. The arrival of Soviet tanks and troops to restore order in the late afternoon of 17 June 1953 effectively signalled the end of the uprising. Protesters could offer little resistance to their machine-gun bullets (Dale, 2005, pp. 27–33). In the course of the demonstrations, approximately 15 SED functionaries, members of the State Security Service (*Stasi*) or policemen had been killed, apparently at the hands of demonstrators (Mählert, 2003, p. 10). Approximately, a further 80 people died while either taking part in the protests or simply passing by the wrong place at the wrong time (Kowalczuk, 2003, p. 104).

The causes of this first uprising in the Soviet Bloc can be traced back to the SED's second party conference in July 1952. At this conference Walter Ulbricht declared that conditions were right for the 'construction of socialism' to begin in the GDR (Hagen, 1992, p. 24). This meant that the SED would take measures to reshape East German industry and society according to the model implemented by Joseph Stalin in the Soviet Union (Loth, 1997, p. 148). Money was poured into heavy industry in order to modernise society, at the expense of investment in consumer goods. Farmers were forced to collectivise, and private entrepreneurs were put under pressure to nationalise. Non-compliance was answered with heavy fines or prison sentences. Moreover, the SED increased the repression of 'class enemies', such as the Church and the middle classes. Citizens' rights in general were also restricted as the Party (SED) took ever-harsher measures to root out suspected opponents (Kowalczuk, 2003, pp. 28–59).

By 1953 the GDR's economy was at breaking point. Not only was the SED investing more and more money in heavy industry, but it was also trying to fund the recruitment and armament of a national army. This had been ordered by Moscow, but not factored into the SED's programme to construct socialism (Hagen, 1992, pp. 24–8). The SED's lack of surplus funds was creating shortages in supplies of fuel (Sperber, 2003, p. 623). Moreover, food was also in short supply because a significant number of those 'voting with their feet' and moving West to escape the SED regime were farmers (Buchheim, 1990, p. 428). A lack of consumer goods was also increasing dissatisfaction amongst citizens. However, instead of easing the pace of its programme, the state decided to put pressure on citizens to work harder under the slogan, 'First produce more, then live better!' (Hagen, 1992, pp. 24–8). On 14 May 1953 the SED decreed that working quotas in heavy industry were to be increased by 10 per cent. This meant that industrial workers would have to work harder to meet their quota and earn their quota-fulfilment bonuses, which many relied upon to get by. Not only did the SED hope that this measure would improve the economy by encouraging more production and increased efficiency, but the Party also hoped that it would save money by bringing down the average wage paid to industrial workers (Buchheim, 1990, p. 429). However, the only thing that this measure achieved was workers' further alienation from the Party that was supposed to represent their interests.

With Stalin's death on 5 March 1953, a troika of leaders comprising Nikita Khrushchev, Lavrenti Beria and Georgi Malenkov took control in Moscow. In April 1953 they attempted to ease the situation in the GDR by relaxing policy on war reparation payments paid by the SED regime to the Soviet Union, as well as relaxing other economic restraints that had been imposed (Hagen, 1992, p. 31). However, conditions in the GDR continued to worsen. On 2 June 1953 Walter Ulbricht, his Prime Minister Otto Grotewohl and fellow Politburo member Fred Oelßner (to act as translator) were called to Moscow to discuss the situation. The Soviet leaders condemned the SED's political course since the second party conference. According to Heinz Brandt, SED secretary for agitation in Berlin at the time, the coercive and repressive means by which these policies were introduced had brought all classes of citizens in the GDR to the verge of revolt (Loth, 1997, p. 149). The Soviet ambassador to East Germany, Vladimir Semenov, warned Ulbricht that if the current state of affairs continued, the GDR would cease to exist by the middle of June 1953 (Haupts, 1992, p. 390). The Soviet leaders demanded that the measures taken against farmers, private entrepreneurs, the middle classes, the Church and other groups be immediately rescinded. Thus a complete political volte-face was ordered (Pritchard, 2000, p. 206).

Upon returning to the GDR, Ulbricht and his Politburo complied with Moscow's orders and drew up the 'New Course', a new political programme that abolished or mitigated the repressive measures of the last 12 months. The New Course was announced to citizens via the state newspaper and mouthpiece *Neues Deutschland* on 11 June 1953. The Politburo statement read that 'on the part of the SED and government a series of mistakes have been made'. It stated that these mistakes had led to the neglect of certain groups in society and that many citizens had left the country as a result (Kowalczuk, 2003, pp. 85–9). The SED then asserted:

> For these reasons the Politburo of the Central Committee of the SED deems it necessary that a series of measures will soon be implemented in connection with corrections to the Plan for Heavy Industry, which will correct the mistakes made and improve the living conditions of workers, farmers, the intelligentsia, craftsmen and other levels of the middle class.
>
> (Jesse and Mitter, 1992, p. 51)

The statement angered many citizens. They had had to suffer under the policies of the SED's attempts to build socialism, but were now being told that these measures had all been mistakes. The fact that the SED and Walter Ulbricht would be remaining in power, despite their declaration of political bankruptcy, also caused a great deal of consternation (Diedrich, 2003, p. 140). Sporadic protests and strikes broke out across the GDR (Kowalczuk, 2003, p. 96).

However, the SED's announcement of its mistakes and the resultant anger on the part of citizens did not lead directly to the uprising of 17 June 1953. The initial spark came on 16 June 1953 from construction workers in East Berlin who were angry that the New Course did not include anything about the increase in working quotas increase that the SED had imposed upon them (Hagen, 1992, p. 35). The SED had not rescinded the increased working quotas because they were now even more necessary for increasing productivity to meet the improved living standards that the New Course promised (Baring, 1957, p. 31). Since the New Course was announced, workers had been discussing the omission of the working quotas issue, and sporadic strikes had taken place (Kowalczuk, 2003, p. 96). On 15 June 1953 construction workers building the Stalinallee in East Berlin even formulated a resolution to Otto Grotewohl complaining that others in the GDR had benefitted from the Party's new policies, while workers had not. They felt that they were being penalised and demanded that the working quotas increase be rescinded immediately (Dale, 2005, p. 19). Although the SED responded the next day by decreasing the quotas to their previous level, workers had become increasingly agitated and impatient at the delay in receiving a response. Moreover, they were further angered by a newspaper article in the trade union newspaper *Die Tribüne* on 16 June 1953, titled 'Yes, of course the decrees about raising the working quotas are completely correct' (Kowalczuk, 2003, pp. 111–2). Despite the fact that the SED sent loudspeaker cars through the streets of East Berlin announcing that the working quotas increase had been repealed, it was too little too late, and the news failed to reach many.

On 16 June 1953 the workers on the Stalinallee in East Berlin could no longer contain their anger with the government. They decided to march to the House of Ministries to demand that the working quotas be decreased. Within a few hours, a crowd of 10,000 people had gathered in front of the building. This crowd consisted not only mainly of workers but also of other citizens who had joined the workers as they marched past. The demonstrators demanded to speak with either Ulbricht or Grotewohl. However, the only functionaries who dared to come out to speak to the crowd were junior officials who were shouted down. The protesters wanted to speak to someone in a position of authority. Nevertheless, when Minister for Mining and Metallurgy Fritz Selbmann finally appeared, he failed to appease the crowds who were mistrustful of anything an SED official had to say (Dale, 2005, pp. 20–1).

Angered by the lack of a convincing response from their government, the scale of the protesters' demands escalated. Calls for the resignation of the Politburo, as well as better living conditions, began to echo around the streets of East Berlin (Fulbrook, 1995, pp. 182–4). A builder addressed the crowd and demanded that the government reduce the working quotas, decrease prices in state-owned shops, improve the standard of living, abandon rearmament, free all political prisoners and hold free pan-German elections. Another worker then spoke and called for a general strike to take place the following day, 17 June 1953. The crowds cheered their approval before dissipating in order to spread the word across East Berlin with the help of several hijacked SED loudspeaker cars (Dale, 2005, pp. 21–2). A few workers made their way to the building housing the radio station RIAS in West Berlin and requested that their demands be broadcast. The radio station complied (Sperber, 2003, p. 628).

On the morning of 17 June 1953 there was only one topic of conversation in factories and other workplaces throughout the country: the strike in East Berlin (Kowalczuk, 2003, pp. 117–9). Workers on the early shifts across East Germany declared solidarity with their colleagues in East Berlin. Moreover, they decided to follow the Berliners' example and protest about the working quotas hike. Other citizens dissatisfied with living conditions and angry with the SED were stirred into action by the sight of the protests and joined the demonstrating workers (Hagen, 1992, p. 201). As had happened in East Berlin, the nature of the protests quickly mutated, encouraged by the participation of citizens from other sectors of society. What had started as a limited demonstration about working quotas developed quickly into a nationwide uprising against the SED and its policies (Diedrich, 2003, p. 143).

As Soviet troops arrived in the late afternoon to put an end to the unrest and restore order, the SED was already formulating its official explanation of what had occurred. The regime rejected any claim that problems within East German society, as well as mistakes on the part of the Party, had provoked protests amongst citizens. Instead, the SED depicted the uprising as an attempted 'fascist-counterrevolutionary putsch' instigated by West German and American 'imperialists'. This official version of events appeared in newspapers, propaganda texts, history books and school textbooks. It remained more or less unchanged until the demise of the regime in 1989. The Federal Republic of Germany (FRG) and its allies rejected the claims made by the SED. In the days that followed 17 June 1953, West German politicians compared the events to the storming of the Bastille in revolutionary France in 1789 and drew parallels with the 20 July 1944 plot to kill Adolf Hitler. They not only equated the demonstrators with Claus von Stauffenberg and his plotters but also equated the SED regime with the Third Reich. West German Chancellor Konrad Adenauer vowed never to rest until East German citizens could live in freedom (Eisenfeld, Kowalczuk and Neubert, 2004, pp. 384–5). On 3 July 1953 all members of the West German parliament (*Bundestag*), except those representing the Communist Party of Germany (KPD), voted in favour of a motion to make 17 June a national holiday and called it the 'Day of German Unity' (*Tag der deutschen Einheit*) in the Federal Republic (Brockmann, 2006, p. 253). Despite some West German academic and political debates regarding the actual extent and participants of the unrest in the GDR, a collective memory of the events of 17 June 1953 as a 'people's uprising' (*Volksaufstand*) against the repressive SED regime passed into popular consciousness in West Germany (see Wolfrum, 1999).

1.2 Remembering 17 June 1953

This book is not a study of the unrest of 17 June 1953 per se. Historical writing on the uprising is dominated by studies detailing the course of the events, examining their protagonists and concluding on the nature of what happened (see, for example, Hagen, 1992; Koop, 2003; Kowalczuk, 2003; Mählert, 2003). Rather, I investigate the existence and nature of memories and awareness of the uprising in GDR society.

When scholars have addressed memories of 17 June 1953 in the GDR, they have focused particularly on the SED and concluded that such memories haunted the Party until the fall of the regime in 1989 (see Mitter and Wolle, 1993, pp. 155–62; Steininger, 2003). Regime policy makers, desperate to avoid angering the populace as they had done in 1953, formulated and adapted state policy accordingly. For example, when isolated strikes broke out in Magdeburg in 1956 one member of the SED city leadership noted in a meeting: 'If you act like they did on 17.6.53, simply trying to regulate the situation by changing the working quotas, then that will create difficulties for us.'[1] Moreover, memories of the unrest influenced the state's internal security doctrine. Permanently afraid that any hint of opposition might lead to a second uprising, the regime took extensive measures to nip any signs of opposition in the bud. These measures included massive expansion of the *Stasi* and the means by which the state could keep tabs on its citizens. Nevertheless, the trauma of the 1953 uprising remained in the back of Party functionaries' minds. Minister for State Security Erich Mielke exemplified this when, in August 1989, he worriedly asked his advisors: 'Do you think that there will be another 17 June tomorrow?' (Mitter and Wolle, 1993, p. 500).

Using oral history interviews with former East German citizens, as well as archive research, this book investigates whether memories and awareness of the uprising of 17 June 1953 were equally prominent in the minds of 'ordinary East German citizens' who experienced the unrest first hand, as well as those born after 1953. It also examines the extent to which the SED regime succeeded in shaping ordinary citizens' memories and awareness of the 1953 unrest. The citizens included in this study were 'ordinary' to the extent that they were not in political office, did not shape policy and were not prominent in the political hierarchy of the GDR. However, these are the only characteristics that they had in common, for there is no such thing as an 'ordinary citizen' in a general sense. As is made clear, the citizens in this study were born at different times, experienced different things and grew up in varying circumstances (Fulbrook, 2011a, p. 3).

Scholars have given little attention to memories of the 1953 uprising amongst ordinary citizens in the GDR. Where this issue is addressed, it is often done so only in passing as part of a broader study of the course and nature of the events of 17 June 1953. Sweeping and general conclusions tend to be drawn. Armin Mitter and Stefan Wolle have written that, despite its best efforts, the SED 'could not eradicate the GDR population's memory of the uprising'. They claim that citizens always remembered the uprising:

> When one posed the question in workers' pubs about what had actually happened on 17 June, one received the whispered answer: 'We gave it to those at the top good and proper...one day it will kick off again, but the next time we will do better.'
> (1993, pp. 155–62)

Others, such as Bernd Eisenfeld, Ilko-Sascha Kowalczuk and Ehrhart Neubert have written that memories of the unrest and the manner of its termination in particular prevented citizens from attempting a repeat of the uprising (2004, p. 361). Mary Fulbrook and Stefan Wolle have concluded that memories of 17 June 1953 were often evoked and/or verbalised every time citizens became unhappy with the regime (Fulbrook, 1995, p. 78; Wolle, 1996, p. 119). However, Kowalczuk has also claimed that eyewitnesses rarely spoke to others about their experiences and that the content and frequency of these conversations depended on the extent of an eyewitness' participation in the unrest (2003, p. 270).

Closer studies of memories of 17 June 1953 amongst East German citizens, while useful, have been limited in scope. The 1987 oral history project carried out by Lutz Niethammer, Dorothee Wierling and Alexander von Plato with citizens of the GDR provides more insight into eyewitness memories of the events (1991). They asked every interviewee how they had experienced 17 June 1953. The youngest of these interviewees was born in 1935. Thus all interviewees were at least 18 years of age in 1953. In his later analysis of interviewees' responses to this question, Niethammer divided the interviewees into three groups. The first group either claimed that they had experienced nothing on the day or refused to respond to the question. They did not want to risk talking about a subject that was recognised as politically controversial. The second group was relatively small and consisted of interviewees who admitted to having taken part in demonstrations. Niethammer concluded that these interviewees had no desire or ability for social advancement. Thus they were not afraid of any possible consequences of talking about the uprising with a West German historian. The third and final group was the largest and consisted of interviewees who had seen and heard a lot on 17 June 1953, but who claimed that they did not want to take part in the unrest. Niethammer called such interviewees 'the informed non-participants' (*die informierten Nicht-Beteiligten*). They portrayed themselves as distanced spectators to the uprising. Niethammer surmised that this may actually be how they experienced the unrest. But he also suggested that the perceptions of at least some of those questioned must have been much more complex before they were filed away to a corner of the mind. Niethammer called this the 'escape into the passive' (*Ausweg ins Passive*). Due to the failure of the uprising and the SED's account of 'fascists' and Western agents, it became necessary for citizens to distance themselves from what had occurred. Thus citizens' memories of the uprising became reports of what others had done. They recast themselves as passive bystanders on the day. Niethammer concluded that the majority of those who experienced the unrest relegated the memories of their experiences to a corner of their minds where they remained unshared, either because the threat of the consequences for speaking about such experiences was too great, or because conditions in the GDR improved after the uprising (Niethammer, 2008).

In 1999 Annette Leo investigated memories of 17 June 1953 amongst workers from the steelworks in Hennigsdorf. Leo asked them what they had told younger colleagues about their experiences of the events. She found that the SED's attempts to restrict information regarding the events had not completely extinguished workers' memories of them.

Workers had passed on fragmentary and vague information about their experiences to younger colleagues. However, Leo found that workers only passed on details that were acceptable within the parameters of the SED's official account. Nevertheless, she writes that the passing on of any information about 17 June 1953 represented a residual rebellious conscience (Leo, 1999). This suggests that, as Mary Fulbrook has written, citizens regarded 17 June 1953 as a 'symbolic talisman' of opposition to the SED, even if they did not dare to contradict openly the regime's claims or carry out their threats of a 'second 17 June' (Fulbrook, 1995, p. 178).

Bernd Eisenfeld has examined further the role of memories and awareness of the uprising amongst East German citizens. In 1999 and 2003 he investigated whether 17 June 1953 served as an inspiration for opposition amongst ordinary citizens toward the regime in the GDR. In 1999 Eisenfeld questioned seven citizens of the former GDR who had been part of the opposition scene between 1978 and 1982. In 2003 he again led discussions with eight former members of various 1980s opposition movements. Of those interviewed, 4 were between 8 and 13 years old in 1953, the others were under 5. Eisenfeld also researched whether opposition groups made reference to 17 June 1953 in *samizdat* publications produced in the 1980s. Eisenfeld concluded that oppositionists in the GDR only felt some sort of connection with the events of 17 June 1953 if the uprising had directly affected them or if eyewitness stories had made some sort of impact on them. Generation does not appear to have played a role in whether or not these oppositionists felt a connection with the uprising. The narratives of the uprising promoted by the governments in East and West Germany also played a role in oppositionists acceptance or rejection of the events of 17 June 1953. Eisenfeld suggests that the West's use of the uprising as a weapon in Cold War politics made his interviewees wary of it. He states further that the SED's account of the uprising as an attempted 'fascist-counterrevolutionary putsch' also influenced opposition members' attitudes toward the event. The lack of conclusive proof that 'fascists' had not been involved led to their rejection of the uprising (Eisenfeld, 2005). Ulrich Mählert has drawn a similar conclusion (2003, p. 24). Eisenfeld also argues that GDR oppositionists could not identify with the 1953 uprising because their goals were different. They did not want the reunification of Germany and the abolition of socialism, as the West German account claimed the protesters in 1953 had desired. They hoped for 'socialism with a human face' and also campaigned on environmental and nuclear disarmament issues. Thus they could not relate to the demonstrators in 1953. Eisenfeld claims that 17 June 1953 only acquired significance for them in the autumn of 1989 against the background of the Tiananmen Square massacre in China on 4 June 1989 (2005, pp. 367–8).

My investigation of memories and awareness of the uprising of 17 June 1953 amongst ordinary East German citizens is much broader in scope than these previous studies, allowing for more detailed and nuanced examination of and conclusions on the existence and nature of such memories and awareness in GDR society. First, I consider the content of two 'frames' of remembering the uprising to which citizens had access or were exposed. I examine the regime's 'official memory' (Bodnar, 1992, pp. 13–14) of the events as an 'attempted fascist-counterrevolutionary putsch' which appeared in the state media, history books, propaganda publications, school textbooks and novels and films in the GDR. I also investigate the 'external collective memory' of 17 June 1953, in other words, the West German version of events as a 'people's uprising' which was presented to East German citizens by the West German broadcast media, more or less annually on the anniversaries of the uprising (Niethammer, 2008, p. 49). Examination of the content, construction and accessibility of these frames shows what citizens were potentially able to learn from a variety of sources about the uprising during the GDR period. Investigation of the regime's official memory indicates how the SED attempted to shape citizens' memories and awareness of the June uprising. Analysis of the West's external collective memory of the uprising not only shows how this might also have shaped citizens' perceptions of the unrest but also the potential extent to which its annual broadcasts maintained the matter of 17 June 1953 in the minds of East German citizens until 1989. Second, I consider the content of eyewitnesses' memories of their experiences, as well as the reasons for, the frequency with which and the circumstances in which they recounted their memories of the unrest to other citizens. Third, I investigate the extent to which citizens born after 1953 were aware of the events. I investigate the content of their awareness of the events, as well as the reasons for, the frequency with which and the circumstances in which the subject was raised amongst these citizens. Finally, I consider traces of the existence of memories or awareness of 17 June 1953 in direct or indirect acts of opposition toward the state. I examine this with regard to the 36 years of 'normal conditions' that prevailed in GDR society before investigating the matter during the 'crisis conditions' of the revolution of 1989.

It is not my intention to identify and conclude on a collective memory of 17 June 1953 amongst East German citizens. Maurice Halbwachs defined collective memory as a socially constructed notion, that is, a recreation and understanding of the past shaped by the context of the social group (Halbwachs, 1992, pp. 22–4). However, the citizens included in my analysis (interviewees, as well as those found in the files) were not a homogenous group. They came from different backgrounds and belonged to different social groups at different times. Thus they were members of several 'mnemonic communities', each with their own collective memories of the past and no single collective memory of the uprising of 17 June 1953 (Kansteiner, 2002, p. 189). I focus instead on citizens' individual memories of 17 June 1953 and investigate commonalities in these memories, without generalising about an all-encompassing collective memory of the events. Thus I examine what James E. Young terms 'collected memories'. In response to collective memory theories, Young has argued that individuals do not share each other's memories. He concedes that groups may indeed 'share socially constructed values that organise memory into roughly similar patterns', but stresses that considering individual memories ensures that 'we remain aware of their disparate sources, of every individual's unique relation to a lived life and of the ways our traditions and cultural forms continuously assign common meaning to disparate memories' (Young, 1993, pp. xi–xii). Furthermore, it is clearly erroneous to talk about the collected memories of the uprising where citizens born after 1953 are concerned, since they did not experience the events and therefore could not have any memories of it. Here, I consider what they learned about the uprising from various sources, which I term their 'collected awareness' of the events.

1.3 Method

1.3.1 Magdeburg

This book focuses on the city and citizens of Magdeburg. Magdeburg was selected because, due to the extent and seriousness of the unrest in the city on 17 June 1953, it could be anticipated that research into memories and awareness of the uprising amongst its citizens would yield rich results. Magdeburg lies approximately 80 miles west-southwest of Berlin and approximately 30 miles east of where the inner-German border divided Germany. Magdeburg was the capital city of the administrative district (*Bezirk*) of Magdeburg (the GDR was divided into 15 such districts), and 1.2 million people lived in the *Bezirk* of Magdeburg, with 250,000–300,000 of these inhabiting the district capital. Throughout the GDR period, Magdeburg was well known as a city of heavy industry.

The largest industrial plant in the city, the 'Ernst Thälmann' Heavy Machinery Combine (SKET), employed some 12,000 people. The *Bezirk* of Magdeburg saw a high proportion of unrest on 17 June 1953 with disturbances in 19 of its 21 districts (Rupieper, 2003, pp. 12–13). The city of Magdeburg itself was the scene of the most serious disorder. Potential for unrest in Magdeburg had actually been simmering below the surface since mid-December 1952, when significant, if short-lived, strikes broke out in a number of the city's large industrial plants. Workers were unhappy with the SED's replacement of their Christmas pay bonuses with a much lower end-of-year premium (Pritchard, 2000, p. 205). After these strikes the SED designated Magdeburg a 'centre of hostile activity' and kept a close watch on the city (Grünwald and Puhle, 1993, pp. 35–6).

In response to the events of 16 June 1953 in Berlin Chief Inspector Herbert Paulsen, commander of the *Volkspolizei* (People's Police) in the *Bezirk* of Magdeburg, ordered his men to be on high alert the following day (Diedrich and Hertle, 2003, p. 315). Meetings were arranged between the city's senior SED functionaries and local police commanders to discuss what might be done in case of emergency. They were ordered to close off factories and prevent the spread of trouble. However, they were numerically too weak to do this successfully as over 200 police officers had been called to Berlin as reinforcements (Koop, 2003, pp. 175–9). Moreover, Paulsen had ordered the remaining officers that they should not under any circumstances draw their weapons (Diedrich, 2003, p. 104). He would later explain that he gave this order because he and his subordinates had no idea what was happening in Berlin as well as no information on the character of the events or the mood of citizens (Diedrich and Hertle, 2003, p. 313).

The first signs of impending trouble were recorded in the 'Karl Marx' plant at 7 a.m. on 17 June 1953. Sixty workers on the early shift had downed tools and were discussing the unrest in Berlin, about which they had heard during the night through RIAS. At approximately the same time, workers in the moulding workshops of the SKET had also stopped work to discuss what was happening (Kowalczuk, 2003, p. 161). By 8.45 a.m. 5,000 workers in the SKET had declared solidarity with the striking workers in Berlin (Grünwald and Puhle, 1993, pp. 38–9). This quickly rose to 10,000 as news spread throughout the vast heavy machinery works. Moreover, the strikers began to make political demands. SED symbols were vandalised, and there were calls for free elections, the resignation of the government, the release of political prisoners and the reunification of Germany (Rupieper, 2003, pp. 114–20).

A short time later, the SKET workers decided to take their protest to Magdeburg city centre. Setting out from their position a few miles to the south, they encouraged others to join them, such as the 2,000 workers at the 'Georgi Dimitroff' plant, with shouts of 'Magdeburgers, follow the Berliners!' At the Dimitroff plant the SED functionaries locked the factory doors, but some demonstrators outside managed to get in around the back and persuade those inside to join them. As the workers broke out, they attacked the factory militia and *Volkspolizei*. Similarly, workers in the 'Karl Marx' plant had also been locked in by regime and trade union officials. They, too, were liberated by demonstrators. There were confrontations between workers and the police at the 'Karl Liebknecht' plant, but police officers there and in other parts of the city were seriously outnumbered and could only stand by while events unfolded. By 9 a.m. all major factories in Magdeburg had stopped work (Kowalczuk, 2003, pp. 161–3).

Moving into the city, demonstrators targeted physical symbols of the SED regime. Party buildings were stormed and ransacked, as were offices of the state youth organisation, the Free German Youth (FDJ) and the state trade union federation (FDGB). Badge-wearing members of the SED were attacked and beaten (Koop, 2003, p. 117).

At 10.50 a.m. the train of demonstrators from the south reached Hasselbach Platz in the heart of the city. Of the 20,000 citizens who were now congregating there, not all were industrial workers. Their ranks had been swelled by citizens from other walks of life unhappy with the SED and inspired, encouraged or simply swept along by the protests (Koop, 2003, p. 177). Moreover, more and more workers and citizens from other corners of the city were arriving in central Magdeburg, having heard about what was happening. In total there were now approximately 100,000 demonstrators congregating in or around the city centre (Rupieper, 2003, p. 116). At this point, smaller groups of protesters broke away from the main body and marched to other corners of the city (Kowalczuk, 2003, p. 164). At around midday, the telecommunications office in the north of the city centre was stormed and occupied (Diedrich and Hertle, 2003, p. 320). At the same time, demonstrators also laid siege to the building housing the *Magdeburger Volksstimme* local newspaper (Kowalczuk, 2003, p. 164).

At approximately 11.30 a.m. a crowd 15,000 strong moved from Hasselbach Platz to Halberstädter Straße on which the main police headquarters and court buildings were to be found adjacent to each other, with a prison and detention centre standing behind the court building (Kowalczuk, 2003, pp. 163–7). Armed with stones, clubs, iron bars and some firearms obtained from disarmed police officers, protesters stormed and ransacked both the court building and the police headquarters. They then attempted to liberate those being held in the prison. Protesters fired shots from the windows of the court building down into the prison yard. They also shot through the door linking both buildings. In the hail of fire the policemen Gerhard Händler and Georg Gaidzik and the *Stasi* officer Hans Waldbach were killed (Koop, 2003, p. 179).

During this battle police in the building telephoned the Soviet military commander in the city (Diedrich, 2003, p. 105). The response of the Red Army was almost immediate. Soviet troops and tanks appeared on Halberstädter Straße at 12.15 p.m. (Rupieper, 2003, p. 123). They were greeted with a hail of stones and other missiles (Kowalczuk, 2003, pp. 168–9). It is unclear whether demonstrators also fired shots at the troops. However, the Soviets did use armed force to disperse the demonstrators. Three Magdeburgers were killed, and none of them were industrial workers (Ahrberg, Hertle and Hollitzer, 2004, pp. 162–8). A further 40 were badly injured as the crowd quickly dispersed (Rupieper, 2003, p. 123).

At 1 p.m. a ten-man strike committee met with mayor of Magdeburg, Philipp Daub, to discuss the situation. This was the only apparent attempt to organise resistance in Magdeburg on 17 June 1953. However, there is no evidence to indicate that this committee represented all of the demonstrators, nor that many even knew of its existence (Hofman and Praschl, 2003, p. 150). A lack of leadership characterised the protests in Magdeburg. Many of the protesters were unsure about what to do once they had reached the city centre. Demonstrations formed while others dissipated as soon as they had begun (Kowalczuk, 2003, p. 164).

At about the same time as this meeting, staff in the detention centre on Moritzplatz to the north of the city centre came under pressure from about 2,000 demonstrators (Kowalczuk, 2003, p. 169). The officers refused to give in to an ultimatum that all prisoners should be freed by 3.30 p.m. (Diedrich and Hertle, 2003, p. 322). The crowd attacked at 3.20 p.m. releasing 221 prisoners (Kowalczuk, 2003, p. 171). This was despite the fact that the Soviet military commander in the city had declared a state of emergency and serious consequences for anyone seen out on the streets after 2 p.m. As elsewhere in the city, Soviet tanks broke up the demonstration (Koop, 2003, pp. 180–4).

The Soviet military needed reinforcements to restore full order in the city, which they only managed at 6 p.m. (Diedrich, 2003, p. 106). In the following wave of arrests 3,500 people were taken into custody (Rupieper, 2003, p. 130). Two of these – Alfred Dartsch and Herbert

Stauch – were tried and executed by the Soviet military authorities on 18 June 1953. Dartsch was charged with having killed the policeman Gerhard Händler. Stauch was charged with organising the revolt because he had been part of a delegation that had demanded to speak with police commanders in Magdeburg. A third Magdeburger was also executed in connection with the events of 17 June 1953. Ernst Jennrich was charged with the murder of the policeman Georg Gaidzik. Jennrich had been at the prison on 17 June and was apparently seen firing shots at the police. In court he claimed he had taken a gun from a young man and emptied the magazine to prevent any violence. Jennrich was sentenced to life imprisonment, escaping the death penalty because it could not be proven conclusively that he had committed the crime. However, on 8 September 1953 the GDR's Minister for Justice Hilde Benjamin cancelled the life sentence and recommended the death penalty for Jennrich in order to make an example of him to others. He was guillotined at 4 a.m. on 20 March 1954 in Dresden (Ahrberg, Hertle and Hollitzer, 2004, pp. 169–80).

Disturbances continued in some Magdeburg factories after the uprising had been put down. On 18 June 1953, 25 per cent of the workforce in the SKET refused to work despite the presence of Soviet troops (Rupieper, 2003, p. 126). Similarly, 3,000 were ready to strike in the 'Karl Marx' plant. But the presence of the Soviet military prevented many from repeating the exploits of the previous day (Koop, 2003, p. 180). Normal service was resumed in the factories of Magdeburg by 20 June 1953 (Kowalczuk, 2003, p. 171).

1.3.2 Oral history interviews

I interviewed eyewitnesses to the events of 17 June 1953, as well as citizens born afterwards (see Appendix A for a list of interviewees, their birth years and political party memberships. All other details about the interviewees indicating their identities, such as their names, birthplaces and workplaces have been anonymised at their request). A target number of 40 interviewees – 20 eyewitnesses and 20 citizens born after 1953 – was set in order to provide a reasonable sample for analysis. The only age restriction set was that interviewees born after 1953 had to have been at least 21 years old in 1989. Thus they had to have reached adulthood in the GDR. No gender stipulations were decided prior to commencement of the project. Interviewees were also not selected based on the political beliefs that they had held in the GDR period. In the event, nine eyewitnesses interviewed had been members of the SED, one a member of the Liberal Democratic Party of Germany (LDPD) and one a member of the

National Democratic Party of Germany (NDPD). Only five interviewees born after 1953 had been members of the SED, and none had joined another party. The target number of interviewees was met in the case of the eyewitnesses. These interviewees comprised 17 men and 3 women whose ages in 1953 ranged from 4 to 32 years. Unfortunately, the target number of 20 citizens of the former GDR born after 1953 was not met. Only 18 willing to participate could be found. These comprised 6 men and 12 women aged between 23 and 39 in 1989. With regard to the social background of the interviewees, I had initially hoped to interview people who had been manual workers. This group had led the unrest on 17 June 1953. For this reason I anticipated that it would be this group that would have had the most to say about their experiences of the day, with each other and with later generations, be they fellow workers or relatives. Yet it proved very difficult to find workers willing to take part in the project (one interviewee suggested that people who had been manual workers in the GDR might have lacked the confidence to take part in an interview with an academic researcher from Great Britain). Consequently, most of the interviewees had not been workers before 1990. However, the majority of the interviewees' parents or grandparents had been manual workers.

The interviews were arranged in a number of ways. First, I contacted the *Gedenkstätte Moritzplatz* in Magdeburg, a museum situated in a former *Stasi* prison. They had a register of former East German citizens willing to take part in interview projects and provided me with names and contact details. Second, I conducted an interview with the *Magdeburger Volksstimme* newspaper in which I talked about my project and requested that interviewees come forward. Finally, I acquired interviewees by asking friends in Magdeburg whether they knew anybody who would be willing to take part. The majority of people born after 1953 with whom I spoke were found using this method.

The interviews took the form of structured life history interviews, usually lasting two to three hours and taking place in the interviewees' homes. I anticipated that life history interviews would not only enable me to establish what role memories or awareness of the uprising did (or did not) play in interviewees' lives but also allow me to ascertain whether other experiences and influences were more significant in their lives. Before the interviews began the interviewees were made aware that they were taking part in a project to investigate memories and awareness of 17 June 1953. During the course of the interviews all interviewees were asked a number of questions about their lives from childhood to present day. Interviewees were permitted to talk as little or as much as they wanted and further questions were asked depending on the issues raised. Each interview followed a similar structure. The interviewees were asked questions about their childhoods and their parents; their time at school; what they did when they left school; their adult relationships with friends and family; where they had worked during their adult life; and how they had experienced the events of 1989 and the time since. Although the aim of these questions was to extract the life history of the interviewees, the questions particularly focused on elucidating the political experiences of the interviewees. Such information enabled evaluation of whether memories or awareness of the uprising played an important role in an interviewee's attitude toward the state, or whether other political influences were at work. Topics were raised such as interviewees' parents' political convictions; their own interest in the subject; the extent to which politics played a role in their school or working life; the political organisations they had joined; and other experiences of politics that they had had. Questions specifically about 17 June 1953 were then posed, if the subject had not already been raised by the interviewee. Eyewitnesses were asked to recount their memories of the day. They were then asked questions about the issue of their experiences in the years that followed, such as how often and why they had spoken to others about their experiences and whether they felt it had been a significant event in their lives. They were also asked what they had learned about the events from other sources. Interviewees born after 1953 were asked what they had known about 17 June 1953 during the GDR period, questioned about the sources of information they had accessed, and whether they had discussed the subject with others, as well as whether the uprising had held any significance for them. Finally, both sets of interviewees were asked whether they had been thinking of 17 June 1953 during the autumn revolution of 1989, and what feelings such thoughts had evoked.

Essential to the analysis of oral testimony is resistance to what Alon Confino calls the 'unbearable lightness of interpretation', that is, the temptation to accept the statements of interviewees at face value, thereby forgoing in-depth examination and allowing oral history sources literally 'to speak for themselves' (Confino, 2008, p. 83). Failure to resist this temptation means failure to recognise the complexities behind individuals' memories. People consciously and subconsciously transform their autobiographies according to a variety of motives such as the desire to present themselves in the best 'light', to elicit praise, avoid blame or argue a certain point of view (Fulbrook, 2011b, pp. 94–100). Moreover, analysis of the results of oral history interviews must take account of the issue of the reliability of interviewees' memories. My interviewees were asked to recount their experiences and feelings from at least 20 years ago to, in some cases, over 60 years ago. Few would have been able to recall every last detail of their experiences or feelings. Thus what was recounted may only be a part of what an interviewee actually experienced or felt.

We must also consider that individuals' memories are shaped by past and current frames of remembering, with regard to which individuals interpret and organise their experiences, as well as their narrations (Schmidt, 2008, pp. 197–200). Consideration of the various ways in which individuals drew upon such frames and the ways in which they interacted with them is paramount to any study of memories of an historical event (Clarke and Wölfel, 2011, pp. 16–22). In the context of this project, pre- and post-1990 debates about the nature of the events of 17 June 1953, as well as post-1990 debates about the nature of the SED regime, constitute the main frames of remembering, against which interviewees' statements ought to be considered. All of these frames will have played some role in shaping interviewees' memories and awareness of the June uprising in the GDR.

Before German reunification the SED's official memory of the events as a 'fascist-counterrevolutionary putsch', as well as the West German external collective memory of the uprising as a 'people's uprising' for freedom and German unity, represented the main frames for remembering the events of 17 June 1953 pushed by politicians on either side of the Berlin Wall. Since German unification in 1990, politicians in the united Germany have promoted the account of the unrest as a 'people's uprising' for freedom, democracy and German unity. Moreover, the German political establishment has recast the events of 17 June 1953 as part of a broader narrative of a German political resistance and the freedom movement. Indeed, on the occasion of the sixtieth anniversary of the events in 2013, Federal President Gauck stated in his speech to the *Bundestag* that the unrest in the GDR was 'one of the greatest days in the German history of freedom...a symbol of the tradition of freedom' (Gauck, 2013). Federal Chancellor Angela Merkel noted that the events of 17 June 1953 constitute a 'significant landmark' in joint German history and also cast the events as part of a much broader narrative of past and current movements for 'freedom and human dignity, democracy and the rule of law' (Merkel, 2013). Consequently, commemoration of the uprising has become a major event in the political calendar of the united Germany, used and promoted by politicians as a means of bringing together all Germans, not just those in the former GDR, in commemoration of an event in a united German history.

Since 1990 there has been much less consensus amongst academics. The opening of the East German archives after reunification allowed new ground to be broken in research on the uprising of 17 June 1953 in the GDR. New light was shed on the causes, course and details of the events (for extensive analysis of post-1990 research into the events of June 1953, see Eisenfeld, Kowalczuk and Neubert, 2004, pp. 657–780). Few scholars disagree that citizens from all sectors of society took part in the unrest and that the events constituted a people's uprising (see, for example, Fulbrook, 1995, p. 184; Kleßmann, 2007, p. 316; Knabe, 2003, p. 431; Koop, 2003, p. 343; Lindenberger, 2003, pp. 121–2; Wolfrum, 2006, p. 125). However, despite the fact that few would also deny that protesters on 17 June 1953 wanted more democratic social structures, as well as policies that would allow them greater freedom in their everyday lives, there is disagreement on whether the demonstrators aimed to achieve the reunification of Germany. Manfred Hagen (1992) and Volker Koop (2003, p. 343) identify Germany unity at the top of the demonstrators' agenda in 1953. Armin Mitter and Stefan Wolle claim that the events of 1953 constituted a failed revolution and hypothesised that the uprising of 17 June 1953 would have led to German reunification, if there had not been Soviet intervention (1993, p. 160). Mitter and Wolle (1993), as well as Rolf Steininger (2003) and Volker Koop (2003) claim further that the aims of the uprising of 17 June 1953 were finally achieved with the fall of the GDR and the reunification of Germany in 1989–1990. However, Mary Fulbrook rejects the notion that the protesters on 17 June 1953 aimed to achieve German reunification. She cites the lack of any serious attempts to gain control of the media, transport, communications or weapons as evidence that the uprising was more a spontaneous outburst of anger at the regime than a serious attempt at revolution and reunification. According to Fulbrook, the calls for unification made by protesters only came late in the afternoon on 17 June 1953 as a result of rumours that the SED regime had fallen (1995, p. 184). Hubertus Knabe echoes this view (2003, p. 432). Gareth Pritchard writes that the protesters' main aim was to remove the SED regime. He recognises that some protesters did call for reunification, but maintains that the only thing that united the many diffuse groups of citizens that participated in the demonstrations was the desire to see Walter Ulbricht removed from office (2000, pp. 217–20). Hermann-Josef Rupieper also underscores the desire for national political reform on the part of the protesters (2003, p. 28).

Consideration of interviewees' statements in the context of how the GDR has been remembered since 1990 is also important. Bill Niven notes that the SED regime has been condemned by conservative politicians and academics as a totalitarian Stalinist state (Niven, 2002, p. 58). Despite the fact that their opponents on the left have called for a more critical remembering of the GDR that does not simply focus on repression, public debates about the nature of the GDR consistently cast the regime in a negative light (Ross, 2002, pp. 19–44). In the context of memories and awareness of the June uprising in the GDR, interviewees could state in light of such negative public debates that they had always rejected the SED's official memory of the uprising, when in actual fact they had given it some credence before 1989. Conversely, such negative public debates about the GDR could be perceived by some as an attack on East German. Consequently, they could reject the account of a 'people's uprising' as simply another condemnation of the GDR and re-evaluate their memories or awareness of the uprising accordingly.

1.3.3 Archival research

To compensate for variables in the oral history interviews and identify possible anomalies, I undertook archival research. I searched for contemporary evidence of the existence of memories and awareness of the uprising of 17 June 1953 amongst East German citizens. My research focused on searching for instances in which ordinary citizens were recorded making reference to and/or expressing opinions on the uprising during the GDR period. The SED, afraid that a second uprising would occur, closely monitored and recorded any reference to the unrest made by its citizens. Examination of these utterances and the circumstances in which they were made elucidate the nature of citizens' memories or awareness of 17 June 1953 as they existed in the GDR period. This can then be compared and contrasted with what the interview results suggest about the nature of such memories and awareness during the GDR period as remembered 20 years later.

Using the records of the Magdeburg branch of the SED, I began by examining the reports composed by local SED functionaries on the mood of citizens (*Stimmungsberichte*) in their wards. These contained the functionaries' own evaluations of the mood, together with reports on comments made by citizens that either had been made directly to the functionaries, or had simply been overheard. The reports were sent to the SED's city leadership in Magdeburg and then passed to the district leadership. Each office discussed what was reported in their weekly leadership meetings. For my purposes, I focused on reports from the last week of May to the first week of July in each year from 1954 to 1989. In this period before and after its anniversary each year, the uprising was most likely to have been on citizens' minds (and perhaps on their lips). Additionally, I examined similar *Stimmungsberichte* covering the same period submitted to the district leadership of the GDR's trade union, the FDGB, by functionaries in Magdeburg. These report on the mood amongst workers. Bearing in mind that low-level SED and FDGB functionaries composed these *Stimmungsberichte* to be passed on to their superiors, the existence of a certain amount of 'spin' (*Schönfärberei*) cannot be discounted. Local officials would certainly have wanted to present to their superiors as pleasant a picture as possible of the mood in the wards or factories for which they were responsible. Thus discontent (including references to 17 June 1953) may not have been fully reported.

In addition to these reports, I examined the files of the *Volkspolizei* and the files of the *Stasi* for reports of crimes referencing 17 June 1953, such as anti-state graffiti or comments referring to the date. Evidence of such crimes and the frequency with which they were committed indicates the extent to which memories and awareness of 17 June 1953 played a role in dissent in the GDR. The *Volkspolizei* in Magdeburg kept reports (*Rapporte*) detailing crimes committed on each day of the year in the city and district from 1961 to 1989. The *Rapporte* from the week before the anniversary of the uprising to the week after the uprising were examined for each year from 1961 to 1989. Again, it could be anticipated that this period around the anniversary was most likely to have provoked relevant actions on the part of ordinary citizens. Unfortunately, no *Rapporte* from each year from 1954 to 1960 have survived, and only occasional *Stimmungsberichte* were able to offer details of crimes related to the uprising committed in these years. Moreover, those *Rapporte* that were available rarely included details on the perpetrators of these crimes, usually because no one was apprehended. However, many *Rapporte* on the crimes committed on the anniversary of the uprising itself included details of security measures taken to stifle any possible unrest related to 17 June 1953 that might occur. This indicates that the SED perceived that memories or awareness of the uprising did have the potential to inspire further opposition from citizens. Access to the files of the Magdeburg *Stasi* was somewhat restricted on data protection grounds. According to current German law one cannot select individual files to view. Key terms, such as '17.6.53', or '17. Juni 1953', must be submitted. The archivists then provide files containing these key terms.

Investigation of the regime's official memory of the uprising of 17 June 1953 included analysis of a range of sources. Articles covering the uprising that appeared in *Neues Deutschland* from 17 June 1953 to 1 July 1953 (by which time references to the events had all but ceased) were examined. Four propaganda booklets produced in the immediate aftermath of the uprising were also analysed. I also examined general histories of the GDR published in each decade of the state's existence. With regard to how the subject was taught in the schools of the GDR, I considered textbooks from 1961, 1962, 1967, 1984 and 1989. Unfortunately, I could find none from the 1970s. I also consulted teachers' guides from 1968, 1971, 1974, 1980 and 1989 for information on how teachers were directed to teach the subject. The accounts in the above sources tend to be heavily biased toward recounting the events in East Berlin, only referring to further centres of unrest with the elusive phrase 'a few other cities'. To investigate what Magdeburgers could learn about the events in their own city, reporting on the uprising in the regional newspaper the *Magdeburger Volksstimme* was examined. Moreover, copies of the *Volksstimme* published in the week preceding and the week following the anniversary of 17 June for each year from 1954 to 1989 were also inspected for references to the events.

With regard to novels featuring depictions of 17 June 1953, Peter Bruhn has identified up to 100 titles (Bruhn, 2003, pp. 57–9). The constraints of this project did not allow for analysis of all of these texts. The novels studied for this book were selected based on their inclusion in previous academic studies as the most prominent examples of literary treatment of 17 June 1953 in the GDR (Mohr, 1978; Pernkopf, 1982; Wichard, 1983; Mohr, 1983). Information on the censorship of these texts was found in the publishing permission (*Druckgenehmigung*) files of the relevant publishing houses in the Bundesarchiv. The first print-run figures were also contained in these files. Details of further editions published were acquired through e-mail contact with the publishing houses that still exist. The two films and one television drama considered constitute the only cinematic representations of the uprising produced in the GDR. Details of the censorship of these films, as well as programmes and press reviews, were found in the DEFA (Deutsche Film-Aktiengesellschaft) files held by the Bundesarchiv. My research into East German citizens' reaction to these novels and films is based on letters nominating or reviewing certain pieces sent to the FDGB for its arts and literature prize in the years from 1954 to 1989, also available in the Bundesarchiv. Despite the fact that citizens may not have written what they actually thought in these letters for fear of censure, they do constitute examples of East German citizens addressing the subject of the uprising. Moreover, they often compare what was included in the relevant literary/cinematic account with their own memories or awareness of the events.

In view of the sheer volume of programmes aired by the West German broadcast media presenting citizens with an external collective memory of the events, as well as issues of their availability, investigation of these broadcasts focused on those documentaries examined by Andrea Brockmann as the most prominent examples of their kind (2006). In order to establish the volume and frequency of these broadcasts over the course of the GDR period, I consulted back-copies of the West German television and radio listings magazine *Hörzu*. I examined copies of this magazine detailing broadcasts in the week preceding and week following 17 June for each year from 1954 to 1989. This not only provided data on which and how many programmes were broadcast but also occasionally provided details of the content of these broadcasts, as well as West German citizens' views on the 'Day of Germany Unity'. As a result of several interviewees recalling that coverage of the West German commemorations was often featured on ARD's (West Germany's main public television broadcaster) nightly news bulletin *Die Tagesschau*, I also studied the running order of each edition broadcast on the anniversaries of the uprising, available from the television station. These not only showed the titles of the news items featured and their running order but also often contained details of accompanying film footage or pictures shown.

1.4 State and society in the GDR

At the core of this study of memories and awareness of the June uprising, and the extent to which the SED succeeded in shaping memories and awareness of it, is examination of the gap between the regime's central policy and citizens' actual experiences. Thus this is a study of the nature of state power in the GDR as well as the extent to which the SED could plan and control the lives of individual citizens.

In the early to mid-1990s, debate about the nature of the SED's power over its citizens was dominated by advocates of the totalitarian model. This view (fed, amongst other things, by revelations about the massive extent of *Stasi* surveillance) held that the Party implemented a totalitarian system in the GDR in which any attempts to resist state power and indoctrination were futile (for an excellent discussion of this interpretation of the GDR, see Ross, 2002, pp. 1–69). Advocates of this view have been criticised for condemning the GDR outright, leading some to regard the application of the totalitarian model as part of a broader conservative strategy to delegitimize socialism (Clarke and Wölfel, 2011, p. 13). Jürgen Kocka adopted the more nuanced term *durchherrschte Gesellschaft* (thoroughly dominated society) nevertheless to describe the GDR as a top-down society in which the power of the regime drenched every last branch (Kocka, 1994, pp. 547–54).

What Eli Rubin describes as a 'backlash' against these top-down histories of the GDR then developed from those who condemned the alleged Orwellian narrative of the 'totalitarianists' (Rubin, 2009, p. 3). This literature sought to assess the extent of state power in the GDR by examining society from the bottom up. Scholars such as Konrad H. Jarausch (1999, p. 57) and Ralph Jessen (1995, p. 100) concluded that examination of the personal experiences of East German citizens shows that the regime's claim to absolute power remained unfulfilled. It could not plan and control the private lives and thoughts of individual citizens. Jeannette Z. Madarász criticised advocates of the *durchherrschte Gesellschaft* theory for ignoring the gap between central policy and the actual experiences of ordinary citizens (2003, p. 8). And Mary Fulbrook has argued that, although the SED did indeed recruit and draw more and more people into structures through which it could attempt to control them, these people also had the chance to construct their own room for manoeuvre within organisations (1996, p. 284). These bottom-up analyses have come to dominate recent historical writing on the nature of the regime's power in the GDR. In fact, Corey Ross argues that analysis of the nature of GDR society must be carried out from the bottom up. He states that while the application of totalitarianism theories to the GDR system appear convincing when one regards the state from the top down, they are less impressive when considering what actually happened on the ground (Ross, 2002, pp. 33–6).

More recently, Mary Fulbrook has adopted the term 'normalisation' to describe power relations in the GDR, specifically for the period 1961–1979. Fulbrook defines 'normalisation' as the stabilisation of domestic political structures and the routinisation of everyday practices. In this period of 'normalisation', life for East German citizens stabilised and became more predictable. Private lives were no longer radically affected by major historical events or ruptures. Moreover, citizens became familiar with the 'rules' of society, consciously or subconsciously internalised them and learned to play by them (or not) in order to achieve personal goals and construct their room for manoeuvre. In this sense, citizens may recall having lived 'normal lives', however abnormal outside observers may consider their lives to have been. Fulbrook emphasises that she employs the term 'normalisation' neither descriptively nor politically, but comparatively and interpretatively as a tool for examining the everyday experiences of citizens in different periods of GDR history. She also states that 'normalisation' in no way implies legitimisation. Just because citizens learned the rules of the game in the GDR, this does not mean that they believed in them, accepted them or were even willing to play by them (Fulbrook, 2009, pp. 15–16).

Fulbrook herself admits that the term 'normalisation' with its implications about what is 'normal' and what constitutes 'normality' is open to attack (Fulbrook, 2009, p. 3). Eli Rubin, in particular, has condemned the use of the term by Fulbrook and 'Fulbrookian' historians of the GDR, such as Mark Allinson, Corey Ross and Esther von Richthofen. He claims that Fulbrookians are wrong to assert that East German citizens were able to bend and manipulate the system to such an extent that they created a 'normal', ideology-free society for themselves. Rubin argues 'in contradistinction to the Fulbrookians...East German society was not normal in any conceivable way' (Rubin, 2009, pp. 6–9). Yet this is not what Fulbrook asserts and she is at pains to ensure that her use of the term is not misinterpreted in this way (Fulbrook, 2009, p. 3). Rubin criticises the Fulbrookians further for their tendency to 'err on the side of downplaying the state and overplaying "society"', to the extent that they effectively depict a regime which was at the mercy of its citizens (Rubin, 2009, pp. 6–7). For Rubin, GDR society was a combination of bottom-up influences and state intervention: 'state power influenced everyday life and was also affected by the demands of ordinary East Germans...a combination of state and society but representing the power of neither over the other' (Rubin, 2009, p. 3).

I conclude that there were limits to the SED regime's power over its citizens. Analysis of the content and practice of the Party's central policy on remembering the unrest of 17 June 1953 – its official memory – shows how the SED hoped to shape citizens' perceptions of the uprising and thereby reduce the perceived potential of citizens' memories and awareness of it to inspire further unrest against the regime. Considering this in light of 'what actually happened on the ground', that is, citizens' actual memories and awareness of the events, demonstrates that the SED failed to control the content of East German citizens' memories and awareness of the uprising of 17 June 1953. However, the SED did succeed in affecting citizens' interaction with their own memories and awareness of the subject, with the result that they altered their behaviour to the extent desired by the Party. The construction of the SED's central policy with regard to memories and awareness of the uprising amongst the populace led citizens to impose a taboo of the subject upon themselves. Citizens apparently altered their behaviour according to this taboo. Few spoke about the subject with people other than their close family, and even this was rare. Consequently, the uprising of 17 June 1953 held little significance for the majority of East German citizens and inspired very few to practice further opposition against the SED regime.

2
Day X: Fascists, Spies and Thugs

With the dust barely settled on the demonstrations of 17 June 1953, the SED began its attempt to shape citizens' memories and interpretations of the uprising through creation of an official version (and thus an 'official memory') of the events. The Party feared that if citizens evaluated the events as an uprising against the regime (an interpretation propagated by West German politicians and the West German media), then this might hold the potential to inspire further unrest in the GDR. The SED constructed an account of the uprising that rejected any claims that problems within the country, as well as mistakes on the part of the Party, had provoked unrest amongst citizens. Instead, the official account depicted the uprising as an attempted 'fascist-counterrevolutionary putsch' instigated by West German and American 'imperialists' with the aim of bringing down the SED regime and triggering a Third World War. The Party claimed that it was only under its leadership that citizens were able to restore order with some help from the Soviet armed forces. This official version of events appeared in newspapers, propaganda texts, history books and school textbooks. It remained more or less unchanged until the demise of the regime in 1989.

The construction of the Party's account and how it was communicated to citizens shows clearly how the SED attempted to shape citizens' memories and awareness of 17 June 1953. The official account provided very limited information about what had happened during the uprising. Description of actual events was vague. Incidents of unrest took place in 'a few cities', and the account underplayed the scale of the unrest. Participants were simply 'fascists', a faceless, generalised mob baying for blood and violently attempting to destroy the 'achievements of the working class'. Such vague description of the course of the uprising served to reduce the unrest to a non-descript event somewhere in the background of the official account that focused instead on revealing the alleged Western plot behind the unrest. This was reflected in interviewees' responses when they were asked to recount their memories of the content of the official version. Their recollections lacked detail about what the official account stated about actual events. They employed stock phrases such as 'counterrevolution' and 'Western agents' but could not recall what the official account included about specific incidents.

2.1   17 June 1953 in national and local print media

In the immediate aftermath of the unrest the quickest means of communicating a full and comprehensive official account of the events to citizens was via the print media. Several key aspects of the Party's official account of the unrest were laid down in the front-page lead of *Neues Deutschland* (*ND*), the SED-controlled national newspaper, on the actual day of the uprising. On 17 June 1953 *ND* reported on the protests of East Berlin construction workers on 16 June 1953. It stated that provocateurs from West Berlin had infiltrated East Berlin, hoping to 'torpedo' the efforts of the SED to create further understanding between both Germanys. This statement was in line with the consistent claims that it was the only German government working toward reunification, while also maintaining that the West German administration repeatedly blocked its efforts. The provocateurs were later followed by 'fascist' youths, again from West Berlin, intent on stirring up trouble amongst construction workers and causing unspecified damage and destruction. According to the article, East German citizens and the *Volkspolizei* worked together to drive out the 'bandits'. Interestingly, the article also mentioned the SED government's poor handling of the working quotas issue that had originally caused construction workers to strike. However, *ND* attributed blame to lower Party functionaries and not the Party leadership. Moreover, reference to this issue was hidden amongst accusations of 'fascists' and warmongering to such an extent that it is quite easy to miss this detail (*ND*, 1953a, p. 1).

The official account of the unrest further developed in the following days. On 18 June 1953 the headline 'Collapse of the foreign agents' adventure in Berlin' was emblazoned atop the front page of *ND*. Below this was an article entitled 'The crimes of the West Berliner provocateurs', as well an order from the Soviet military commander of East Berlin, Major General Dibrova, banning all demonstrations and threatening contraveners with military justice. *ND* claimed that the West had attacked in order to prevent the success of the New Course introduced by the SED. It stated that West German Chancellor Konrad Adenauer and American 'agencies' were working to delay German reunification and planning for war, but that the success of the New Course had disrupted these plans and forced the West to act (*ND*, 1953b, p. 1). The newspaper stated that US Army officers in East Berlin had been directing bands of 'fascists'. The head of the CIA, Allan Dulles, was alleged to have masterminded the 'putsch' (*ND*, 1953c, p. 1). *ND* also quoted readers' letters – whose authenticity cannot be confirmed – which mentioned 'the shadow of 1945' (*ND*, 1953d, p. 1), 'fascist hooligans' (*ND*, 1953e, p 1) and warned 'no one would forgive us for supporting fascism for a second time' (*ND*, 1953f, p. 6). On 19 June 1953 *ND* used the term 'Day X' (*Tag X*) to describe the uprising for the first time: 'For years Western agencies have prepared for "Day X" ... when the GDR is to be rolled back beginning with Berlin.' The SED employed this term to describe the events of 17 June 1953 until 1989. *ND* also stated that workers ought to have displayed 'the required high level of awareness' to repel the provocateurs themselves (1953g, p. 1). Conspicuous in their absence were reports detailing the intervention by Soviet troops. *ND* went no further than arguing that Soviet troops had prevented a Third World War.

Between 23 and 26 June 1953 articles reported on the case of a woman called Erna Dorn. *ND* claimed that she was 'the SS Commander of Ravensbrück concentration camp' and that Western agents in Halle had liberated her from jail on 17 June 1953. She was alleged to have addressed the crowds on Halle's main market square, jubilantly hailing the return of 'fascism'. Dorn was arrested and executed shortly after the termination of the uprising. The SED continued to use Dorn in its propaganda for many years, claiming that she was proof of 'fascist' involvement in the uprising. The veracity of the Party's claims has never been successfully established (see Gursky, 2003, pp. 350–81).

The regional press in the GDR also presented citizens with the official account of the uprising. Regional SED-controlled newspapers, such as the *Magdeburger Volksstimme* (*MVS*), reproduced the reports that appeared in *ND* with only occasional mention of unrest in their respective cities or regions. In fact, the only explicit reference to unrest in Magdeburg made in the *MVS* of 18 June 1953 was in an appeal by the town council to the citizens of the city. The council members appealed to all of the 'peace-loving citizens' of Magdeburg to support the measures to restore order and hand over 'criminal agents' to the authorities (*MVS*, 1953a, p. 1).

Despite a striking lack of detail regarding the course of the unrest on a local level, it was possible to glean certain details about events in Magdeburg from reports in the *MVS* which occasionally mentioned specific factories or workplaces. For example, one report indicated that there had been unrest in the SKET. The article quoted a worker who employed terms extremely similar to the official account. He condemned the 'attacks on our democratic institutions' and described the perpetrators as 'enemies of German unity' (*MVS*, 1953b, p. 1). In another article, a worker from the Karl Liebknecht plant recounted how none of his colleagues had taken part because 'the government has just introduced measures to improve living conditions' (*MVS*, 1953c, p. 1). The *MVS* further reported on trouble in the railways head office in the city centre (*MVS*, 1953d, p. 2), the police headquarters (*MVS*, 1953e, p. 2) and the offices of the Young Pioneers (*Junge Pioniere*), the junior division of the FDJ (*MVS*, 1953f, p. 3). There was even a report detailing how the inmates of the prison on Moritzplatz had actually helped their guards to repel provocateurs (*MVS*, 1953g, p. 1). On 6 July 1953 a photograph showed 'provocateurs' fighting in front of the *MVS* publishing house in central Magdeburg. The caption underneath read: 'These were the "arguments" of the provocateurs of 17 June. Whoever opposed their terror was beaten according to the tried and tested methods of the SA and SS, as our picture shows' (*MVS*, 1953h, p. 2).

The *MVS* did report on one very specific case relating to the events of 17 June 1953 in Magdeburg. On 27 August 1953 the newspaper reported on the trial of Ernst Jennrich. The *MVS* described Jennrich as a 'submissive tool of the imperialists' who had committed 'a most reprehensible and despicable crime'. It described him as 'one of those bandits with whom they [the West] hoped to carry out "Day X" in order to trigger a civil war'. Throughout the article the journalist made clear that Jennrich had committed the crime. However, he or she concluded by stating (somewhat ridiculously given the earlier claims) that there was no conclusive evidence and that Jennrich was sentenced to life imprisonment for attempted murder (*MVS*, 1953i, p. 2).

Most striking about the newspaper reports that appeared in the national and regional press in the immediate aftermath of the uprising was the fact that they contained very few specific details. Herbert Binkert (born 1930) recalled, 'The newspapers reported about it, but there were no details or such things.' *ND* rarely reported on actual incidents, instead focusing on the Party's claims that Western secret services and 'fascists' had planned the unrest and that East German citizens, the *Volkspolizei* and 'resolute' action on the part of the Soviet troops had restored order (Eisenfeld et al., 2004, pp. 288–9). Similarly, articles referring to the unrest in the *MVS* depicted the events in such vague terms that they communicated no real detail. For example, on 19 June 1953 the *MVS* reported that 'the criminals destroyed workplaces, houses and facilities, stole money from workers' organisations and committed terroristic attacks and murder against peaceful, working people'. One is left to wonder which workplaces were destroyed, what is meant by 'terroristic attack' and who was murdered (*MVS*, 1953j, p. 1). This lack of actual detail about specific events in the articles meant that perpetrators, victims and occurrences became faceless, anonymous and generalised entities. *ND* also underplayed the scale of the events. Articles covering specific incidents in East Berlin were rare; details of other localities affected did not appear. Thus *ND* gave the impression that the uprising was not a national event at all. Perhaps most striking about the initial reporting of the events is how little coverage there was. At most, 20 per cent of *ND* covered the uprising each day. Not even the whole of the front page on 18 June 1953 was devoted to it. By 26 June 1953 reports had all but disappeared.

After the initial storm of press coverage following the uprising of 17 June 1953 (and before the events appeared in history books and school textbooks for the first time in 1960) mention of the unrest in the official media in the following years was rare (see Eisenfeld et al., 2004, pp. 295–317). Consistent with earlier reports, no details of actual incidents or the course of the uprising were given. It continued to be a vague event, hidden somewhere in the background. Instead, *ND* and the *MVS* focused their attention on attacking the Western commemorations of the uprising. On 17 June 1954 the newspaper reported on commemorations of the first 'Day of German Unity' in West Germany. It stated that these had been poorly observed: '17 June 1954 failed just as 17 June 1953 had. Only a fascist mob supported the politicians of the frontline city [West Berlin]' (cited in Eisenfeld et al., 2004, p. 296). *ND* was particularly vitriolic in its condemnation of the commemorations a year later: 'Those who supported 17 June are the same people who a few years ago gassed the Jews and beheaded and strung up the socialists' (cited in Eisenfeld et al., 2004, p. 298). In contrast to *ND*, the *MVS* only referenced 17 June 1953 again six years later when it, too, attacked the West German commemorations of the uprising and stated that the 'working people' in the FRG were not interested in the commemorations (*MVS*, 1959, p. 2). Similarly, at the end of the decade the newspaper concluded that the 'Day of German Unity' constituted nothing more than West German politicians playing a 'Pied-Piper melody without resonance' (*MVS*, 1960, p. 2).

2.2 17 June 1953 in propaganda publications

In the months following the uprising of 17 June 1953, four propaganda brochures addressing the events appeared in the GDR. *Wer zog die Drähte? Der Juni-Putsch 1953 und seine Hintergründe (Who Pulled the Strings? The June 1953 Putsch and its Origins)* produced by the SED's Committee for German Unity (*Ausschuß für Deutsche Einheit*), the state institution tasked with preparing for any future reunification of Germany. *Berlin im Juni 1953*(*Berlin in June 1953*) was published by 'Friedenspost'. This journal was published by the Society for German-Soviet Friendship (DSF), which hoped to promote friendship between East German citizens and their Soviet occupiers. In 1953 'Friedenspost' had a monthly print run of approximately 185,000.[1] *Der Tag X. Zusammenbruch der faschistischen Kriegsprovokation (Day X. Collapse of the Fascist War Provocation)* was composed by the National Front – the coalition of all political parties and mass organisations in the GDR. It could be bought for 20 pfennigs from these parties and organisations (*MVS*, 1953k, p. 3). Finally, *Verratener Verräter (Traitor Betrayed)* was published by the East German trade union federation. The author of this piece, Günther Eckstein, was involved in the uprising in Halle on 17 June 1953 and fled to West Germany the day after. He returned to the GDR some months later and wrote this 'confession' about his experiences, stating: 'What I once considered freedom has shown itself to be a world of dirt and corruption, crime... degradation and prostitution' (Eckstein, 1953, p. 1). Over 700,000 copies were printed, with a further 4,000 copies in English, 4,000 in French, 4,000 in Russian, 5,000 in Swedish and 5,000 in Spanish. No information could be found as to whether these non-German language editions were sold abroad or in the GDR.[2] All of the propaganda brochures were in booklet format, except *Der Tag X*, which was a magazine similar to a Sunday newspaper supplement.

As was the case with newspaper reporting of the unrest, these brochures presented little about the actual events of the uprising, underplayed their scale and focused on revealing the Western figures and organisations allegedly behind the unrest. The analyses of those who were allegedly behind the 'failed fascist putsch' differed little from brochure to brochure. The authors most often blamed West German Chancellor Konrad Adenauer, West German and American industrialists, US Army generals and West German anti-communist organisations, such as the *Ostbüro* (East Bureau) of the West German Social Democratic Party (SPD) (Ausschuß für Deutsche Einheit, 1953, pp. 13–60). The texts claimed that these figures had helped 'Tango-Bubis' (literally

'Tango lads' – a derogatory term for young male enthusiasts of Western music and culture) and 'fascists' from West Berlin to cause unrest. While the brochures played down the scale of the uprising as a whole, the booklet *Berlin im Juni 1953* particularly focused on downplaying the armed Soviet intervention. The author thanked the Soviet soldiers for their actions, but gave no details of these actions. He or she also claimed that even after a state of emergency had been declared on 17 June 1953 Soviet troops were inviting East Germans to dance in the streets and asking them to bring out their accordions. The booklet also sought to encourage East German citizens to approach troops with questions about the unrest. It claimed that 'Lieutenant Sergei' or 'Captain Vassia' were willing to discuss what had happened (1953, pp. 5–25). Perhaps most striking about this brochure is that, of the 32 pages, 25 included a picture of Soviet troops laughing or dancing with citizens. Thus the brochure did not underplay the Soviet presence in the GDR.

These brochures indicate that the SED perceived that its citizens might reject the official account of the uprising in favour of a less desirable (for the Party) interpretation. This is evident in the authors' attacks on the West's account of the unrest as a people's uprising for freedom and German unity. *Wer zog die Drähte?* claimed that 'fascists' in the West were trying to characterise what happened as a 'people's uprising' and stated that such lies had turned the 'former SS responsible' into 'heroes of freedom'. The Committee for German Unity also heavily criticised the decision by the FRG to name 17 June 'the Day of the National Uprising' and likened this to the commemoration of Horst Wessel by the Nazis (1953, pp. 25–32). Why the name of the West German national holiday has been altered is open to debate. Most probably the author did not want to mention that the day was actually named after the unity in which he or she had earlier proclaimed that the FRG was not at all interested.

Comparison of these accounts of the uprising with what appeared later in historical publications shows that the SED further limited its account in later years. In contrast to later historical publications that simply stated that there had been unrest in 'Berlin and a few other cities', *Wer zog die Drähte?* listed Halle, Jena, Leipzig, Köpenick, Görlitz, Niesky and Magdeburg as sites of unrest (1953, pp. 66–7). But it did not describe what occurred in these cities, simply stating that there had been 'fascist-inspired' unrest. Moreover, the author of *Verratener Verräter* was in Halle on 17 June 1953 and he detailed his experiences there. Thus these two brochures did not present the uprising as an event exclusive to Berlin as later historical accounts did. The brochures *Berlin im Juni*

1953 and *Wer zog die Drähte?* also made direct links between the persecution of the Jews before the Second World War and the uprising of 17 June 1953. *Berlin im Juni 1953* presented readers with a picture of a devastated shop. The caption underneath related the destruction in the picture to that seen on *Kristallnacht* (1953, p. 4). The same photograph and caption appeared in *Wer zog die Drähte?*, this time accompanied by photographs of the actual *Kristallnacht* and SA (1953, pp. 48–53). In later historical accounts of the uprising, although 'fascists' were indeed mentioned, no such comparisons to the persecution of the Jews was drawn. This would not have fitted into the Party's attempts in later years to underplay more and more the significance of the uprising.

2.3 17 June 1953 in history books and schools

Only in 1960 did the uprising of 17 June 1953 make its first appearance in the history books and school history textbooks of the GDR. Werner Horn was the first East German historian to include the events in an account of the state's history thus far. His version became the benchmark for GDR historical analysis of the uprising in the Ulbricht era, 1949–1971. Horn classified the uprising as a 'fascist putsch' instigated by West Germany and the United States in order to bring about the fall of the SED regime. Yet he played down the scale of the events and presented few details about the unrest. The account stated that the Party had conceded that it had made mistakes, but that its new political programme was intended to improve living standards and consolidate socialism in the GDR. Horn claimed that this affected the plans of the 'Bonn Ministry of Espionage' to take over the GDR and provoked their attack. He asserted that the 'imperialist warmongers' had hoped to unleash a Third World War. Horn also wrote that the working class and the vast majority of the East German population, under the leadership of the Party and with the support of the Soviet troops, put an end to the unrest. He described the intervention of the Soviet troops as necessary to protect the 'achievements of German workers and peasants' but gave no details of their actions. Horn wrote that only 272 boroughs out of 10,000 in the GDR were affected by the unrest. The only cities mentioned were 'Berlin and a few other cities', but Horn did state that workers resisted provocations in Espenhain, Schwarza, Lauchhammer and Brandenburg. According to Horn, some workers in the GDR were incited to demonstrate by Western agents but no more than five per cent of the total workforce did so and those that did soon returned to work once they had realised the true nature of the events (1960, pp. 46–54).

Also in 1960 the first account of 17 June 1953 to appear in school history textbooks was published. It contained even fewer details than Horn's text, taking up only six paragraphs. Only one lesson was allocated for its teaching. The author of the textbook described the uprising briefly as a 'fascist putsch' and claimed that 'hooligans from fascist organisations, workshy and criminal elements' had instigated the unrest, under the leadership of 'American secret services and Bonn governmental agencies'. A joint effort from the state organs, class-conscious workers and Soviet troops (who prevented a Third World War) successfully ended the 'putsch' (Autorenkollektiv, 1960, pp. 317–8). Advice given to teachers in the 1960s about how to handle the subject shows that the SED was most concerned about how its citizens perceived the uprising. Instead of teaching their pupils about the uprising itself, teachers were to ensure that their pupils clearly understood the 'character of and masterminds behind the attempted putsch of 17 June 1953' (Autorenkollektiv, 1968, pp. 191–6).

Descriptions of the uprising in subsequent historical works and textbooks differed little from Horn's 1960 account (see Horn, 1963; Doernberg, 1964; Schöneburg, 1968). However, in 1966 *Geschichte der deutschen Arbeiterbewegung* (*History of the German Workers' Movement*) became the standard text for historical study in the GDR. This work classified the uprising not as an 'attempted fascist putsch', but as an 'attempted counterrevolutionary putsch'. This change apparently occurred as the GDR sought international recognition and took a more cautious approach to political expression, particularly toward West Germany. Yet this measure was purely cosmetic. The accounts still depicted overwhelming 'fascist' involvement in the 'counterrevolutionary putsch' (Eisenfeld et al., 2004, pp. 338–9).

The only account of the events of 17 June 1953 in Magdeburg to appear in a history book in the GDR was published in 1975 in *Geschichte der Stadt Magdeburg* (*History of the City of Magdeburg*). The account comprised less than two paragraphs and drew exclusively from the reports that appeared in the *Magdeburger Volksstimme*. The text stated that 'imperialist reaction' had instigated the unrest. The author claimed that in the SKET workers handed over the 'ringleaders' to the security services. In the '7. Oktober' plant, workers apparently defended their machines from 'fascists hooligans'. Moreover, the author claimed that in the 'Karl Liebknecht' plant several workers moved machinery in front of the doors in order to prevent the 'provocateurs' outside from gaining access. The account then stated that, while work in Magdeburg's factories and plants was briefly halted during the disturbances, workers soon started up production again, showing that they supported the SED. This concluded the text's description of 17 June 1953. There was no mention of unrest in the city centre, the deaths that occurred or how the uprising was put down (Asmus, 1975, p. 387). Comparison of the final text with the original manuscript shows that description of the SED's introduction of a new working quota in the months immediately prior to the uprising was removed. Moreover, the agents and saboteurs mentioned were originally from 'West German' and not 'imperialist' secret services.[3]

In 1978 *Geschichte der SED. Abriß* (*History of the SED. Overview*) replaced *Geschichte der deutschen Arbeiterbewegung* as the standard history tome in the GDR. Its account of 17 June 1953 featured several amendments to previous versions. The SED's admission that it had made mistakes prior to the uprising was not included. 'Counterrevolutionary forces and fascists' were now solely to blame for the uprising. However, the text also mentioned the working quotas issue. Previous histories had given this only cursory mention, if at all. In an apparent attack on Walter Ulbricht, who had been replaced in 1971 as leader of the SED by Erich Honecker, this account now implicitly laid the blame for the working quota increase at the door of Ulbricht and his Politburo. Any allusion to the scale of the events, numerical or otherwise, was also deleted. Moreover, private businessmen and private farmers in the GDR now found themselves amongst those who were responsible for the unrest. Honecker's 1971 policy of nationalisation and collectivisation had negatively affected the standing of these two groups in GDR society. Finally, this account of the unrest further played down the importance of the intervention of the Soviet troops by giving most credit to the GDR's own security forces for ending the uprising (cited in Eisenfeld et al., 2004, pp. 349–62). It is interesting to note that this revision of the official account occurred at a time when reports on the Western commemorations of 17 June 1953 in *ND* lacked even the most basic detail of the uprising – its date. From the beginning of Erich Honecker's reign as leader of the SED in 1971 reports on West Germany's commemorations of the uprising that appeared in *ND* did not actually feature the date. For example, on 18 June 1978 the newspaper reported on a demonstration in West Berlin to commemorate 'the day 25 years ago on which cold warriors from West Berlin were dealt a miserable defeat' (cited in Eisenfeld et al., 2004, p. 314). The date of the uprising was not printed, nor was it made clear that West Germany was commemorating an event that took place in the GDR. *ND* might have perceived a general awareness of the uprising amongst citizens that was sufficient enough to allow omission of the date. However, it also suggests that the SED was trying to eliminate the event from public consciousness. The uprising had to be included in the history volumes in order to provide a rebuttal to the West's version. But in the medium that arguably reached the most citizens daily – the print media – reference to the uprising was scaled down considerably.

As was the case for the propaganda brochures published in 1953, these history books and school textbooks show that the SED was most concerned that the Western interpretation of the events might shape citizens' perceptions of the uprising. The texts focus on debunking the Western account, rather than informing about the actual events. In 1960 Werner Horn attacked the attempts by 'imperialist falsifiers of history' to prove a 'people's uprising' had taken place (p. 49). In 1963 Horn again wrote about the West's 'falsification of the historical facts' of 17 June 1953 (pp. 215–16). In 1979 Hans Teller claimed to expose the 'legend of a "people's uprising in the Soviet occupation zone" created by the Federal Chancellor' (p. 38). And in 1988 Joachim Heise and Jürgen Hofmann claimed: 'No one can call this a "People's Uprising"' (p. 111). In school history lessons teachers were directed to encourage class discussions based on the statement: 'Western historians and ideologues maintain that the events of 17 June 1953 were a "People's Uprising", caused by the mistakes of the SED. Discuss this claim!' (Autorenkollektiv, 1971, pp. 157–9; Autorenkollektiv, 1974, 158–9). In 1980 teachers were to challenge their pupils to 'Give reasons why the counterrevolutionary putsch was not a people's uprising!' Teachers then had to lead discussion of the 'class interests and political-ideological...intentions...behind the bourgeois falsification of the character of 17 June' (Autorenkollektiv, 1980, pp. 196–8). In 1989 the first point of discussion was to be the increasing criticism from parts of the West German population of 17 June as a national holiday in the FRG (Autorenkollektiv, 1989, pp. 35–7). There had indeed been debate in the FRG about whether 17 June should remain a national holiday (see Eisenfeld et al., 2004, pp. 383–436). The fact that school pupils in the GDR had to discuss this shows how closely linked the teaching of 17 June 1953 in East German schools was to West German attitudes toward and interpretations of it.

GDR school history textbooks and accompanying teaching guides show in theory how the SED wanted teachers to deal with the subject of the uprising and what it wanted school pupils to learn about the matter. But what happened in practice? Doris Ritter (born 1956) and Horst Thiel (born 1958) worked as history teachers in the GDR, which included teaching about the events of 17 June 1953 in the 1970s and 1980s. Both stated that they kept strictly to what was printed in the textbooks. Frau Ritter explained that she was very cautious about such areas of GDR history because she did not want to say anything that could get her into trouble: 'You tried to teach it as briefly and painlessly as possible. Simply teach it, done, tick it off the list.' Herr Thiel also stated that he more or less rushed to get the subject out of the way: 'I did it strictly by the book. Read it, present it, done.'

Both interviewees stated that, despite the school history syllabus advising teachers that they could use supplementary sources to help with teaching the subject, such sources were not made available to them. The suggested materials included the minutes of an interview with an alleged ringleader of the uprising and the portrayals of the events in 'Die Kommandeuse' ('The Commander', 1954) by Stefan Hermlin and *Auf der Suche nach Gatt* (*Searching for Gatt*, 1973) by Erik Neutsch (Autorenkollektiv, 1980, p. 198; Autorenkollektiv, 1989, pp. 36–8). Frau Ritter stated that these suggestions were merely for appearances' sake. Herr Thiel thought that even if these sources had been available, there was no means of copying them for a class of 30. Moreover, contrary to what the syllabus advised, no discussions on the subject were held in the classes and the pupils never had to produce related pieces of written work. Herr Thiel stressed that when teaching about the Nazi period the pupils were encouraged to go home and ask their grandparents about their experiences. This was never advised when teaching about the early years of the GDR.

Frau Ritter and Herr Thiel both claimed to feel very uncomfortable when they taught the subject. The cause of their unease was their pupils', as well as their own, knowledge of other versions of the events. This confirms that the Party was right to be concerned by the potential of alternative accounts to shape its citizens perceptions of the uprising. Frau Ritter stated that, because she knew that her pupils watched West German television and were aware of the account of 17 June 1953 as a 'people's uprising', she was afraid that they would ask questions that she could not answer in a way that adhered to the SED's account of the events, and that then the *Stasi* would somehow learn of this. Herr Thiel claimed that the fact that he could not form his own opinion on the nature of the events, because the sources of information to which he had access varied so drastically, made him uncomfortable teaching the subject. Though he was a member of the SED, he claimed to be critical of the Party and wanted to 'change' it for the better. This attitude apparently made him more open to alternative versions of 17 June 1953. He said that he had heard contradictory accounts from his grandfather who told him of the violent suppression of the unrest, from his father who was an SED hardliner with whom he fell out on numerous occasions because he had chosen to be a teacher and not a factory worker, from Western television and at school. As a result, Herr Thiel maintained that it was impossible for him to form his own evaluation of the events and to be confident enough about it to feel comfortable teaching it. But Herr Thiel also stated that he would not have been brave enough to contradict the SED's official account in class, even if he had been happy with his sources. He knew that the parents of a lot of his pupils worked for the police, the army or the *Stasi*.

Yet school pupils in the GDR apparently showed very little enthusiasm for the subject of 17 June 1953. Frau Ritter claimed that pupils knew from their parents and grandparents that what was in the history textbook was ideologically coloured and was not the whole story. Herr Thiel was of the opinion that no pupils were interested because of the content of the syllabus. He called the class ten history syllabus a 'punishment for teachers and pupils alike'. Both teachers said that the syllabus up to this point had been full of interesting subjects like the Nazi period and regional events, like the destruction of Magdeburg during the Second World War. But from class ten onwards, when the syllabus focused on the post-1945 period, teaching was informed by Party documents and the results of Party conferences, which, Herr Thiel recalled 'made the history of the country repellent. It was a real catastrophe.' According to Herr Thiel, the only aspect of the syllabus that interested the pupils was the Space Race. He stated that the only pupils who worked hard in the history classes were those who wanted to become officers in the security forces because they knew that a political-historical education was essential.

The recollections of interviewees who had attended history classes as pupils after 1960 were varied. However, the majority denied outright that the subject of 17 June 1953 had been taught at all. Anika Rosenkranz (born 1963), Nadine Weber (born 1960), and Gerhard Siedel (born 1966) and his wife (born 1967) emphasised that, according to their own recollection, the subject did not exist in the school history lessons of the GDR. Katja Müller (born 1962) was convinced that 'that date wasn't in our school books'. Manfred Ebert (born 1965) also declared: 'That subject didn't officially exist at school. It was completely hushed up.' Significantly, not only their words but also the tone of their responses indicated that, in their opinion, the mere suggestion that the subject had been taught was ridiculous. Many laughed at the suggestion that the subject might have been broached. They clearly perceived that the topic had been a taboo subject in the schools of the GDR. It is possible that these interviewees were misremembering or had forgotten. Indeed, Alexandra Brendel (born 1950) and Brigitte Schneider (born 1956) stated that they could not confirm or deny that the subject had been broached at school. Alternatively, as Katrin Heidinger (born 1957) explained, although there was something in the textbook about 'evil people' who had tried to overthrow the regime on 17 June 1953, the subject was simply not taught.

However, several interviewees did recall that the subject was addressed at their school. Christina Heinemann (born 1953) stated that the uprising was taught as a 'putsch steered by the West'. Doris Ritter (born 1956) said that the subject was covered in one lesson: 'I learned the classic version, the version in the GDR's history books. 17 June was steered from abroad by imperialists in the West. They goaded the workers into demonstrating to bring down the government.' But the extent to which the subject was taught apparently varied. Werner Prauss (born 1958) remembered that his history teacher spoke briefly about it but that the subject was very much a side issue. Similarly, Karl Schirra (born 1958) stated that the uprising was not a major subject at school. Christel Schlachter (born 1957) also recalled the subject being dealt with 'only very briefly. They really didn't go into much detail at all.' And Dorothea Freichel (born 1953) said that the subject was treated very superficially.

Monika Klein (born in 1948) and Susanne Dobrat (born 1965) remembered teaching of the subject very differently to other interviewees. Frau Klein recalled that the subject was taught comprehensively in history lessons. Similarly, Frau Dobrat stated that it had been treated as a completely normal historical subject and that at least one to two hours had been spent studying it. In stark contrast to other interviewees, both women responded in a tone that suggested that, in their opinion, to propose that the subject had not been taught was ridiculous. Examination of both interviewees' upbringings suggests several reasons for this. The parents of both women had been particularly strict SED supporters. Frau Dobrat's father was a member of the SED District Party Control Commission in Magdeburg, the Party body that regulated members' political discipline. Her mother was SED secretary in her workplace. Frau Klein stated that her father was politically active for the SED and that the family moved around several times as he was sent on political assignments. Her mother, also an SED member, worked for the *Volkspolizei*. Both interviewees were raised to support the SED and the GDR. Watching West German television was forbidden in their family homes and when they moved out they continued to watch GDR television almost exclusively (by her own account Frau Dobrat admitted to watching a Western film occasionally, but never the West German news or anything political). With no access to the West German account of the events during their school years, both interviewees grew up to regard the subject of 17 June 1953 and the SED's account thereof as unproblematic and as Frau Dobrat recalled 'a completely normal historical subject'. Their responses also apparently confirm Horst Thiel's recollection that it was only pupils brought up to be committed supporters of the state who paid attention in school history lessons. This suggests further that other interviewees did not recall learning about the subject at school because their parents, while not active opponents of the SED, were not active supporters either, and had not raised their children to support the Party.

By the interviewees' accounts, teaching of the subject of 17 June 1953 became less common from the mid-1970s. Nineteen interviewees were old enough to have attended school in the GDR when 17 June 1953 was on the curriculum. Twelve were born in the late 1940s and 1950s and would have been in class ten between 1963 and 1975. Seven of these were born in the 1960s and would have been in class ten between 1976 and 1983. Of the 19, eight insisted that the subject had been taught at their school. Seven of this eight were born in the late 1940s and 1950s. Only one was born in the 1960s. The fact that the older interviewees remembered teaching of the subject better than their younger counterparts also implies that 17 June 1953 was more meaningful to them than those born later.

2.4 Television

Despite the SED making no secret of the fact that the uprising had taken place by consistently including it in historical publications and history textbooks (albeit from 1960 onward), treatment of 17 June 1953 on GDR television reveals a more ambivalent attitude to communicating the events to citizens. The uprising was rarely mentioned on GDR television and never featured as the central topic of a historical documentary, suggesting that the SED was not happy to promote the uprising via a medium to which more and more citizens gained access and which became more and more popular as a means of informing oneself. Apart from propaganda broadcasts to counter the West's annual commemorations of the unrest, the uprising hardly featured in the GDR's television history programmes.

On the one occasion on which the uprising featured in a documentary, it was part of a much broader examination of the GDR's history in 1984's 'Unser Vaterland die Deutsche Demokratische Republik' ('Our Fatherland the German Democratic Republic'). In this broad historical account, which traced the roots of the GDR back to the fifteenth century, pictures briefly showed protesters on 17 June 1953 throwing stones at Soviet tanks and tearing down the Soviet flag atop the Brandenburg Gate. The commentary stated: 'On 17 June 1953 thousands gather at the symbol of German division. Anger is centred on the Red Flag. The uprising is put down.' Despite the brevity of this segment, it is interesting that reference to the number of protesters was made at a time when the history books were playing down the scale of the uprising. Moreover, there is no mention of the official 'fascist-counterrevolutionary putsch' terminology. The events are referred to as a 'revolt' (*Aufruhr*) instead (Brockmann, 2006, pp. 236–9).

2.5 Public commemoration

Examination of official public commemoration of the events in the GDR also reveals ambivalence in the SED's attitude to communicating the events to citizens. This is evident in the commemoration of three members of the security forces who died during the unrest in Magdeburg. On 17 June 1953 police officers Gerhard Händler and Georg Gaidzik and *Stasi* officer Hans Waldbach were shot dead as they tried to prevent the storming of the prison behind the police headquarters in Magdeburg (Ahrberg et al., 2004, pp. 156–61). The *Magdeburger Volksstimme* announced their deaths on 29 June 1953: 'Gerhard Händler...Georg Gaidzik and...Hans Waldbach...were brutally killed by Adenauer's murderous bandits. They fell as true patriots...they gave their lives for the interests of the working class and the preservation of peace' (1953, p. 2). On 23 June 1954 the *Stasi* in Magdeburg applied to the city council for a street to be renamed in honour of Waldbach. It was decided that the renaming should take place on 1 July 1954.[4] Before the next meeting of the city council the *Volkspolizei* in Magdeburg also requested that two streets be renamed in honour of the dead policemen. They requested that this also take place on 1 July 1954 because this was the national 'Day of the *Volkspolizei*'.[5] The city council proposed that Schäfferstraße be renamed Hans-Waldbach-Straße; Seehäuser Straße become Georg-Gaidzik-Straße; and Hohendodeleber Straße become Gerhard-Händler-Straße. None of these streets were important or significant thoroughfares in Magdeburg. In fact, the selection of these streets apparently contradicted the SED's own guidelines regarding the renaming of streets in honour of people. These guidelines stated that the street selected must have been in some way connected with the person in whose honour it was to be renamed.[6]

None of the men killed had lived in these streets. Hans Waldbach had lived in Wienerstraße, a major road in Magdeburg, but which was perhaps too prominent to be named after someone connected with 17 June 1953.[7] The streets were renamed on 1 July 1954. There was no indication on the street signs as to who these men were and no clue to link the names to the uprising of 17 June 1953. The regime apparently only wanted to commemorate the men, not the uprising. The executive of the city council only actually officially granted the requests to rename the streets on 27 July 1954.[8] The streets were therefore renamed without the official permission of the city authorities, demonstrating that the applications for such permission were merely for appearances' sake.

Only in March 1975 did the SED city leadership add detail to these street signs that explained something about the men. However, this was highly misleading. The Party decreed that, on the occasion of the thirtieth anniversary of the end of the Second World War, all streets named after 'antifascist resistance fighters' should receive plaques explaining who the individuals behind the street names were and what they had done. Such plaques were placed under the signs on Hans-Waldbach-Straße, Georg-Gaidzik-Straße and Gerhard-Händler-Straße. However, the plaques made no mention of 17 June 1953. The shield in Hans-Waldbach-Straße simply read: 'Waldbach, Hans. 1920–1953. Antifascist Resistance Fighter'.[9] Plaques in Gerhard-Händler-Straße and Georg-Gaidzik-Straße featured the same inscription. Although the term 'antifascist resistance fighter' is, according to the SED's account of the events of 17 June 1953, technically correct, it is also misleading. The SED's political dictionary defined the 'antifascist resistance movement' as the 'entirety of the various forms of political, military and ideological fight against the fascist hegemony. The antifascist resistance movement arose in the 1920s and 1930s.' The definition cited several key dates in the history of the movement, the last of which was 20 July 1944 (Autorenkollektiv, 1978b, pp. 46–8). None of the three security officers killed on 17 June 1953 in Magdeburg had been active in this movement. These plaques led citizens to believe that these men had been part of the 'antifascist resistance' during the Second World War and were being commemorated because of the role they played in that movement. Katja Müller (born 1962) stated with regard to streets named after certain men or women that 'the most simple explanation of streets named after people was that that person could have been an antifascist resistance fighter during the Nazi period'. Similarly, Alexandra Brendel (born 1950) recalled, 'I associated them with the antifascist resistance. I didn't know that they were connected to 17 June.'

In 1984 the SED city leadership commissioned the composition of a guide to the street names of Magdeburg in which the origins of the names were to be explained. In the original manuscript Gerhard-Händler-Straße and Georg-Gaidzik-Straße were included and each accompanied by the following short commentary: 'People's policeman, shot defending the achievements of the GDR on 17 June 1953.'[10] Hans-Waldbach-Straße was not included in the manuscript. In the final published text none of the three streets appeared (Buchholz, 1985).

Only Peter Momber (born 1938) and Erwin Strempel (born 1932) stated that they had known who the men behind the street names were. Herr Momber lived in a street very close to Georg-Gaidzik-Straße and Gerhard-Händler-Straße. He knew that both men had been shot and killed on 17 June 1953. He also knew of Hans-Waldbach-Straße and stated: 'The MVS reported that the streets were renamed "in honour of the comrades who were killed by counterrevolutionary bandits".' However, no such announcement appeared in the *MVS*, not even on the 1 July 1954 when the streets were renamed. It is possible Herr Momber was simply remembering the announcement of the deaths of the men which were reported in the *MVS*.

Of the interviewees born after 1953, Susanne Dobrat (born 1965) knew most about the streets. While working for an FDJ youth group in 1988 Frau Dobrat took charge of a that involved researching the lives of the two policemen who were killed in the prison behind the building on 17 June 1953. Only research into the circumstances of the deaths was required. No research into the course of the events in Magdeburg was requested. The FDJ group then produced a booklet in honour of the two men. Frau Dobrat thought that this booklet might have been presented to the parents of the dead men, but was not entirely sure. After the booklet was written, a retired policeman who had been in the police headquarters on 17 June 1953 visited the FDJ group and talked about his experiences of the uprising. Frau Dobrat and the FDJ group then attended a wreath-laying ceremony at the grave of one of the policemen, whose mother was also present. Before undertaking this project Frau Dobrat had never heard of the policemen killed on 17 June 1953.

The majority of interviewees who recognised the street names stated that they had not known anything about the men commemorated. The city authorities also struggled at times to identify the men. In 1962 the city council commissioned a study of the street names in Magdeburg. The authors of the study could not find out who Georg Gaidzik.[11] Moreover, in the late 1960s the city council composed a list of street signs to be granted a plaque explaining to citizens who the individuals behind the street names were. Gerhard-Händler-Straße was included in the list of streets 'whose origin is still unclear'.[12]

The regime's attitude to public memorials linked to 17 June 1953 is exemplified in the files of the Magdeburg branch of the *Stasi*. In 1983 the *Stasi* in Magdeburg proposed that a plaque commemorating the death of Hans Waldbach be placed on the wall of the prison close to the entrance where he had been shot. The plaque was intended to contribute to the 'historical education' of *Stasi* officers. When considering the inscription on the plaque, the first two suggestions – 'In honourable memory of Lieutenant Hans Waldbach who was killed by counterrevolutionaries on 17 June 1953' and 'In honour of the murdered fighter of the attempted counterrevolutionary putsch of 17 June 1953' – were rejected. The preferred inscription read: 'In honour of the fighter for the construction of socialism who was murdered on this spot by counterrevolutionaries.'[13] Thus the inscription chosen gave no hint that Waldbach had died during the uprising. Once again, the man, not the events, was to be commemorated. However, the plaque was never installed, probably due to the somewhat ridiculous stipulation that it should be on the wall of the prison but should be visible neither to public nor prisoners. Instead, a Hans Waldbach 'corner of tradition' (*Traditionsecke*), book of honour and award were produced and kept strictly for *Stasi* eyes only in their prison on Moritzplatz in the north of Magdeburg (see Schulz, 2008).

2.6 Conclusion

The SED successfully embedded some of the terminology of its official memory of 17 June 1953 into the minds of East German citizens, even if these citizens did not accept the Party's version of events. When asked to recount the SED's version of the uprising, many of the interviewees reproduced exact words and phrases from the Party's account, such as 'American and West German counterrevolutionary forces'; 'the West instigated the counterrevolution'; '17 June was steered from abroad, by imperialists in the West'. Interestingly, no interviewee needed time to think about his or her answer. They reproduced these stock phrases instantaneously. This suggests that interviewees were either often exposed to the SED's official account, or that they were often exposed to the kind of rhetoric employed and were stating how they think the Party would have viewed the events. These responses demonstrate that the SED's account impressed only two things upon citizens – the alleged instigators of the events and the SED's classification of the uprising. Interviewees offered no more details other than these stock phrases about 'counterrevolution'. They could and did only learn very limited information and details about actual events and incidents on 17 June 1953 from the Party's account. Even such details as the case of Erna Dorn, one of the few specific incidents detailed in the account and appearing in many publications, were apparently not communicated with as much emphasis as these stock phrases. Only Horst Thiel (born 1958) knew about Dorn and his knowledge of the episode may only be due to the fact that he had worked as a teacher and had had to teach the subject of the uprising.

Despite absorbing much of the official terminology, East German citizens apparently rejected the credence of the SED's account of the events as a 'fascist-counterrevolutionary putsch'. Only Franz Immig (born 1941) mentioned this term. In fact, he and Christina Heinemann (born 1953) were the only interviewees who used the word 'putsch', even though this term was used extensively by the SED to describe the events. The manner in which interviewees responded when asked to recount the SED's version of the events was also indicative of their rejection of it. Many laughed or adopted a mock authoritative tone, ridiculing the Party's account, though it must be kept in mind that interviewees may only have adopted such an attitude to the SED's official account since 1990. By interviewees' own accounts, awareness of the Party's official version of events decreased over time. All 11 interviewees who were born in the 1950s stated that during the GDR period they had been aware of the SED's official classification of the uprising as a 'counterrevolutionary putsch' instigated by the West. In contrast, only two of the seven interviewees born in the 1960s stated that they had known about the SED's official classification of the uprising. This apparent decrease in awareness is concomitant with the SED's scaling down of the official account in the late 1970s and 1980s. The Party deleted references, numerical or otherwise, to the scale of the uprising in its revision of its version of events in 1978. It was also during the period 1971 to 1989 that no explicit reference to the date of the uprising appeared in GDR newspapers.

3
Tales of That Day

The account of the uprising of 17 June 1953 found in the state media, history books and school textbooks of the GDR was not the only version of the events officially available to citizens. Up to 100 novels featuring scenes of the unrest or making reference to it were published in the GDR (Bruhn, 2003, pp. 57–9). Two films and one television drama also depicted the unrest. The very nature of these accounts as works of 'historical fiction' sets them apart from the history books. In contrast to the history books, they present the thoughts, feelings and emotions of their characters during or in reaction to the events. However fictitious these may be, they contribute to the creation of an historical narrative that penetrates the imagination of the reader. In other words, these aspects add a human quality to the historical narrative, bringing it to life and making it more real to the reader or viewer than a dry textbook account. For many this makes history more accessible, meaning that works of historical fiction are often regarded as 'extremely influential and effective transmitters of historical understanding' and the 'most potent shapers of the general historical consciousness' in societies (Wills jnr., 1984, pp. 38–46). The availability of these works in the GDR also sets them apart from the sources previously examined. In comparison to the history books, whose older editions were periodically removed from circulation, these novels remained available to citizens in libraries and bookshops from the date of their publication to the end of the SED regime (see Appendix B for publishing and distribution details of the novels and films considered in this chapter). Furthermore, the fact that historical fiction is not only widely available but also relatively

---

Sections of this chapter appeared in Millington, R. (2013). 'The Limits of Control: The "Public Discourse" about the Uprising of 17 June 1953 in Novels and Films in the German Democratic Republic', German History 31.1, 42–60.

inexpensive, means that it is often a prime source of historical understanding for many. Once bought, a book can be 'read and re-read; the reader absorbs its richness of information and many levels of meaning as he or she is ready for them'. This is in sharp contrast to visiting a museum, historic site or attending a school history lesson where 'what is learned... is largely dependent on the knowledge, imagination, and curiosity brought along on one visit' (Wills jnr., 1984, p. 40). These qualities of historical fiction contribute to the fact that 'more people... are led to history by way of fiction than through lectures and monographs' (Whiting, 1949, p. 95).

The individuals who composed these works of historical fiction also differed from the historians and propagandists who produced the official accounts of 17 June 1953. Unlike the latter, these authors and film-makers were not in the employ of the Party. In fact, many artists in the GDR fulfilled the role of mediators between the private and public spheres. According to David Bathrick, this allowed them to enjoy a certain amount of political independence, often enabling them to articulate a more pluralist public discourse in their works. Moreover, in a society in which official historical accounts often consisted of little more than 'tautologies, empty formulae and metaphors', there was sufficient scope for these artists to expand on the content of official communication (Bathrick, 1995, pp. 42–3).

Analysis of the scenes of 17 June 1953 that appeared in works of historical fiction in the GDR shows that, although authors and film-makers all ultimately portrayed the uprising as a 'fascist-counterrevolutionary putsch', they did expand on the SED's account of the unrest. In particular, they provided more detail of the geographical scale of the unrest. Moreover, they often did not make explicitly clear that all those involved in the demonstrations were exclusively 'fascists' or Western agents and several even depicted workers striking with just cause. The variations between the content of these fictional depictions and the Party's official account were due to inconsistencies in the censorship process, to which these works were subjected before being granted permission for release. There were apparently no rigid guidelines limiting the content of literary and cinematic portrayals of the unrest, or, if such guidelines did exist, they were not consistently enforced. Rather, the evidence indicates that the harshness of the censor varied between authors and depended upon factors that apparently had little to do with ideology.

Contemporary reaction of East German citizens to these films and novels shows that they stimulated discussion of the uprising amongst them, confirmed their experiences of the day, reawakened personal memories and informed subsequent generations about the subject. Significantly, citizens reacted with surprise when they encountered the subject of 17 June 1953 in these works. Similarly, when asked about their knowledge of scenes of the uprising in GDR novels or films, the majority of interviewees immediately dismissed the possibility that the SED would ever have permitted such pieces to be published. They were equally surprised to find out that many works did exist. Citizens laboured (and still do) under the misapprehension that the subject of the uprising of 17 June 1953 was a taboo in GDR literature and society. Although it was certainly taboo to mention details that contradicted the Party's official account, citizens believed that the entire subject, including the official version, was a taboo.

3.1 Literary and cinematic depictions of the uprising of 17 June 1953

The artists who included depictions of 17 June 1953 in their works were from varying generational cohorts and political backgrounds. The authors or film-makers of 7 of the 21 pieces considered here were born between 1899 and 1915. Moreover, this seven (Anna Seghers, Stephan Hermlin, Werner Reinowski, Inge von Wangenheim, Eduard Claudius, Wolfgang Joho and Fritz Selbmann) had been active in the communist movement before the Second World War. During the Nazi period they had either chosen to emigrate, or had remained in Germany and were actively involved in resistance movements, for which Joho, Selbmann and Claudius spent time in prison. Given the political convictions of these 'old communist' authors and their experiences during the Second World War, it is hardly surprising that their pieces are partisan in their support of the SED's official account. Hermlin's 'Die Kommandeuse' ('The Commander', 1954) and Reinowski's *Die Versuchung* (*The Temptation*, 1956) are particularly venomous in their portrayals of the West. The narrator in Joho's *Die Kastanie* (*The Chestnut*, 1972) likens the demonstrators to baying anti-Semitic mobs that she had seen before the Second World War (pp. 271–2). Of this cohort, only Fritz Selbmann goes somewhat against the grain of the official account in his depiction of striking workers in *Die Söhne der Wölfe* (*The Sons of the Wolves*, 1966). Minister for mining and metallurgy in 1953, Selbmann achieved notoriety with regard to the uprising by being the only top SED official to confront the crowds gathered before the House of Ministries in Berlin (Kowalczuk, 2003, p. 116). Despite the fact that a few days after the unrest he likened the uprising to the Nazi invasion of the Soviet Union in 1941, Selbmann's later depiction of the unrest may have been influenced by his 1958 dismissal from political office, when he was accused of supporting a faction against Walter Ulbricht (Roth, 2002, p. 469).

The other 14 authors and film-makers whose works are examined here were born between 1926 and 1944. Most were active supporters of the regime. Hermann Kant worked as an informer for the *Stasi* from 1963 to 1976 (Müller-Enbergs, Wielgohs and Hoffmann, n.d.). Bernhard Seeger informed for the state security service from 1953 to 1972, too, and also became a member of the SED's Central Committee in 1967 (Müller-Enbergs, Wielgohs and Hoffmann, n.d.). Erik Neutsch belonged to the SED leadership in Halle (Müller-Enbergs, Wielgohs and Hoffmann, n.d.). Harry Kampling had even emigrated to the GDR from the Federal Republic in 1956.[1] Yet authors who often wrote critically about life under the regime, such as Werner Heiduczek and Christoph Hein, also depicted the uprising according to the official account. Though one might explain such artists' apparent compliance with the official account as a result of self or state censorship, it is possible that they did believe the SED's account. Even if this were not the case, few would have been willing to contradict the SED's version of events, if not in order to avoid censure, then in order not to appear to support the 'fascists' who the Party claimed were involved. The author Christa Wolf has asserted that the SED's claim that it was an extension of the pre-war antifascist resistance discouraged many from opposition, especially as many of the Party's leading functionaries, such as Erich Honecker, had suffered for their political allegiance during the Nazi period. People were reluctant to organise opposition against self-proclaimed 'antifascists' and thereby expose themselves to accusations of 'fascism' (Bathrick, 1995, p. 12).

The small number of works of historical fiction available in the GDR whose main plots focus on the events of 17 June 1953 suggests that authors and film-makers were reluctant to produce pieces that dealt exclusively with the uprising. The unrest is at the centre of only 4 of the 21 works of historical fiction considered in this chapter (Hermlin, 1954; Reinowski, 1956; Seghers, 1968; von Wangenheim, 1957). It is notable that the authors of these four pieces were all 'old communists', suggesting that the events held more meaning for them than authors of later generations. In the remaining novels, coverage of the uprising varies in length from only a few paragraphs (Joho, 1972, pp. 271–2), to several pages (Kant, 1972, pp. 143–5; Bastian, 1974, pp. 320–5), to over 10 pages in some instances (Seeger, 1981, pp. 381–407) and over 20 in others (Neutsch, 1978, pp. 339–74). Scenes of the uprising in the films *Schlösser und Katen* (*Castles and Cottages*, 1958) and *Geschichten jener*

Nacht (*Tales of the Night*, 1967) and the television drama *Auf der Suche nach Gatt* (*Searching for Gatt*, 1976) made in the GDR do not last longer than a few minutes. Yet despite the brevity with which the uprising often appeared in these works, the fact that scenes of the unrest featured at all implies that authors were not averse to including it in their stories if they deemed it necessary. In fact, authors often devoted more coverage in terms of words and pages to the unrest than the regime's own history books. The fact that even in the 1980s authors addressed the subject suggests that the uprising still held meaning for citizens.

In the majority of the works authors and film-makers include the events of 17 June 1953 as a vehicle for a change in political attitude of their characters. They depict the day of the uprising as one upon which the heroes of their pieces make a decisive choice in favour of socialism. Thus the unrest serves as a moment or day of truth for the characters (Braun, 2007, pp. 107–21). The character Materna in *Geschichten jener Nacht* (1967) states in his narration that, after his experiences in the German army during the Second World War: 'No power in the world would ever make me put on a uniform again or take up a rifle.' However, after being attacked by provocateurs on his building site on 17 June 1953 Materna joins his workplace militia. He concludes the narration by stating: 'When I came home from the war, I made up my mind never to go to war again. I have had to change my mind.' Similarly, in Karl-Heinz Jakobs' novel *Beschreibung eines Sommers* (*Account of One Summer*) the main character Tom undergoes a change in his attitude on 17 June 1953. Previously depicted as someone who cares little for socialism and the GDR, Tom refuses to denounce either, even when physically abused by West Berlin police officers during the unrest (1961, pp. 205–7).

While none of the portrayals evaluate the events as anything other than an 'attempted fascist-counterrevolutionary putsch', several do expand on the official account in terms of the geographical scale of the unrest. This is perhaps unsurprising given that the only allusion to centres of unrest in the official account was the empty phrase 'Berlin and a few other cities'. Artists took it upon themselves to name these 'other cities'. Joachim Knappe (1966) and Erik Neutsch (1973) depict the uprising in Eisenhüttenstadt and Mansfeld, respectively. Werner Reinowski (1956) portrays the events in Berlin, but the Western spies in his novel also receive reports of unrest from colleagues in various other cities such as Dessau, Bitterfeld, Sangershausen, Magdeburg and Halle. Eduard Claudius (1957), Werner Heiduczek (1977), Christoph Hein (1982) and Rudolf Scholz (1981) make more of a break with the official version of the uprising by depicting events in rural towns and villages. Unrest in such locations was hardly implied by the phrase 'a few other cities'. Moreover, the pieces by Hein and Scholz appeared after the Party had deleted allusion to the scale of the events from its account in 1978. In Scholz's *Mein lieber alter Lukowski* (*My dear old Lukowski*), which is set in a country village, the character Hentschel recounts: 'Actually, the events played out mostly in the cities. But there were people here who also thought their time had come. A few of them are still doing time' (1981, p. 149).

Analysis of the protagonists of the uprising in these depictions shows that authors presented the demonstrators vaguely. The Party's official account also did not offer much detail about specific individuals or incidents, other than that those involved in the demonstrations were 'hooligans from fascist organisations, work shy and criminal elements' under the leadership of 'American secret services and the government in Bonn' (Autorenkollektiv, 1960, pp. 317–8). However, whereas the official account employs explicit terms such as 'fascists' or 'Western provocateurs', authors use neutral words such as 'they', 'people' or 'someone'. Such terms leave room for the interpretation that the protagonists might also have been East German citizens. In the city centre in 'Die Kommandeuse' Stephan Hermlin writes that 'a few people had started to sing the Horst Wessel song' ([1954] 1983, p. 227). These 'people' could be Western agents or East German citizens. Similarly, Werner Heiduczek does not indicate the identities or origins of the crowd of 'perhaps ten thousand... baffled faces, angry faces, apathetic faces, laughing faces' (1977, p. 268). And Erik Neutsch is equally vague about who attacks his main character: 'Suddenly someone pointed from the crowd. He pointed at the Party badge on Gatt's lapel and shouted: "You Russian lackey. Take that thing off!"' (1973, p. 96).

The most striking deviation from the official account of the uprising comes when several authors depict workers taking part in the strikes and having just cause to do so. Despite several changes over the years to the SED's account of the unrest of 17 June 1953, the assertion that the events did not consist of justified strikes remained constant. The Party claimed that the few workers who might have joined the protests did so because they had been duped by Western agents and quickly returned to work. However, in *Die Söhne der Wölfe* Fritz Selbmann writes of two demonstrations. The first comprises 'young lads, yobs in leather jackets, thugs from the "Junge Union"... There were even a few American soldiers in uniform.' The 'Junge Union' was the youth wing of the West German conservative Christian Democratic Union party (CDU). The second protest consists of workers. Selbmann suggests that these workers are protesting because they are unhappy with their working conditions: 'A real workers' demonstration...like they used to do it...Orderly, calm, clear demands, resolved to the fight, how the union orders it and what the German worker is used to.' Upon witnessing this, the character Lorenzen thinks of the factory where he works: 'Sure, there were unhappy workers there, too. Not everything was hunky-dory with the working quotas...There had been complaints' (1966, p. 140). Horst Bastian also writes of two separate protests in *Gewalt und Zärtlichkeit* (*Violence and Tenderness*) and implies that, although provocateurs were causing much of the unrest, workers were also striking over their dissatisfaction:

> A chorus of voices rang out: 'Down with the SED!' Placards read: 'Kill dead what's red!' Somewhat to the side there was another group, sombre, silent. Their placards read: 'Stop the quotas!', 'Lower the quotas!', 'Work, yes – work yourself to death, no!'
>
> (1974, p. 325)

Though history tomes published after 1978 made no mention of possible inner causes of the unrest, Harry Kampling in *Der Mann aus der Siedlung* writes that workers are striking because of their working quotas: ' "The miners are striking", said Renneberg...Wallhauer nodded. "We ought to strike with them, because of the working quotas" ' (1981, p. 273). Given that Kampling emigrated to the GDR from West Germany in 1956, it is surprising that he was permitted to publish an account of 17 June 1953 that directly mentioned strikes. One also wonders what his depiction of the events is based upon. Though he does adhere to the SED's account of the uprising in as far as he describes the involvement of 'provocateurs' on the day, his mention of strikes indicates that he drew upon sources that lay outside of the official narrative of the uprising.

Authors and film-makers did, however, toe the regime line exactly when it came to depicting the intervention of Soviet troops on 17 June 1953. The Party's official account, while praising the conduct of the Red Army and thanking the troops for their intervention, never detailed exactly what this had entailed. Artists' strict adherence to this aspect of the official account suggests that they (or the censors) felt that this was one detail that could not be left open to interpretation. In many of the pieces of historical fiction the Soviets only arrive after citizens of the GDR have helped the SED to retake control of the situation. Workers and SED members in *Das Vertrauen* (*Trust*) successfully defend their factory themselves, long before Soviet tanks arrive: 'They are putting a stop to the uprising. Our best people are doing it, themselves. They have already done it. Alone' (Seghers, 1968, p. 354). Similarly, in the film *Schlösser und Katen* (1958) villagers arrest the main provocateur before any tanks arrive. In several of the portrayals the Soviets are present during the demonstrations, but still take no action. In *Beschreibung eines Sommers* Karl-Heinz Jakobs writes of a solitary Soviet tank patrolling Unter den Linden in Berlin, but it takes no action, even when provocateurs pelt it with stones (1961, p. 205). Likewise, tank crews remain stoical when insulted and stoned by demonstrators in *Die Kastanie* (Joho, 1972, p. 271). The tanks present on the market square in 'Die Kommandeuse' merely rev their engines, although there is something ominous in Hermlin's use of the word 'thundered' to describe their sound ([1954] 1983, p. 229). The noise of tanks is also referred to in *Am Morgen ist der Tag ein Kind* (*In the Morning the Day is a Child*). The sound of approaching tanks (and not machine gun bullets) is enough to disperse the provocateurs (von Wangenheim, 1957, p. 393). One rare instance in which Soviet troops actually intervene in the demonstrations can be found in Horst Bastian's *Gewalt und Zärtlichkeit*. However, there is no violence involved. A solitary Soviet soldier addresses the crowds and announces that whoever is still on the streets in 14 minutes time will be arrested. The protesters soon disperse (1974, p. 334).

The manner in which authors and film-makers reference the date of the uprising when introducing their depictions of 17 June 1953 suggests that these artists assumed a certain amount of prior knowledge and awareness about the events from their readers or viewers. Several of the depictions make no explicit or only partial reference to the date of the events. This might have been an attempt to dupe the censor. But it also indicates that authors expected audiences to be able to identify what was being depicted from a few vague details. Eduard Claudius makes no specific mention of the date of the uprising in *Von der Liebe soll man nicht nur sprechen* (*One Ought Not Simpy Talk About Love*) writing: 'On that morning when strikes broke out in the fields – in the cities something was also afoot' (1957, p. 506). Claudius' allusion to the uprising by mentioning strikes in the countryside, directly contrasts two details of the SED's account. Yet it was not just authors writing in the years immediately following the uprising who perceived enough awareness of the events on the part of readers to omit the date completely. Christoph Hein also made no direct reference to the date in *Der fremde Freund* (*The Distant Lover*). Moreover, Hein's depiction of the unrest suggests that he perceived that readers would be able to identify the uprising from the mention of tanks, which made no appearance in the SED's account: 'On that day, when the tanks came...on that day the boys ran to the window in the middle of the lesson and shouted: The tanks are coming, the tanks are coming' (1982, p. 122). Yet many of the works do state that what they depict occurs on 17 June 1953 (see Selbmann, 1966; Joho, 1972; Bastian, 1974; Heiduczek, 1977). Significantly, it is one of the few specific dates (along with 8 May 1945) to which such pieces actually make explicit reference; they usually only refer to seasons or years. This indicates that authors perceived it as a historically significant date for the GDR. In several of these cases, there is somewhat of a break with official discourse with regard to the events. *Das Impressum* (*Imprint*, Kant, 1972); *Die Kastanie* (Joho, 1972); *Auf der Suche nach Gatt* (Neutsch, 1973), as well as its 1976 television adaptation; *Gewalt und Zärtlichkeit* (Bastian, 1974) and *Tod am Meer* (*Death by the Sea*, Heiduczek, 1977) all appeared during the Honecker era when the state newspaper *Neues Deutschland* was apparently forbidden from printing the date '17 June 1953'. This shows that, although this ban certainly could not and did not extend to the history books, novels and films were also exempt.

As opposed to the history and propaganda publications, these historical fiction accounts of 17 June 1953 presented the thoughts and emotions of their characters in reaction to the events, as well as for the rest of their lives. At the end of his depiction of the events in *Der Friede im Osten. Zweites Buch: Frühling mit Gewalt* (*Peace in the East. Second Book: Violence in the Spring*), Erik Neutsch writes that 17 June 1953 was 'a day...which would stay in the memories of those who experienced it for a long time' (1978, p. 374). A number of authors address the long-term effects of memories of the unrest upon their characters' lives. In so doing they suggest that memories of the uprising continued to affect the lives of real life citizens. In several works personal memories of the uprising affect characters' political lives. The character Elisabeth in *Die Kastanie* recalls that her experiences of the unrest made her realise that she wanted to belong to the new society being created in the GDR. Recounting her experiences of the June unrest, Elisabeth comments: 'I will never forget my terror, when I came upon a jeering mob.' The sight of demonstrators stoning and insulting Soviet troops reminded her of how a Jewish childhood friend had been subjected to the same sort of treatment before the Second World War. Elisabeth states that this scene and the memories it evoked 'made me suddenly and very clearly aware of my affiliation... back then I grasped completely where I belonged and what I didn't want to lose and would not give up' (Joho, 1972, p. 271-2). Thus her experiences of the uprising determined her political allegiances for the rest of her life and continue to do so. Similarly, personal memories of the events of June 1953 influence politically the character Materna in *Geschichten jener Nacht* (1967). At the beginning of the film we see Materna patrolling the border between East and West Berlin on 13 August 1961 as a member of a workplace militia unit. This image contrasts with his narration, in which he states that he had decided after his experiences of the Second World War that no one could ever force him to take up arms again. Materna then recounts what has happened in his life since 1945. This culminates with his recollection of a strike on his building site on 17 June 1953: 'Someone was giving a speech. And someone grumbled something about fat cats and Bolsheviks. Somewhere, someone was singing "Deutschland über alles".' The scene ends with Materna being knocked unconscious by a demonstrator while attempting to stop the strike. Returning to Materna in his militia uniform he tells us that his memories and experiences of the uprising led him to decide to join the armed forces again.

Significantly, Christoph Hein suggests in *Der fremde Freund* that the subject of 17 June 1953 was a taboo in GDR society. The character Claudia explains: 'Father said to me, I ought not to ask questions in school [about the uprising] and ought not to discuss it'. Hein also suggests that the fact that eyewitnesses did not speak about the subject also communicated to younger generations of citizens that they should not discuss it either and should not ask eyewitnesses about it. Claudia perceives that her parents' silence on the matter indicates that the subject is loaded with some sort of threat 'because none of the adults spoke about the tanks, I realised that a conversation could be something threatening. And I kept quiet, so that they didn't have to talk.... I learned to keep quiet' (1982, p. 124).

Despite the considerable number of literary and cinematic depictions of the uprising of 17 June 1953 available in the GDR, the SED's particular promotion of several depictions implies that it regarded these as exemplary. In 1989 the short story 'Die Kommandeuse' by Stephan Hermlin (1954) was recommended as a further source of information about the uprising to teachers of class ten in GDR schools. The SED advised them that they could use the story to 'prove' to their pupils that 'fascists' had been involved in the events of June 1953 (Autorenkollektiv, 1989, p. 37). Similarly, Erik Neutsch's (1973) *Auf der Suche nach Gatt* was recommended to teachers of class 11 in 1980 to help them with teaching their pupils about 17 June 1953 (Autorenkollektiv, 1980, p. 198). In 1988 the history book *Fragen an die Geschichte der DDR* (*Questions on the History of the GDR*) also reproduced several pages of the novel's portrayal of 17 June 1953 in its section detailing the course of the uprising (Heise and Hofmann, 1988, pp. 117–8). Moreover, in 1976 a two-part television adaptation of Neutsch's novel *Auf der Suche nach Gatt* was aired on GDR television. This production also featured scenes of the uprising. Harry Kampling's (1981) depiction of 17 June 1953 in *Der Mann aus der Siedlung* (*The Man from the Estate*) was also reproduced in a format other than a novel. The story was serialised in the *Magdeburger Volksstimme* in the first six months of 1982. Interestingly, the scenes featuring 17 June 1953 in the work were printed in the editions of the newspaper from 12 to 18 June 1982.

Even in these portrayals of the uprising contradictions are evident. The depictions of the protagonists of the uprising differ to a certain extent. Both Erik Neutsch (1973) and Stephan Hermlin ([1954] 1983) present 'fascists', Western agents and hooligans as the main instigators and protagonists of the unrest. Neutsch's demonstrators are wearing Western fashions: 'Lads with cropped hair, lemon-yellow shirts and hooped socks on their feet' (p. 100). He writes further: 'From Berlin's Western sector more and more mobs of rampaging youths entered the East' (pp. 196–7). It is later reported that former concentration camp guards also played a vital role in the unrest (p. 106). Hermlin's tale is based upon the story of Erna Dorn and uses details and quotes from the trial that saw Dorn sentenced to death. On the day of the uprising in the story, two Western spies liberate former concentration camp guard Hedwig Weber from prison so that she can help the Americans to restore 'fascism'. This excites Weber, who enthuses that 'soon we will be wearing out beloved SS uniforms again' (p. 222). Later in the portrayal Hermlin also includes youths dressed in Western fashion and burning books in the street (p. 222–9). However, in *Der Mann aus der Siedlung* Harry Kampling (1981) does not explicitly state that 'fascists' or Westerners were involved in the unrest. The appearance of a man wearing a leather jacket instead of overalls addressing a crowd of miners is the only indication that there might be something more sinister to the protests than simple dissatisfaction with working conditions. This man addresses the miners: 'We workers demand the unification of Germany. We won't be exploited any longer. We want democracy and freedom. Everyone to the town hall! To the market square!' (p. 277). Suspicion of this man is reinforced by the thoughts of Kampling's main character Renneberg: 'Where did he come from?... no proletarian speaks like that' (p. 275). The only hint of 'fascists' comes later when Renneberg hears drunks singing 'Deutschland über alles' (p. 277).

In neither *Auf der Suche nach Gatt* nor 'Die Kommandeuse' do the authors explicitly state that citizens of the GDR are involved in the demonstrations. In Neutsch's (1973) novel East German citizens look at the demonstrators and stand quietly and paralysed (p. 96). The television adaptation (1976) of the novel also shows East German citizens (mostly old men and women – there are no workers to be seen) confused and horrified by the sight of the demonstrations. The only ones involved in the unrest are youths in leather jackets and brightly coloured t-shirts. Hermlin ([1954] 1983) writes that the crowd of citizens gathered on the market place in (fictional) Saalstedt are simply strolling around and chatting. None are involved in the protests (p. 225). Yet Kampling's portrayal does not follow suit. He depicts workers involved in the demonstrations: '"The miners are striking," said Renneberg... Wallhauer nodded, "We should strike with them, because of the quotas".' Moreover, Kampling apparently justifies their participation. After hearing about the 10 per cent increase in working quotas, the character Renneberg thinks 'if that really is correct now, the thing with the quotas, They [the SED] will have everyone against them' (1981, pp. 272–3).

These portrayals also differ in their presentation of the SED regime's reaction to the crisis of the uprising. Neutsch (1973) adheres to the SED's account of 17 June 1953 by depicting the SED as being in control of the situation. Gatt learns that the local SED leadership 'were advising on the situation since the early morning hours. Messages were arriving incessantly from the central offices, one after the other' (p. 97). On the streets of Mansfeld, Gatt also finds other SED members with whom he organises resistance to the rampaging youths. Moreover, at midday they receive news from the Politburo that 'peace will be defended with all means necessary' (p. 99). Yet Kampling's (1981) description of the actions of the forces of the state is highly critical: ' "Where's the factory militia then?", asked Renneberg. "Not one bastard to be seen", said Wallhauer... "...And the Party Secretary?" "Nothing, nothing at all. The office is empty. They have all bolted"' (pp. 273–4). Interestingly, Hermlin ([1954] 1983) does not actually mention the Party once throughout his story.

The only aspect of the official account to which all three texts adhere is that of the Soviet intervention. All refer to the presence of Soviet tanks and troops without explicitly mentioning the violence of their intervention on 17 June 1953. Neutsch's (1973) reference to the Soviets' role in ending the uprising is fleeting. Gatt learns that, even though hordes of West Berlin youths are crossing the border 'on Potsdamer Platz Soviet tanks were patrolling already' (p. 97). Gatt later states that 'The Red Army intervened, gun turrets and Soviet stars' (p. 112). His use of 'gun turrets', however, implies that some sort of armed action was required.

Hermlin ([1954] 1983) gives a little more coverage to the presence of Soviet troops. Soviet tanks are present in the city centre in his portrayal, but the troops are relaxed, leaning on their tanks and laughing (p. 229). In *Der Mann aus der Siedlung* the only mention of the Soviet intervention comes when the character Renneberg awakes on 18 June 1953: 'Outside, directly in front of his garden gate stood a tank, a T-34' (Kampling, 1981, p. 280). This is the only portrayal to refer to the specific model of the Soviet tanks. T-34 tanks were renowned for the role that they played in the liberation of Berlin in 1945. Kampling's reference implies that as they had done eight years earlier, so these tanks again rid the GDR of 'fascists' on 17 June 1953.

The SED's promotion of these portrayals in particular suggests that the Party judged them to be especially favourable. The fact that Hermlin's and Neutsch's depictions were promoted in the schools of the GDR implies that the details from the official account included in these texts were the ones that the SED considered to be most important. As the GDR's school textbooks, history books and propaganda publications do, both texts emphasise the involvement of Western agents and 'fascists' in the uprising of 17 June 1953. But Kampling's portrayal only loosely adheres to the SED's official account of 17 June 1953 and is critical of the Party's handling of the uprising. One might have assumed that these facts would have blocked publication of the novel, let alone its serialisation in the *Magdeburger Volksstimme*, above all over the anniversary of the events in 1982. This fact suggests further that the Party's control over these cinematic and literary portrayals of 17 June 1953 was by no means absolute.

3.2 Censorship of literary and cinematic depictions of 17 June 1953

Despite the fact that the SED denied the existence of censorship, all artistic works were assessed before being granted permission to be released to the general public. In the case of literary works this process went by the name of 'publishing approval procedure' (*Druckgenehmigungsverfahren*) (Barck, 2002). This was to ensure that artists were toeing the Party line. Cultural production in the GDR was subordinated to the tenets of the Party. The regime decreed that it was an artist's duty to educate citizens to become better socialist citizens. Works of art were to support the construction of a socialist society by promoting socialist virtues, a socialist work ethic and the idea of the collective. Moreover, artists were to 'take a stance against all forms of ideological co-existence and against the infiltration of reactionary and revisionist views' (Emmerich, 2000, pp. 40–4).

Artists active in the GDR have identified themselves as the first censors in this process. They were aware of which subjects were acceptable and unacceptable to the Party. The extent of the influence on the creative process of an artist's perception of which themes could jeopardise publication of their work cannot be underestimated. The author Christlieb Hirte recalled that whenever she wanted to have a work published, she first had to consider how best to present it to meet the ideological requirements of the her publishing house and the Ministry of Culture: 'Everything had to be formulated so that it pleased the right people... it was always a bit calculating.' Hirte had to take the 'scissors in her head' (*Schere im Kopf*) to each formulation (Hirte, 2005, pp. 392–3). However, the author Gabriele Eckhart claims that the process of self-censorship was a subconscious one – artists automatically omitted subjects that they knew might be an obstacle to having their work released, often rendering official censorship further down the line superfluous (Zipser, 1995, p. 28).

Once a work had been prepared, artists submitted it to their publishing house or film studio for assessment. The in-house assessors (*Lektoren*) were often also authors or academic experts and were responsible for identifying and reporting the ideological shortcomings of the works (Barck et al., 1997, pp. 232–4). An in-house committee comprising 'ideologically reliable and respected experts' undertook final review of the work (Zipser, 1995, p. 16). The piece was then sent to the Ministry of Culture for further assessment.

In the case of literary works the *Hauptverwaltung Verlage und Buchhandel* (*Main Administration for Publishing and Bookselling*, HV) at the Ministry of Culture was responsible for the final assessment of manuscripts. It was the HV's main task to 'raise the quality of literature through the assessment (*Begutachtung*) of the planned works'. Manuscripts were processed in the Assessment Division (*Abteilung Begutachtung*). This sub-department regulated, assessed and set the conditions for the granting of publishing approval slips (*Druckgenehmigungen*) (Barck et al., 1997, pp. 19–21). If works did not fulfil the Ministry of Culture's requirements, they would be returned with a list of changes to be made. When works were satisfactorily corrected, permission would usually be granted and release could go ahead (Zipser, 1995, pp. 16–7).

However, the assessment process was uneven and inconsistent. Officials at the Ministry of Culture did not have absolute control over submitted works, meaning that there was some room for manoeuvre for artists. This was often due to the individual assessors themselves. 'Open and educated' individuals who held assessment posts could manipulate the guidelines to ease the controls (see Barck et al., 2001; Klötzer and Lokatis, 1999). Other variables included the generation of the censors and the strength of their political conviction (Rüther, 1997, p. 35). The author Karl-Heinz Jakobs has described the system of censorship as a team effort of authors, publishers and officials, rather than a centralised system of repression. He recalled that, in the case of in-house assessors at least, friendly negotiation was usual: 'Once initial mistrust had been overcome, longstanding friendships developed' (Zipser, 1995, p. 188).

The severity of the Ministry of Culture's official policy on censorship also varied throughout the 40 years of the GDR. In the late 1950s the SED encouraged artists to depict East German society as it was (not as it should be), in order to make culture more appealing to ordinary people (von Richthofen, 2009, p. 160). Accordingly, artists produced works depicting everyday problems within society, frequently focussing on youth (Feinstein, 2002, pp. 179–80). This cultural 'thaw' came to an abrupt end in December 1965 with the Eleventh Plenary of the Central Committee of the SED. Minister of Culture Kurt Hager criticised the period of cultural liberalisation, claiming that it had given artists free reign to attack socialist society. Ulbricht's crown prince, Erich Honecker, claimed that cultural production in the GDR was now beset by moral and sexual depravity (von Richthofen, 2009, p. 164). Consequently, the Party reverted to a course of cultural repression. Another period of cultural liberalisation was instigated in 1971 when Honecker replaced Ulbricht as leader of the SED. He announced that there should be 'no taboos' for artists (Fuhrmann, 1997, p. 42). However, as artists grew bolder and censorship slackened, so the Party became more and more alarmed at the number of works critical of the regime being made available to the public (Zipser, 1995, pp. 21–2). This period of cultural liberalisation ended with the forced exile of dissident poet Wolf Biermann in 1976.

Censors in the GDR clearly had no problem with artists including scenes of the uprising of 17 June 1953 in their works. In fact in the censorship documents of the pieces considered here no censor criticised an author for addressing the events or demanded the removal of scenes simply because they depicted the uprising. In many of the censorship assessments officials did not even acknowledge that scenes of the events featured in the works. And in those where assessors did acknowledge inclusion of the uprising, they often only did so when detailing the content of the work or the time period in which it was set. Only once did an official apparently show their surprise at the inclusion of the uprising. Scrawled in the margin of an early manuscript of Erik Neutsch's *Auf der Suche nach Gatt* (1973) is the exclamation 'The putsch of 17.6.53?!'[2]

Yet, if all of these works were subjected to the censorship process, how can one explain the publication of historical fiction accounts that included details which clashed with the official history books? Why were accounts which left room for interpretations not in line with the Party's version of events granted permission to be distributed to the public? The evidence shows that the censorship of these works was highly inconsistent. It is not possible to establish from the censorship documents a definitive list of details that the SED did not want included in these portrayals. Censors demanded the deletion of aspects of the depictions of June 1953 in some works, but permitted their appearance in others. Thus there was a varying degree of control over which details of the events were presented to citizens.

Comparison of the censorship of Erik Neutsch's six-page portrayal of 17 June 1953 in *Auf der Suche nach Gatt* (1973) with other published depictions of the uprising starkly underscores inconsistencies in the assessment process. Reviewing Neutsch's manuscript in 1969, Ministry of Culture officials advised Neutsch to remove passages that might lead readers to conclude that the unrest was caused by dissatisfaction amongst East German citizens and not instigated by 'fascists' and Western agents:

> It would be desirable for the author to avoid rash conclusions such as jam or the cost of 20 pfennigs for a tram ticket <u>had led to 17 June</u> [underlined in original], so that <u>his political concern</u> [underlined in original] to present 17 June as a struggle for power can be fully realised.[3]

Yet in *Tod am Meer* Werner Heiduczek writes of citizens' negative opinions of the SED's policies:

> Some thought the West was sabotaging our construction... Others felt that the domestic policies pursued by the Party's leadership and the government were wrong... Socialism was simply breaking the workers' bones differently to capitalism.
>
> (1977, p. 249)

And in *Am Morgen ist der Tag ein Kind* angry workers confront a leader of the FDJ on 15 June 1953 about how the state treats them:

> You love us! All of you with your badges and declarations. You cherish us in your newspapers and festivals! And then you squash us like fleas between the pages of your files because we own a boat, or a farm... all out of love for us, of course! That is your justice, your state!.
> (von Wangenheim, 1957, p. 111)

The fact that this passage appeared at a time when SED cultural policy was promoting depictions of real life and everyday conflicts may explain why it was permitted to remain in the work. Yet although Neutsch's and Heiduczek's manuscripts were reviewed during periods of cultural clampdown in the GDR (1969 and 1977, respectively), Heiduczek's arguably stronger criticisms were permitted, while Neutsch's were not.

Suggestions in *Auf der Suche nach Gatt* that the SED reacted negatively to the uprising were also removed, though it is not clear at what stage in the process this occurred. Neutsch's original account did not reflect the Party's official version that it had led the working class to victory over the provocateurs. In the manuscript Gatt makes his way to the SED district headquarters in Mansfeld in order to find out 'what ought to happen today and tomorrow. Whether we ought to dance to the music playing on our radio station or whether we ought to protect the revolution.' This comment on the lack of directives coming from the SED did not appear in the published novel. Moreover, in the original manuscript Neutsch suggests that when the Party finally took action, it was confused: 'From the central offices directives arrived incessantly, one after the other, but one contradicted the other'.[4] The final clause did not appear in the published novel (Neutsch, 1973, p. 97). In other portrayals of the uprising though, negative comments regarding the SED's reaction to the crisis were left uncensored. For example, in the factory in *Der Mann aus der Siedlung* the SED committee is nowhere to be found during the uprising and the characters assume that the committee members have run away (Kampling, 1981, pp. 273–4). The SED's reaction to the uprising in *Tod am Meer* actually descends into the ridiculous. In the town of Ronnburg SED secretary Imme attempts, and fails, to shout over a loud speaker calling citizens to strike. Heiduczek writes in veiled criticism of the Party: 'As long as Imme shouted, he was the loser' (1977, p. 269).

Comparison of Neutsch's manuscript with the final novel shows that suggestions that the SED lacked support from its own citizens during the uprising were deleted. In the manuscript Gatt complains: 'Fascists on the streets and no counter-demonstration'.[5] Thus citizens were not taking action to support the Party. But in the final novel this line was altered to imply that citizens were simply helpless to do so: 'Fascists on the streets, but we had no weapons' (Neutsch, 1973, p. 106).

Yet in other works it was not made clear that citizens and workers of the GDR stood with the Party against the 'fascists'. In Erik Neutsch's depiction of the uprising in the later novel *Der Friede im Osten. Zweites Buch: Frühling mit Gewalt* the narrator heavily criticises citizens of the GDR for not supporting the Party:

> Disappointment with the German working class was disparately bigger. They did nothing. They didn't defend themselves. They stuck their hands in their pockets and watched as the FDJ offices were set alight... THEY DID NOTHING – 1525, 1848, 1933... The German working class leaves me so cold.
>
> (1978, p. 365–6)

And In *Das Impressum* Hermann Kant writes of the crowds: 'the worst thing about their faces was that not all of them were those of the enemy' (1972, p. 144). Kant later depicts a crowd of workers calling for an SED minister (modelled on Fritz Selbmann and named Fritz Andermann) to be lynched (1972, p. 277).

These apparent anomalies in the censorship process were due to the fact that individual authors were subjected to varying levels of censorship. This is exemplified in the cases of Erik Neutsch's *Auf der Suche nach Gatt* (1973) and Hermann Kant's *Das Impressum* (1972). Neutsch's depiction of the events of 17 June 1953 adhered fairly closely to the Party's official account. On the morning of the uprising in *Auf der Suche nach Gatt*, Gatt arrives in Mansfeld to find the tram network has ground to a halt. Outside the FDJ headquarters he sees a group of men armed with knuckledusters ransacking the building and burning its contents. Gatt runs through the streets gathering together fellow SED members to form opposition to the 'hooligans'. Suddenly, a car races through the crowd. It is driven by former concentration camp guards who have escaped from prison. Behind the car they are dragging the bloodied corpse of a policeman. Upon seeing this, Gatt is filled with rage and jumps onto the running board of the car. The scene ends with Gatt being shot and left for dead in the street, mumbling 'My life is over... but the Revolution has been saved'. Gatt survives and we later learn that the Soviets had some hand in calming the unrest, though this is not detailed

(Neutsch, 1973, pp. 95–101). The depiction of the unrest in Kant's *Das Impressum* is much more ambiguous. The narrator David is in Berlin on 17 June 1953. He sees groups of men dressed as workers attacking a man wearing a 'Victim of Fascism' badge (the 'Victims of Fascism' were East German citizens officially recognised as having suffered under the Third Reich and were entitled to certain financial and medical benefits.). But David notes of the attackers that 'the worst thing about their faces, was that they were not all those of the enemy' (Kant, 1972, pp. 143–4). Later in the novel, David finds a photograph taken by his wife of the demonstrations in Berlin. It shows workers forcing SED minister Fritz Andermann against a wall. David recalls that the workers were shouting for Andermann to be hanged. He describes the crowd of workers as 'a mix of carpenters' ribs, foremen's elbows, hod carriers' muscles, shoulders from building sites'. But he comments, 'the more they shouted, the less they understood what had happened to them and what they had let happen'. Kant does not make clear how the events were resolved, though he does mention the street being torn up by tracked vehicles (1972, pp. 277–80).

Neutsch's and Kant's manuscripts were reviewed in the late 1960s and thus ought to have been subjected to the same level of assessment according to cultural policy. Initially, it appears that this was the case. In 1969 the Ministry of Culture censor returned Neutsch's manuscript to his publishers and advised in relation to the scenes of 17 June 1953 that 'differentiation between the <u>duped</u> [underlined in original] masses and the <u>consciously acting</u> [underlined in original] fascist groups ought to be strengthened'.[6] In the same year the Ministry censor was similarly critical of Hermann Kant's depiction of the uprising in the manuscript of *Das Impressum*:

> There are...places where one asks the question: what prompts the author to write meekly on decisive questions. For example, in the description of 17 June, where his keen attention to detail is lacking in his depiction of the KgU [Die Kampfgruppe gegen Unmenschlichkeit – an anti-communist group based in West Berlin.] and the mob steered by its puppet masters.[7]

Both Neutsch and Kant refused to make the suggested amendments. Neutsch's publishers submitted the manuscript of *Auf der Suche nach Gatt* again in 1973 (perhaps hoping that Honecker's announcement of 'no taboos' might help its cause). But the censor noted that the changes suggested in 1969 had not been made because, as the publishers remarked, there had already been more than half a dozen rewrites since 1965 and Neutsch was now working on other things.[8] Hermann Kant made some alterations to his manuscript, but upon receipt of the amended text, Ministry officials complained that 'the changes do not signify a completely satisfying solution'. Moreover, Kant had not made any alterations to his depiction of 17 June 1953.[9] Yet Ministry officials reacted differently to each author's refusal. In the case of Neutsch's text, the Ministry of Culture censors took it upon themselves to make the desired 'Deletions, adjustments and insertions' to the text, including the scenes of the 1953 uprising. The novel was then granted publication permission in 1973.[10] However, officials did not amend Kant's text at all. Despite the fact that in the final assessment, Ministry officials complained that 'the author did not take on board our suggestions to make his presentation of the enemy, its role and physiognomy on 17 June 1953 clearer', the manuscript was granted permission for publication.[11]

Sylvia Klötzer and Siegfried Lokatis have concluded that the degree of control to which artistic works were subjected in the GDR often depended upon the artist's prestige and political influence (1999, p. 255). There is certainly compelling evidence to suggest that the difference in prestige and influence between Hermann Kant and Erik Neutsch played some role here. In 1969 Kant was vice president of the GDR's Academy of the Arts. His first novel *Die Aula* (1965) had sold over one million copies in the GDR and the FRG (Anon, 2011). Thus he was a hugely popular author. Kant also apparently had political connections. In response to the recommendations regarding his manuscript, Kant threatened to complain directly to Walter Ulbricht and Erich Honecker.[12] The fact that the Ministry of Culture officials apparently perceived this as a threat that ought to be taken seriously hints at the extent of Kant's political influence. Furthermore, Kant also worked as an informer for the *Stasi* from 1963 to 1976 (Müller-Enbergs, Wielgohs and Hoffmann, n.d.). Erik Neutsch was a successful author in the GDR in his own right, but could not compete with Kant's sales figures or international recognition. And although a member of the SED district leadership in Halle, Neutsch's political influence did not stretch as far as Kant's (Müller-Enbergs, Wielgohs and Hoffmann, n.d.). However, prestige, political influence and ideological failings in his depiction of 17 June 1953 do not completely explain why Neutsch had to wait so long for *Auf der Suche nach Gatt* to be published. In fact, in 1969 Fritz Selbmann judged Neutsch's depiction of the uprising to be 'outstanding'. However, Bruno Haid, head of the *Hauptverwaltung Verlage und Buchhandel* in 1969, had taken a personal disliking to Neutsch and consequently questioned the author's 'political development'. For this reason, he refused to grant permission to publish *Auf der Suche nach Gatt* until all suggested amendments had been made (Barck et al., 1997, pp. 241–2).

3.3 Contemporary reaction

How did ordinary East German citizens react to the works discussed here? Over the period of the GDR's existence the FDGB literature and arts prize committee received at least 370 letters from workplace libraries and workers' reading groups discussing the merits of 19 novels featuring portrayals of 17 June 1953 and the television drama *Auf der Suche nach Gatt*. Only 57 of the letter writers directly mention the scenes of 17 June 1953 in the piece they discuss. This is hardly surprising, as scenes of the unrest constitute only a small episode in most of the works.

All of the letter writers who addressed the depictions of the uprising are overwhelmingly positive about such scenes in the work that they are nominating. Given that these letters were sent through official channels, this suggests that citizens were aware of how they were supposed to talk about the events in an official public setting. Perhaps these workers were convinced by the official account of the unrest. But few would have dared to pen anything that could be interpreted as critical of these portrayals of the events as a 'fascist-counterrevolutionary putsch'. In 1956 a reader commented that *Die Versuchung* (1956) had 'written so convincingly about 17 June 1953'.[13] Another wrote: 'The book describes the true background to the riots of June 1953. Capitalist agents will always try to disturb peaceful progress, not only in our GDR, but also in all of the people's democracies, as it happened in Hungary.'[14] Twenty years later a reader praised highly the level of historical realism in *Der Friede im Osten* (1978):

> these years, marked by bitter and unrepeatable revolutionary struggle (for example 17 June), acquire, for the reader of today young and old, the character of a vivid book about contemporary history.[15]

Other letter writers claimed that the depictions confirmed their own experiences. In 1958 one worker stated after reading *Am Morgen ist der Tag ein Kind* (1957):

> What is decisive, is that we experienced something similar in the factories on 17.6.53, that is, that workers – even those who were

fickle – recognised in the face of the criminal activities the puppet masters and supporters of 17.6.53 and made up their minds for their own interests, for their own state.[16]

Novels continued to provoke a similar reaction decades later. Referring to *Der Friede im Osten* (1978) one worker commented in 1979: 'Reading this one can confirm again and again, "Yes, it was like that." '[17] In 1982 a reader of *Der Mann aus der Siedlung* (1981) stated that 'not many people understood back then, that the attacks would lead to the destruction of everything we had made sacrifices for'.[18] In the same year a reader of the same novel wrote, 'I was working in the mines in Calbe at the time and experienced something similar'.[19]

A considerable number of those who wrote letters considered these portrayals of 17 June 1953 important enough for them to recommend that they be accessed by more people in the GDR, particularly younger generations. Letters from the 1950s recommend the portrayal of the unrest in *Die Versuchung* (1956): 'The book must be read by as many young people as possible, so that they can learn about the treachery with which unscrupulous agents work to win new victims for their criminal ends.'[20] Letter writers in the 1970s and 1980s also insisted, 'this book [*Gewalt und Zärtlichkeit*] is to be recommended to our young people'[21]; 'the content [of *Der Friede im Osten*] is particularly important for younger generations... for example, the depiction of 17 June 1953'[22]; '[the] presentation [of 17 June 1953 in *Auf der Suche nach Gatt*] has historical worth for everyone, but more so for those born later'.[23]

In only one letter is there evidence that some workers rejected the portrayal of the uprising as an attempted putsch instigated by the West. In 1957 a nomination letter stated with regard to *Die Versuchung* (1956): 'one colleague condemned the book but did not want to commit his thoughts to paper... We will do everything to convince him of his false point of view.'[24] This novel deals exclusively with the uprising and depicts the unrest attempted putsch, led by a fictional Western spy agency which trains 'fascists' for the 'invasion' on 17 June 1953 with the help of the US Army. The fact that this one worker 'did not want to commit his thoughts to paper' suggests that East German citizens knew that there was an acceptable and an unacceptable way of talking about the uprising in public.

Despite the fact that citizens may not have written what they actually thought in these letters for fear of censure, reluctance on their part to use the official terminology of the SED's account suggests that they did actually reject the Party's version of events. The official classification of the uprising as an 'attempted fascist-counterrevolutionary putsch' appears in only two of the 57 letters that address scenes of the unrest. These letters date from 1957 and 1958. 'Day X' ('Tag X'), as the SED often referred to 17 June 1953, is cited twice in letters also from 1958. And just seven use 'counterrevolution' in relation to the events. Six of these date from 1975 to 1983, but one dates from 1958. Many letter writers prefer simply to use the date '17.6.53' when referring to the events. Others favour the euphemistic term 'events' (*Ereignisse*), while several completely avoid mentioning the events, only referring to the 'past' or the 'difficult early years of the Republic'.

Significantly, some letter writers stated that they were happy that the works that they were evaluating were breaking the 'literary taboo of 17 June 1953'. Given that none of these works contradicted the official account of the events, the taboo that these works were apparently breaking was not the taboo of the events as a 'people's uprising'. These workers perceived that any mention of the uprising (even one that adhered to the Party's official account) was taboo in the literature of the GDR. In 1975 a worker praised *Gewalt und Zärtlichkeit* (1974) because it included '17 June 1953 for the first time in our literature'.[25] The uprising had in fact appeared in a large number of novels before 1975. This misapprehension could be attributed to the ignorance of the letter writer. But other workers expressed similar thoughts. In 1979 a letter writer stated regarding *Der Friede im Osten* (1978):

> The book covers the problems of the 1950s. Particularly the events of 17 June 1953 are very openly addressed. A subject, that for years has remained a literary taboo, is addressed here. The events are evaluated truthfully and very critically.[26]

Other letter writers implied that the entire matter of the uprising, including the official narrative thereof, was a taboo in GDR society in general. This was despite the availability of these literary and cinematic works and of the SED's account of the events in newspapers, history books, propaganda and school textbooks. Their perception of the uprising as taboo apparently stemmed from their perception of the official account as too brief and from their doubts about its credibility. One letter writer praised *Gewalt und Zärtlichkeit* (1974) because it included 'Truths...that formerly were preferably hushed up or only alluded to (17 June, Stalin, KVP)'.[27] Another letter in 1979 more explicitly claimed the same when it referred to the depiction of 1953 in *Der Friede im Osten* (1978): 'the older colleagues of the council...expressed the desire for such problems to be addressed more often and honestly, not just in literature, but also in other areas of life'.[28] The fact that these workers commented that the uprising had only been 'preferably hushed up or alluded to' and had not been addressed often enough indicates that they felt the official account of the events did not deal with the unrest adequately enough. Moreover, the call for such matters to be dealt with 'more honestly' suggests that these workers did not completely believe the Party's version of the uprising. Perhaps it clashed with their experiences of the day. Ultimately, workers' disappointment with the official version in terms of its detail and of its credibility led them to believe that the subject was officially taboo in the GDR.

3.4 Interviewees

When asked whether they had ever read a novel or seen a film in the GDR featuring scenes of 17 June 1953, only one interviewee stated that he could remember doing so. Horst Thiel (born 1958) recalled that the uprising featured in *Gewalt und Zärtlichkeit* (1974). When prompted with a list of the works, Herr Thiel also remembered reading *Der Friede im Osten* (1978), *Beschreibung eines Sommers* (1961), *Der fremde Freund* (1982), *Das Impressum* (1971), *Die Kastanie* (1972), *Der Harmonikaspieler* (*The Harmonica Player*, 1981), *Die Söhne der Wölfe* (1966) and having watched *Schlösser und Katen* (1958). Eight other interviewees also realised that they had accessed some of the material when prompted with a list of the novels and films. Wolfgang Scholl (born 1933) had read Brigitte Reimann's *Das Geständnis* (*The Confession*, 1969). Erwin Strempel (born 1932) had watched the television production of *Auf der Suche nach Gatt* (1973) and had also read *Das Impressum* (1971). Theodor Puff born (1949) had read *Auf der Suche nach Gatt* (1973) and also thought he had read *Der Friede im Osten* (1978). Alexandra Brendel (born 1950) was surprised to find that the items on the list that she had accessed featured scenes of the uprising. She had read *Das Impressum* (1971), *Auf der Suche nach Gatt* (1973), *Der Harmonikaspieler* (1981), *Das Vertrauen* (1968), *Am Morgen ist der Tag ein Kind* (1957) and had also seen *Schlösser und Katen* (1958). Doris Ritter (born 1956) remembered reading *Gewalt und Zärtlichkeit* (1974); Brigitte Schneider (born 1956) had read *Der fremde Freund* (1982); Christel Schlachter (1957) thought she had read *Auf der Suche nach Gatt* (1973); and Katrin Heidinger (born 1957) remembered reading *Gewalt und Zärtlichkeit* (1974) and *Tod am Meer* (1977).

Several interviewees explained that they had read none of the novels on the list because of their aversion to East German authors. Franz Immig (born 1941) stated:

> I rejected books by Eastern authors, because I knew that what was written wasn't true. I didn't want to read that at all. I have nothing against Erik Neutsch, but I know that what he writes must be nonsense. It can only be nonsense if it was published in the GDR.

Peter Momber (born 1938) said something similar: 'I have to say that what came out in the East was so subjective, you just condemned it immediately, without bothering to look into it further.' Neither Herr Immig nor Herr Momber claimed to have supported the SED or its policies. They regarded themselves as opponents of the Party, even though they never expressed this opposition verbally or tangibly. This attitude toward the SED regime led them to reject novels and films produced, as they saw it, by this regime.

The majority of interviewees (including those who later found that they had actually accessed one of these works) were initially convinced that the SED would never have permitted scenes of 17 June 1953 to be included in novels or films. They immediately dismissed the notion that such works existed and reacted in a manner that indicated that they felt that to suggest such a thing was naïve. By their own accounts, the subject of 17 June 1953 was a taboo. Erwin Strempel (born 1932) commented that literary and cinematic portrayals of the uprising would have been banned: 'There was no freedom of speech or freedom of opinion in the GDR. The GDR regulated the arts.' Theodor Puff (born 1949) simply stated that there was no such thing and reacted incredulously ('Really?! Novels that were published in the GDR?!'), when prompted with the list. Anika Rosenkranz (born 1963) stated: 'We never read any novels about it...And there weren't any. There was nothing at all like that here, literature like that.' When prompted with the list, Albert Keck (born 1959) had expected to see only West German publishers. He was surprised to see that all of the pieces were East German in origin. And before seeing the list of works, Katrin Heidinger (born 1957) had exclaimed that 'such books would never have been allowed'. These interviewees could simply have been misremembering. However, their responses echoed in retrospect the FDGB letter writers who had perceived that 17 June 1953 was a taboo in the GDR.

Werner Otto (born 1942) and Christina Heinemann (born 1953) also echoed a number of FDGB letter writers when they stated that they would have liked to have been able to learn more about 17 June 1953 during the GDR period. These interviewees and several FDGB letter perceived that the information about the uprising available to them in the GDR was inadequate. Upon seeing the list of novels and films featuring scenes of the uprising that had been available in the GDR, Herr Otto was shocked. He stated that he would have liked to have been able to read more about the unrest and commented: 'They would have interested me very much.' Frau Heinemann claimed that she simply did not know that she had had the opportunity to read about 17 June 1953 in the literature of the GDR and commented: 'I definitely would have read them.'

Horst Thiel (born 1958) was the only interviewee who stated that the subject of 17 June 1953 was not a taboo in the GDR. He had accessed nine of the works featuring scenes of the uprising and was the only interviewee who could remember having done so. When this fact was commented to him, he stated: 'The scenes of the uprising certainly entered somewhere into my subconscious. But, because it wasn't a taboo, it didn't strike me as anything much at all.' Herr Thiel's response suggests that the fact that interviewees could not recall having read or seen anything about 17 June 1953 might not have been a case of their forgetting. It implies that they did not remember because reading about the unrest was actually nothing out of the ordinary in the GDR. However, Herr Thiel worked as a school history teacher in the GDR who annually taught about the events of 1953. Thus reading and talking about the uprising was nothing unusual for him. However, this was apparently not the case for the FDGB letter writers and the majority of interviewees who did not encounter the subject as regularly as Herr Thiel did and therefore concluded that it was a taboo subject in the GDR.

3.5 Conclusion

With its guidelines on censorship and the long process of assessment through which novels and films had to pass before being granted public release, the SED planned that only works which adhered to official narratives and policy would be made available to its citizens. However, in the case of these portrayals of 17 June 1953, a gap did develop between official policy and what happened on the ground. Extra details, some of which presented certain aspects of the events rather ambiguously, slipped through the net. That this was the case was apparently not due to carelessness on the part of individual censors. In some cases, it mattered little whether an artist was prepared to jump through all of the correct political hoops or not when depicting the uprising of 17 June

1953 in their work. Whether a work was granted permission for release depended not only upon ideological soundness but also upon the artist's standing in GDR society, political influence and even whether the censor personally liked the author or not. Thus the system of censorship in the GDR was governed less by ideology and more by the whim of the Party and/or the censor (Barck et al., 1997, pp. 241–2).

Examination of these portrayals does not support David Bathrick's claim that artists were permitted to present a more pluralist public discourse. Although, as Bathrick claims, the artists here did indeed expand on the content of official communication, all of them did ultimately portray the events as an attempted fascist putsch instigated by the West. For Bernd Eisenfeld, Ilko-Sascha Kowalczuk and Ehrhart Neubert, this fact renders any deviations insignificant (2004, pp. 589–620). Any real attempts to open a pluralist public discourse about 17 June 1953 in GDR film, and literature were simply not granted permission to be released. The best-known attempt to do so is Stefan Heym's 5 *Tage im Juni* (*5 Days in June*, 1974), which was repeatedly denied publication permission over a period of 30 years. Though Heym depicted Western involvement in the uprising, this did little to appease censors and Party officials unhappy with his portrayal of striking workers. Heym's portrayal of Western involvement in the uprising could not mitigate for censors or Party officials his depiction of unhappy workers striking, a regime unwilling to change and learn from its mistakes and the quelling of the unrest by Soviet troops. Heym simply went too far against the grain of the official account, and no amount of political petitioning or prestige could alter the view of the regime that the novel could not be released to the general public. Published in the West in 1974 (to the intense displeasure of the Party), the novel was finally granted permission for publication in the GDR in 1989 after the SED regime had all but collapsed (Hutchinson, 1992, p. 93; see also Krämer, 1999).

Significantly, the Party did, however, apparently remain in control of citizens' public contributions to this 'public discourse' about the uprising. Analysis of citizens' reaction to these portrayals of the uprising of 17 June 1953 shows that there was (and still is) a discrepancy between what information about the uprising was officially available and what citizens believed to be officially available. Citizens praised works for breaking what they perceived as the official taboo of the entire subject in GDR society, not just a taboo of details that the Party might have found undesirable. Yet the subject (at least in the Party's terms) was not officially taboo – the SED's account of the uprising was available, as were a large number of historical fiction depictions of 17 June 1953. Citizens' statements about this perceived taboo are often followed by comments about the inadequacy or credibility of the official account. They were unhappy with the vagueness and brevity of the official account, as well as a perceived unavailability of sources of information about the uprising. This led them to believe in a taboo of the subject in the GDR. The fact that their perception of the taboo stemmed from their dissatisfaction with the Party's account supports Melani Schröter's conclusion that people perceive an enforced silence from above when their expectations of what will be officially said about a subject are disappointed (Schröter, 2008, p. 117).

4
Watching the West

While the SED kept a tight rein on the content of its official account of 17 June 1953, it could not control the West's evaluation of the uprising. West German media and politicians quickly seized on the uprising as a positive event amongst many negative ones in recent German history, as well as an invaluable weapon in the propaganda war with the SED. On 23 June 1953 West German Chancellor Konrad Adenauer declared in West Berlin that he regarded the unrest as a plea from the citizens of the GDR to the Federal Republic not to forget them. The executive committee of the opposition SPD also stated that the 'demonstrations for freedom' in the GDR had shown that German unity in freedom was the most pressing concern for all Germans (Eisenfeld et al., 2004, pp. 384–5). The preamble of the law that accompanied the declaration on 4 August 1953 of 17 June as a national holiday in West Germany stated that 'on 17 June 1953 the German people in the Soviet Occupation Zone [GDR] rose up against communist tyranny... in an expression of their desire for freedom. Therefore, 17 June has become a symbol of German unity in freedom' (Brockmann, 2006, p. 253). The 'Day of Germany Unity' was observed as a national holiday on each 17 June up until and including 1990.

The SED would not have perceived the Western claims about a 'people's uprising' and West Germany's annual commemoration of the events as a major problem had it been able to control the extent to which East German citizens were exposed to them. However, the majority of citizens could access this West German 'external collective memory' (Niethammer, 2008, p. 49) of the uprising via West German television and radio programmes aired to commemorate the anniversary of the uprising each year. In fact, from the year of its founding in 1954, the Advisory Board of Indivisible Germany (*Kuratorium unteilbares Deutschland*, KUD) petitioned television and radio directors and producers to promote and publicise the commemorations. The KUD was a cross-party organisation committed to keeping hopes of German reunification (on Western terms) alive. It aimed to mobilise West German citizens and prevent stagnation of the concept of reunification amongst them (Wolfrum, 1999, pp. 115–6). The SED's attempts to block its citizens' access to the West German broadcast media, including ordering all aerials pointing westwards to be torn down in 1961, ultimately failed. The regime simply had to accept that its citizens watched Western television and listened to Western radio, however ideologically undesirable this might have been (Holzweißig, 2002, pp. 53–4). The West German broadcast media annually aired coverage of speeches and tributes made in the *Bundestag*, as well as vigils and demonstrations across West Germany on the occasion of the *Tag der deutschen Einheit*. Documentaries often also featured prominently in the television and radio schedules with many including interviews with eyewitnesses and invariably presenting the unrest in the GDR as an uprising against the SED regime.

The West German media broadcasts on or around the anniversaries of 17 June 1953 provided East German citizens with the opportunity to learn more about the uprising than they could do from official sources in their country. In fact, interviewees claimed that accessing these programmes enriched their knowledge of the uprising and many maintained that they learned much of what they knew about the June uprising from these programmes. The programmes also created the possibility that citizens would be annually prompted to recall the uprising or informed of the fact that it had occurred. Interviewees confirmed this with their recollections that the programmes had prompted discussion of the events with fellow citizens during the GDR period. However, the number of programme hours dedicated to such broadcasts decreased from highs in the 1950s and 1960s to much lower numbers in the 1970s and 1980s. Thus in the latter two decades of the GDR's existence the West German broadcast media presented citizens with fewer opportunities to watch or listen to programmes about the uprising. Yet the possibility that they would be prompted to recall the uprising or learn of its occurrence still existed in the 1970s and 1980s in the form of news reports on the commemorations of and occasional review programmes about the 'Day of German Unity'. And although fewer programmes were broadcast in the 1970s and 1980s, interviewees born after 1953 were no less aware of these broadcasts than those who had been able to access a larger quantity of similar programmes in the 1950s and 1960s.

4.1 Peak in coverage, 1954–1967

The large number of broadcast hours dedicated by the West German media to programmes about 17 June 1953 per anniversary in the 1950s means that there was a good probability of East German citizens listening to or watching at least one of these programmes, intentionally or by chance, in this decade. In these years 77 per cent of GDR households owned a radio (Staatliche Zentralverwaltung für Statistik, 1989, p. 291), giving them access to approximately seven and a half hours of West German radio programmes commemorating the uprising on each anniversary. One per cent of households owned a television set in the mid-1950s (Staatliche Zentralverwaltung für Statistik, 1989, p. 291) and an average of approximately one hour of relevant television programmes was aired.

On the first anniversary of the events documentaries aired tended simply to recount the events of one year previous. These included SFB's television production *Der 17. Juni 1953* (*17 June 1953*) and the radio programmes *Vor einem Jahr* (*One Year Ago*) on RIAS and *Berlin – 17. Juni 1953* (*Berlin – 17 June 1953*) on NWDR. The latter was based on a book by Curt Riess, which claimed to be 'the history of an incomplete revolution' and consisted exclusively of eyewitness reports (Riess, 1954). Furthermore, SFB's radio programme *Aufstand der Arbeiter* (*Uprising of the Workers*) simply rebroadcast the station's news bulletins from 17 June 1953 (*Hörzu 24, 1954*, pp. 27–39).

Over the next few years, documentaries included not only the Western account of the uprising but also analysis of its nature and consequences. These documentaries presented East German citizens with accounts of the uprising that were richer in detail about the causes, course, termination and consequences of the uprising than official sources in the GDR. They also directly contradicted the SED's official account. Such programmes portrayed the events as a 'people's uprising' with mainly political, but also social and economic goals (Kowalczuk, 2003, p. 271). For example, on 17 June 1957 NDR/WDR broadcast the television programme *Das grosse Elend der Diktatur. Der 17. Juni und seine Folgen* (*The Great Misery of the Dictatorship. 17 June and its consequences*), presented by journalist Klaus Harpprecht (*Hörzu 25, 1957*, pp. 48–9). The programme was based on a study of 17 June 1953 that Harpprecht had published under the pseudonym 'Stefan Brant' in 1954 (Brant, 1954). Harpprecht portrayed the uprising as a GDR-wide 'people's uprising' with political causes and goals. He traced these causes back to the political measures taken by the SED in 1952 and claimed that these had led to a worsening of living conditions and an intensification of political repression in the GDR. Harpprecht cited these two factors as the main causes of the uprising. He identified 'freedom' and German unity as the main aims of the demonstrators and emphasised that the protagonists of the uprising consisted of citizens from all levels of society. For him there was no 'fascist' element; protesters had simply wanted to live in a 'free' and united Germany (Eisenfeld et al., 2004, pp. 452–4).

In the 1950s, the West German broadcast media also aired extensive coverage of the political commemorations taking place in West Germany. The number of broadcast hours devoted to covering such commemorations was considerably more than the number dedicated to documentaries. Thus citizens in the GDR were presented with far more political evaluations and interpretations of 17 June 1953 than actual information about the uprising itself. On 17 June 1954 RIAS broadcast coverage of a rally taking place in West Berlin (*Hörzu 24, 1954*, pp. 27–39). This was staged on Rudolf-Wilde-Platz (later John-F.-Kennedy-Platz) in front of the West Berlin House of Representatives in Schöneberg, West Berlin, and became an annual event. This rally was by far the best-attended public event commemorating 17 June, with an average of between 80,000 and 100,000 people in attendance annually between 1954 and 1968 (Wolfrum, 1999, p. 158). West German politicians and political thinkers spoke at these rallies, giving their thoughts on the matter of 17 June 1953 and the divided Germany. This rally was broadcast in each following year of the decade.

In 1955 West German radio broadcast for the first time the official ceremony (*Feierstunde*) in the West German parliament in commemoration of the uprising (*Hörzu* 24, 1955, pp. 46–54). This was also broadcast on each remaining anniversary of the decade, sometimes on radio or television, or both. At this event speakers from political parties represented in the West German parliament communicated their views on the events of 17 June 1953, their consequences for the two Germanys and the prospect of German unity. For example, in 1955 Jakob Kaiser, Federal Minister for Joint-German Affairs, declared 17 June 1953 a symbol for the Germans' desire for unity. In 1956 President of the *Bundestag* Gerstenmaier spoke of his hope that reunification would soon be realised. However, from 1958 speakers tended not to address the possibility of reunification as German division persisted and the prospect of a united Germany became less and less likely. Instead, speakers praised the fortitude of the West German political course and called for the population to have patience (Eisenfeld et al., 2004, pp. 390–2). In addition to this *Feierstunde*, the laying of a wreath in the presence of the mayor of West Berlin at the memorial to those West Berliners killed on 17 June 1953 was also often aired (*Hörzu* 25, 1956, pp. 35–9). This took place in the cemetery on Seestraße in Berlin-Wedding. In 1958 and 1959 ARD's televised evening news bulletin *Die Tagesschau* also reported on the speeches in the West German parliament, as well as the rally in West Berlin, at which 80,000 people were apparently present (*Die Tagesschau* 1079, 1958; *Hörzu* 24, 1959, pp. 60–73). In the 1950s, *Die Tagesschau* was only aired three days a week, and before 1958 none of these broadcasts had been on a day close enough to the anniversary of the uprising to report on the commemorations taking place in West Germany.

In comparison to the 1950s, more East German citizens had access to more West German media broadcasts commemorating the uprising of 17 June 1953 on its anniversaries in the 1960s. In 1960 16 per cent of GDR households owned a television set. This figure increased steadily to over 60 per cent by the end of the decade (Staatliche Zentralverwaltung für Statistik, 1989, p. 291). From 1960 to 1969 there was now an average of approximately two hours of television programmes per year that commemorated the uprising. In this decade 90 per cent of GDR households (Staatliche Zentralverwaltung für Statistik, 1989, p. 291) were able to access an average of approximately seven and a half hours of relevant radio programmes aired on each anniversary of the uprising.

However, in the first few years of the decade no documentaries about the uprising were aired on either television or radio, suggesting that West German broadcasters' enthusiasm for commemorating the events every year was waning. Only on the tenth anniversary of the events in 1963 did relevant documentaries appear again. Yet the content of these documentaries and their analyses of the uprising presented contradictory evaluations of what happened on 17 June 1953 in the GDR. These documentaries were broadcast as part of extensive commemorations consisting of over 16 hours of radio programmes and two and a half hours of television programmes. Matthias Walden's highly politicised SFB television production *Der Aufstand vor zehn Jahren* (*The Uprising Ten Years Ago*) portrayed the unrest as an 'anti-totalitarian people's uprising'. In the first section of the programme, Walden recounted his memories of the day. In 1953 he was working as an editor for RIAS. He claimed that the American heads of RIAS instructed their broadcasters to react in a restrained manner in order not to stir further unrest. Walden's commentary in the 1963 programme concentrated on describing the strikes in East Berlin and the resultant demonstrations there. But Walden did make clear that the unrest spread throughout the whole of 'the zone' (*die Zone* – a derogatory term applied to the GDR, indicating non-recognition of it as a state in its own right) where, he claimed that 'despotism' reigned. Pictures of Soviet tanks, wounded citizens, and demonstrators fleeing Soviet troops accompanied the voiceover. Additionally, the documentary presented pictures of the material destruction of 17 June 1953, such as stills of broken propaganda billboards. Walden concluded with three points. First, the uprising demonstrated that the citizens of the GDR wanted 'freedom'. Second, they showed that they had been willing to make sacrifices in pursuit of this. Finally, Walden claimed that the events of 17 June 1953 demonstrated that Soviet imperialism was only as strong as the armour on Soviet tanks (Brockmann, 2006, pp. 215–9).

By contrast, the hour-long documentary *Wie es gewesen ist – der 17. Juni 1953* (*How It Was – 17 June 1953*), written by the historian Arnulf Baring, described the unrest as a localised 'workers' uprising'. In 1957 Baring had published a study of the events that became one of the benchmarks of the West German historical interpretation of 17 June 1953. His conclusions in *Der 17. Juni 1953* (*17 June 1953*) largely defined West German academic interpretation of the uprising until 1989. Baring portrayed the unrest as a 'workers' uprising' and emphasised that East Berlin was the only site of real disorder. Thus he refuted the hitherto common West German claim that 17 June 1953 had constituted a 'people's uprising' that had taken place across the GDR. By concluding that the uprising was a socio-economic conflict whose main cause was the working quotas issue Baring countered the conclusion of previous West German publications that the demonstrators had hoped to achieve political 'freedom' and national unity. Baring emphasised that RIAS had played a major role in triggering the uprising by broadcasting pieces designed to aggravate the situation. He also underplayed the role of the Soviet armed forces, concluding that the uprising had failed before the intervention of Soviet tanks (Eisenfeld et al., 2004, pp. 458–64). Significantly, his evaluation of the events influenced more and more publications and documentary makers in West Germany. From the mid-1960s documentaries tended to reduce the significance of the uprising by evaluating it, following Baring, as a 'workers' uprising' involving only workers in a few big cities. Any political demands that demonstrators might have made were neglected, reducing the causes of the uprising further to purely social and economic dissatisfaction (Kowalczuk, 2003, p. 271).

Coverage of West German political commemorations increased in the 1960s. The *Feierstunde* in Bonn continued to be broadcast. On 17 June 1960 Federal President Heinrich Lübke addressed 12,000 young people on the Hohe Meißner mountain near Eschwege on the inner-German border. He called on the international community to give Germans the right to self-determination and unity. The following year the majority of speeches also addressed the right to self-determination of all Germans. On the first anniversary of the events after the construction of the Berlin Wall in 1961 politicians called on West Germans to recognise the Federal Republic as representative of the German state. The rallies in Schöneberg continued to enjoy annual coverage, too. On 17 June 1966 the mayor of West Berlin (and future Federal Chancellor) Willy Brandt declared that the time had come to stop talking about a united Germany and to start acting without illusions within the bounds of what was possible (Eisenfeld et al., 2004, pp. 393–9). In addition to these events in Schöneberg, further rallies were broadcast. On 17 June 1960 RIAS aired three hours of live coverage of a rally organised by the KUD at the inner-German border (*Hörzu* 24, 1960, pp. 52–3). In 1962 RIAS also broadcast coverage of another KUD-organised rally, at which Federal President Lübke was in attendance (*Hörzu* 24, 1962, pp. 66–7).

In the 1960s ARD's *Die Tagesschau* continued to report on the West German parliament speeches, rallies and wreath-laying ceremony in Berlin-Wedding. Significantly, its coverage on 17 June 1960 included a film showing scenes of protesting workers and Soviet tanks from 17 June 1953 (*Die Tagesschau* 1684, 1960). The report the following year included details of fires being lit in several locations across the Federal Republic in memory of 17 June 1953 (*Die Tagesschau* 1989, 1961). These 'June fires' (*Junifeuer*) or 'freedom fires' (*Freiheitsfeuer*) were central elements of the commemorations of the uprising until the mid-1960s. The bonfires were normally lit in locations along the inner-German border which made them visible to East German citizens (Wolfrum, 1999, pp. 166–7). However, in 1967 the running order for ARD's *Die Tagesschau* indicated that attitudes in the West German media toward the 'Day of German Unity' were changing. In previous years its reports on the speeches in Bonn, the rally in West Berlin and the wreath-laying in Berlin-Wedding had always been the first items featured in the programme. In 1967 they were items six, seven and eight, respectively. In the final programme a report from the rally in Schöneberg was dropped (*Die Tagesschau* 4112, 1967).

4.2 'Cold War relic', 1968–1982

On the final two anniversaries of the uprising in the 1960s the number of hours of commemorative programmes broadcast decreased sharply.

On 17 June 1968 there was no coverage of the ceremony in the *Bundestag* in Bonn because no such event took place and the annual rally in West Berlin was also cancelled. In 1968 the grand coalition government of the CDU and the SPD had tabled a motion to keep 17 June as a national day of remembrance, but to strip it of its status as a national public holiday. The coalition increasingly perceived the ritual of the 'Day of German Unity' as a Cold War relic and troublesome in light of moves for closer political relations with the GDR. Federal Economics Minister Karl Schiller stated in 1967 that with the commemorations in their current form: 'we won't advance one step further in the "Germany question"'. The motion was unsuccessful, opposed by trade unions and members of the CDU mistrustful of the SPD (Eisenfeld et al., 2004, pp. 402–4). In place of the annual *Bundestag* ceremony in 1968 Federal Chancellor Kurt-Georg Kiesinger chose to make a special address which was broadcast on West German television and radio. ARD's *Die Tagesschau* did not, however, include any kind of report relating to commemorations of 17 June 1953. A feature on the wreath laying in Berlin-Wedding had been planned, but was omitted from the final bulletin (*Die Tagesschau* 4472, 1968). On the decade's last anniversary of the uprising there was again no *Feierstunde* in the West German parliament. Instead, Kiesinger again broadcast a special address (Wolfrum, 2005, p. 420). This featured on *Die Tagesschau* on the same day. The bulletin also reported on the laying of a wreath at the memorial in Berlin-Wedding by mayor of West Berlin Klaus Schütz (*Die Tagesschau* 4831, 1969).

Though, the overall decrease in broadcast hours dedicated to commemorations in 1968 and 1969 can be linked to changing West German political attitudes toward the national holiday, enthusiasm on the part of West German citizens for the commemorations was also dwindling. As early as the late 1950s their participation in the commemorations had fallen, suggesting a reason why broadcasters had also apparently lost enthusiasm for 17 June documentaries in the years directly preceding the tenth anniversary of the uprising in 1963. By the mid-1960s the national holiday for many West German citizens had become a day for relaxation, day trips and free-time activities, not for mourning or reflection on the division of their homeland and the possibility that this would continue indefinitely (Wolfrum, 2005, p. 420). This was made clear in a survey carried out in 1967 which concluded that, though a majority of West Germans wanted to keep 17 June as a public holiday and have a day off work, they also felt that the rallies and ceremonies should be stopped (Eisenfeld et al., 2004, p. 405).

Throughout the 1970s the commemoration of 17 June 1953 continued to be the subject of political debate. The 'Day of German Unity' and its celebration embarrassed the ruling coalition government of the SPD and the Free Democratic Party (FDP), which had come to power in late 1969 and governed until late 1982. In line with his statement made in 1966 as mayor of West Berlin, Federal Chancellor Willy Brandt preferred to focus on what he felt was achievable in German–German relations, instead of on a quest for German unity. The commemorations presented a stumbling block in Brandt's attempts at rapprochement with the GDR, which nevertheless succeeded in 1972 with the two countries officially recognising each other as sovereign states for the first time. The opposition CDU meanwhile vehemently defended the commemorations of the uprising and blocked government attempts to switch the 'Day of German Unity' to 23 May – the day on which the Federal Republic's constitution came into effect in 1949. The conservative media also campaigned in support of 17 June, with the *Bild* tabloid newspaper bemoaning a 'national historical amnesia' and the betrayal of the victims of 17 June 1953 (Wolfrum, 1999, pp. 286–7).

Media coverage of the commemorations and promotion of the 'Day of German Unity' nevertheless continued to decrease in the 1970s. Thus in comparison to the two previous decades, there were considerably fewer opportunities for East German citizens in the 1970s to access (intentionally or by chance) West German radio or television programmes featuring 17 June 1953. This was despite the fact that only a minority now did not have some sort of access to the West German broadcast media. In 1970 almost 70 per cent of households in the GDR owned a television set. This increased to 88 per cent by the end of the decade. Radio set ownership in the GDR also increased in the 1970s to 99 per cent of households by 1980 (Staatliche Zentralverwaltung für Statistik, 1989, p. 291). However, on 17 June 1970, 1972, 1974, 1976, 1977 and 1979 no programmes informing about or commemorating the uprising were broadcast on West German television. On 17 June 1972, 1976 and 1977 no relevant radio programmes aired either. On the anniversaries when relevant television programmes did air, the average number of broadcast hours did not increase from the two hours it had been in the 1960s. But the average number of hours of relevant radio programming decreased from its 1960s average of seven and a half hours per anniversary to approximately two and a half hours per anniversary in the 1970s.

Far fewer documentaries about the uprising were aired in the 1970s. Those that were broadcast, although considerably richer in detail than the SED's own account of the events, again presented viewers with mixed messages about the nature of the uprising. On 31 May 1970 ARD aired the programme *Gedenktag* (*Day of Remembrance*). This docu-drama presented viewers with a portrayal of an organised 'people's uprising' on 17 June 1953 in the GDR. The programme used documentary material, interviews and dramatisations of the events to investigate what had happened in Bitterfeld. Bitterfeld was one of the few places in the GDR on 17 June 1953 where there was an organised attempt at revolution. A democratically elected strike committee directed the uprising in the town and under its leadership citizens successfully took over the main centres of state power in Bitterfeld (Kowalczuk, 2003, pp. 203–5). The programme showed workers forming protests before being joined by other citizens. Viewers were presented with dramatised scenes of citizens storming state buildings, throwing documents out of windows and setting newspaper kiosks alight. Significantly, the documentary portrayed the intervention of Soviet troops as the decisive factor in the termination of the unrest (*Hörzu* 22, 1970, p. 54).

Yet on the 20th anniversary of the events in 1973 another ARD television documentary titled *Ein Mittwoch im Juni. Was geschah am 17. Juni vor 20 Jahren im Osten Berlins?* (*One Wednesday in June. What Happened on 17 June 20 Years Ago in East Berlin?*) contradicted much of what *Gedenktag* had presented about the uprising (*Hörzu* 24, 1973, pp. 54–81). This documentary, authored by the journalist Lutz Lehmann, investigated whether a 'people's uprising', a 'workers' revolt' or a 'secret services putsch' (*Agentenputsch*) had occurred, but did not draw a final conclusion on the nature of the events. Lehmann began by deconstructing the SED's claims about an attempted 'fascist-counterrevolutionary putsch', notably mentioning Erna Dorn. In his analysis of the uprising Lehmann considered its long-term causes in depth. He examined the economic and social problems that followed the SED's decision in 1952 to increase the pace of the construction of socialism in the GDR. He then detailed the progress of the unrest from its early beginnings with workers in East Berlin on 15 June 1953 to its spread to 300 localities throughout the GDR. Lehmann questioned whether the intervention of the Soviet troops that ended the uprising had really been so brutal. Answering this question was Arnulf Baring who stated that the Soviet troops acted to avoid bloodshed. Lehmann concluded that the uprising saved Walter Ulbricht and consolidated his position. In his conclusion Lehmann also criticised FRG policy toward the events of 17 June 1953 and their commemoration. In light of Willy Brandt's recent policies and the resultant measures taken to strengthen West and East German political relations,

Lehmann stated that 17 June 1953 should have been an indicator for the FRG that politics of détente toward the GDR was needed. Instead, Lehmann claimed, the gap between the two Germanys had widened since the uprising took place (Brockmann, 2006, pp. 219–27).

With no *Feierstunde* taking place in the West German parliament and no rally staged in Schöneberg, the West German broadcast media also aired less coverage of political commemorations of the uprising in the 1970s. However, there were occasional reports of rallies and some speeches were still made in Bonn, several of which were broadcast (*Hörzu* 24, 1974, p. 84). On 17 June 1970 Federal Chancellor Willy Brandt's parliamentary address was aired (*Hörzu* 24, 1970, pp. 66–7). He stated that 17 June 1953 had shown that the Germans' wish for the conservation of peace was more important than their wish for national unity (Eisenfeld et al., 2004, p. 407). The following year RIAS aired President of the *Bundestag* Kai-Uwe von Hassel's address on the occasion of the 'Day of German Unity' (*Hörzu* 24, 1971, pp. 74–5). He stated that 17 June was, above all, a day for German democracy and called for the realisation of all Germans' right to self-determination (Eisenfeld et al., 2004, p. 410). On the 25th anniversary of 17 June 1953 in 1978 the West German broadcast media aired over three hours of relevant television programmes and four hours of relevant radio programmes, including coverage of the first official *Feierstunde* in the West German parliament for over a decade.[1]

Despite the low number of programmes broadcast in the 1970s and the years in which no relevant programmes were aired, it was still possible East German citizens might annually be informed about the occurrence of the uprising or might be prompted to recall it. West German radio stations annually broadcast short segments, usually lasting five minutes and variously titled *Kommentar zum 17. Juni* (*Commentary on the 17 June*) or *Thema des Tages – 17 Juni* (*Topic of the day – 17 June*). These were broadcast several times per anniversary and often followed the radio news bulletins. Moreover, ARD's evening television news bulletin *Die Tagesschau* reported annually on commemorations of the events taking place. In 1971 and 1972 it reported on the wreath-laying ceremony in Berlin-Wedding (*Die Tagesschau* 5559, 1971; *Die Tagesschau* 5820, 1972). In 1974 the bulletin featured the KUD's commemorations of the uprising in Bonn and West Berlin. *Die Tagesschau* also reported on a speech addressing 17 June made by the chairman of the CDU/CSU parliamentary group Karl Carstens (*Die Tagesschau* 6655, 1974). The following year *Die Tagesschau* included President of the *Bundestag* Annemarie Renger's speech addressing the 'Day of German

Unity', as well as again reporting on the wreath-laying ceremony in Berlin-Wedding (*Die Tagesschau* 7020, 1975). In 1976 it covered the wreath-laying ceremony in West Berlin, as well as a silent march through Lauenburg on the inner-German border in memory of the uprising (*Die Tagesschau* 7386, 1976). And on the following anniversary ARD's evening news bulletin covered Federal Chancellor Helmut Schmidt's speech in the West German parliament (*Die Tagesschau* 7751, 1977). He stated that relaxation of tensions in Europe required not only relaxation of tensions between the two Germanys but also the realisation of human rights for all Germans (Eisenfeld et al., 2004, pp. 413–4). On 17 June 1978 the show featured the events taking place in commemoration of the 25th anniversary of 17 June 1953 as its first news item *Die Tagesschau* 8116, 1978). However, on the final anniversary of the decade the only reference to 17 June 1953 came in item 14 of *Die Tagesschau*, which was a report on the wreath-laying ceremony in Berlin-Wedding (*Die Tagesschau* 8481, 1979).

Although the number of West German media broadcasts relating to 17 June 1953 decreased significantly in the 1970s, it was in this decade that history teachers in the GDR were directed more and more to debunk the West's claims about a 'people's uprising'. The sources suggest that the SED was now greatly concerned about how the West German account of the events might shape its citizens' perceptions of them. The SED may have felt it was easier to counter the West's narrative when it was no longer being presented so regularly and under such intense political scrutiny in West Germany itself. Teachers were to pose the following question to their pupils: 'What conclusions can be drawn about the fact that the Federal Republic celebrates 17 June as a holiday?' (Autorenkollektiv, 1971, pp. 157–9; Autorenkollektiv, 1974, pp. 158–9). The fact that such concerns apparently grew in a decade when West German broadcast media programmes commemorating 17 June 1953 were few and far between also suggests that the SED was aware of the few programmes that were being broadcast and perceived that citizens were accessing them.

At the turn of the decade there was little change in the positions of the major political parties regarding the commemorations of the 'Day of German Unity'. The governing coalition of the SPD and FDP continued to ponder the suitability of the holiday. SPD politician Jürgen Schmude called in 1982 for 23 May to replace 17 June as a national holiday. In his opinion 'no one would miss the meaningless holiday on 17 June', which he considered to be 'washed out' (Eisenfeld et al., 2004, p. 419). The CDU on the other hand, led by Helmut Kohl, stressed the importance of the national holiday and the 1953 uprising's legacy for current national policy on reunification. On 17 June 1980 Kohl declared in the *Bundestag*: 'Whoever asks about the meaning of 17 June, here is the answer: It was and still is about the right of 17 million people to self-determination... and freedom. That is and remains at the centre of German domestic policy' (Eisenfeld et al., 2004, p. 418). This speech was reported on *Die Tagesschau* on the same day (*Die Tagesschau* 8847, 1980).

4.3 Revival, 1983–1989

In May 1983 Federal Chancellor Helmut Kohl stated that he and his governing CDU party would 'do everything to strive for and complete German unity in peace and freedom' (Eisenfeld et al., 2004, p. 420). With German reunification now central to the political agenda of the West German government, new life was breathed into celebration of the 'Day of German Unity'. Concomitantly, the West German media renewed its interest in broadcasting coverage of the commemorations. In contrast to the 1970s, television programmes commemorating the uprising were now screened on each of its anniversaries, with the exception of 1984. On these anniversaries an average of just under two hours of relevant television programmes were broadcast. At this time 93 per cent of GDR households owned a television set (Staatliche Zentralverwaltung für Statistik, 1989, p. 291). In the same period, radio programmes commemorating 17 June 1953 were broadcast on each anniversary. An average of just over two and a half hours of relevant radio programmes was aired. Ninety-nine per cent of GDR households now owned a radio set (Staatliche Zentralverwaltung für Statistik, 1989, p. 291).

The documentaries aired about 17 June 1953 continued to offer viewers contradictory evaluations of the uprising that were nevertheless richer in detail than and contradicted the SED's own version of the events. To commemorate the 30th anniversary of the uprising in 1983 the West German broadcast media aired relevant programmes in a quantity similar to that seen in the 1960s. The schedules featured two major television documentaries: ZDF's *Der 17. Juni 1953: Arbeiteraufstand in Ost-Berlin und der DDR* (*17 June 1953: Workers' Uprising in East Berlin and the GDR*) and ARD's *Jene Tage im Juni* (*Those Days in June*).

Der 17. Juni 1953: Arbeiteraufstand in Ost-Berlin und der DDR concluded that the events of 17 June 1953 constituted neither a 'people's uprising', nor a revolution. The programme categorised 17 June 1953 as nothing more than a spontaneous strike movement with no organisation. In an interview a man claiming to have been one of the leaders of the strikes asserted that the main aims of the demonstrators were for working quotas to be reduced, free pan-German elections and the release of political prisoners. More participants interviewed stated that hooligans from West Berlin had also been heavily involved. The authors of the documentary claimed that most of the demonstrators, described as 'heroes of freedom' by the West, were simply 'thrill-seeking hooligans'. They further stated that such hooligans were the only ones amongst the demonstrators who perpetrated violence against the state forces. The makers of the documentary attributed the fact that the unrest quickly spread across the GDR, encompassing 270 localities, to the broadcasts of RIAS on the day. Arnulf Baring appeared and repeated his opinion that Soviet troops had acted cautiously (Brockmann, 2006, pp. 227–35).

By contrast, ARD's *Jene Tage im Juni* concluded that what had occurred on 17 June 1953 was a 'people's uprising' whose participants had hoped to achieve freedom and German reunification. The programme detailed the increasing repression and hardship in the lives of citizens of the GDR since the SED's decision to 'construct socialism' in the summer of 1952. It claimed that despite the SED's New Course after Stalin's death, working quotas unrest amongst workers led to the outbreak of a nationwide uprising, helped in no small part by RIAS. The documentary explicitly stated that 272 localities in the GDR were affected by the unrest. Interviews with leaders of the strikes in Bitterfeld, Leuna, Merseburg, Rathenow, Jena, Leipzig, Dresden and Görlitz were included. Contemporary photographs of the demonstrations and the intervention of Soviet tanks accompanied stories of the storming of prisons and Soviet action (Brockmann, 2006, pp. 186–8).

In comparison to the previous decade there were also more broadcasts covering the West German political commemorations of the uprising. In 1984 RIAS and *Deutschlandfunk* offered live coverage of the speeches in the West German parliament. In this year speakers focused on the West German population's support for the national day of remembrance (Eisenfeld et al., 2004, p. 424). On the anniversary of the uprising in 1986 ARD televised the entire *Feierstunde* in the West German parliament for the first time since 1978.[2] And on 17 June 1987, 1988 and 1989 ARD, ZDF, RIAS, SFB and *Deutschlandfunk* broadcast the commemorations in the West German parliament.[3]

ARD's evening news bulletin also continued to cover the political commemorations of the events. Significantly, in 1983 the programme reported on the Green Party's opposition to any sort of commemoration of the day (*Die Tagesschau* 9942, 1983). The Greens felt that the day had for years been celebrated with false pathos (Eisenfeld et al., 2004,

p. 423). Similarly, in 1985 the only item about 17 June 1953 to feature on *Die Tagesschau* reported on the non-participation of the Greens in the commemoration ceremony in the *Bundestag* (*Die Tagesschau* 10673, 1985). The following year the bulletin reported on the speeches made in the West German parliament and also featured the wreath-laying ceremony in Berlin-Wedding for the first time since 1979. And there was once again a report about the fact that 'The Greens describe 17 June as an anachronism' (*Die Tagesschau* 11038, 1986).

The rejection of the national holiday by some parts of the West German political scene was the subject of several discussion programmes aired by the West German broadcast media in the 1980s. On 15 June 1983 the historians Arnulf Baring and Ernst Nolte discussed whether 17 June was 'a reason to celebrate' on SFB's weekly *Mittwochsforum* (*Wednesday Forum*) programme (*Hörzu* 23, 1983, pp. 68–75). In 1985 ARD televised Federal President Richard von Weizsäcker's discussion of the matter with school pupils in West Berlin. In the same year ZDF's weekly *Reportage am Montag* (*Report on Monday*) investigated what West Germans would be doing on the anniversary:

> This holiday is for many, or even for the majority, just a day off work. There will be memorial ceremonies and the laying of wreaths but few will pay them any attention. For years people have complained that so many Germans do not know the origins of this holiday, the workers' uprising in East Berlin and the GDR on 17 June 1953.[4]

It was not just on the West German airwaves that the matter of the commemoration of 17 June 1953 was being discussed in the 1980s. School pupils in history lessons across the GDR were also debating it. This further indicates that the West German broadcast media's commemoration of 17 June 1953 influenced the SED's policy on how it communicated the events of June 1953 to its own citizens (Autorenkollektiv, 1989, pp. 35–7).

4.4 Interviewees

Of the 38 former citizens of the GDR interviewed only Monika Klein (born 1948) claimed that she, as a strict supporter of the Party, had never tuned into West German radio or television programmes during the GDR period. The remaining interviewees stated that they were fully aware that the West German broadcast media aired programmes on the anniversary of the uprising each year that informed about or commemorated the events of 17 June 1953 in the GDR. Manfred Ebert (born 1965) claimed that it was inevitable that people were exposed to something because there was so much broadcast. He felt that this was intentional on the part of West German politicians. Similarly, Albert Keck (born 1959) felt that the West German media broadcasts guaranteed that the uprising 'could not fade into obscurity'. However, none of the interviewees could recall a specific programme that they had listened to or watched.

The majority of interviewees who had experienced the uprising first hand claimed that they did not learn anything about the uprising from the West German broadcast media that they thought they had not already learned from their own experiences. Franz Immig (born 1941) asserted:

> I didn't need to learn anything because that was a part of my life. I knew there had been unrest in Berlin, Dresden, Leipzig, Chemnitz. In Burg, where my grandmother lived, nothing happened. It was only in the big cities. I didn't need to learn that. Word got about.

Yet Herr Immig seemingly contradicted himself immediately after stating the above by saying 'one heard it through propaganda: RIAS, SFB, NWDR'. Other eyewitness interviewees maintained that they were already aware of the main details of the uprising because they had experienced the events first hand, while also citing Western propaganda as a supplementary source of their knowledge. Thus they made a distinction between the Western propaganda to which they were exposed in the immediate aftermath of the events and that which was broadcast in the years that followed.

By contrast, several interviewees born after 1953 stated that they had had no prior knowledge of the uprising before watching or listening to one of the West German broadcasts. Anika Rosenkranz (born 1963) heard about the uprising for the first time from West German television. She had not learned about 17 June 1953 at school. Likewise, Brigitte Schneider (born 1956) stated:

> The Western commemorations of 17 June were broadcast every year. There were reports about it every now and then. I can't remember anything exactly, but I think my entire knowledge about the uprising at the time came from Western television.

Similarly, Manfred Ebert (born 1965) felt that most of what he knew about the uprising came from the West German broadcast media. Before accessing these sources Herr Ebert said he had talked about the uprising with his grandfather, who was an eyewitness to the events, but who had only wanted to discuss it very briefly.

Several interviewees born after the uprising claimed to have learned more about the actual details and specifics of the unrest from the West German broadcast media than from sources in the GDR. This supports the conclusion that the SED's account of the events communicated only the fact of the uprising and no real details about what had happened. Horst Thiel (born 1958) stated that he supplemented what he had learned as a history teacher in the GDR with what was presented on West German television:

> I knew almost all of the facts. Most of it came from Western television. There was always the holiday, the 'Day of German Unity', that was in the news. I knew about that, and it always showed pictures. We permanently watched Western television. And when the 17 June holiday came round, then the information was there, the pictures of the Brandenburg Gate, of Leipziger Straße, where the tanks were.

Werner Prauss (born 1958) claimed that he first learned that the uprising had affected cities other than Berlin through the television programmes broadcast in the 1980s. And Albert Keck (born 1959) said that after watching the West German broadcasts: 'I learned that the scale of the uprising was much larger than what we had been told in school.' Dorothea Freichel (born 1953) had also learned about the SED's official account at school but said that what was taught was very superficial. She asserted that she learned more from West German television:

> It came from the reports in the Western media. I more or less knew the Western version of what had happened – that the workers here had fought against the norms, against dissatisfaction. The large protest came from the construction workers in Berlin. They had to do more work for less money. There were also a lot of shortages. That's what I knew from the Western media.

Furthermore, Frau Freichel stated that she learned about the actual scale of the events and about the unrest in Magdeburg from the West German programmes.

Karl Schirra (born 1958) suggested that some East German citizens accessed the West German broadcast media programmes expressly to learn more about what had happened in the GDR in June 1953. He had done so because he was not satisfied with what he had learned about 17 June 1953 from his school history lessons. He recalled that the topic had been covered, but that little time had been spent on it before the teacher moved onto the next subject. Herr Schirra remembered watching documentaries about 17 June 1953 on West German television because: 'I wanted to see how they presented it and I was curious about such things, just because it was officially a taboo here.' Thus, as several letter writers to the FDGB implied, so the perceived dearth of information about the uprising of 17 June 1953 available from official sources in the GDR led Herr Schirra to perceive that the subject was a taboo.

There was a marked difference in interviewees' perceptions of the veracity of what they heard about 17 June 1953 from the West German media. No interviewees born after 1953, even those who had been supporters of the SED, claimed to have questioned what they saw or heard about the uprising from the West German media. In fact, learning about the West German account of the unrest actually led them to question the SED's version of events, indicating that the Party's official account was not convincing enough for them. When asked whether he had believed what he learned at school about 17 June 1953, Albert Keck (born 1959) responded:

> At first, yes, at first, yes. And later when I was older and I heard all about it on Western television every year again and again... Then I said, it must have happened differently, because they are saying one thing and they are saying another. So something in the history that they [the SED] told us mustn't have been right.

Dorothea Freichel (born 1953) experienced something similar. When asked to recount what she had heard about the SED's official account of the uprising, she stated that, upon seeing the West German television programmes about 17 June 1953, she thought about the account she had heard at school and realised: 'No, it can't have been like that.'

By contrast, the first reaction of several interviewees who had witnessed the unrest first hand to questions about the West German broadcasts was to condemn them as weapons in the propaganda war between the two Germanys. They declared that this had influenced their decisions on whether to watch the programmes or not, as well as whether to believe everything that was asserted about the uprising in these broadcasts. Former policeman and member of the SED Heinz Kurtsiefer (born 1945) stated: 'Basically, I learned that both sides used the uprising for political aims. That's what I concluded from it. The

West turned it into a big people's uprising.' Yet it was not exclusively eyewitnesses close to the regime who claimed to have held such opinions of the West German broadcasts. Peter Momber (born 1938) was not a member of the SED, nor, so he claimed, did he support its policies. But he explained that he had also been critical of the West German programmes: 'We didn't believe everything that the West broadcast. We said, "no, that's not true". It was of course propaganda, too. Objectivity fell by the wayside.' Similarly, Wolfgang Scholl (born 1933) and Heinrich Schmidt (1926) were neither members of the SED, nor, so they claimed, supporters of the regime. Both recalled having regularly watched West German television, but refused to watch the programmes about 17 June 1953 because they regarded them as propaganda. Herr Scholl held a view similar to that of Herr Kurtsiefer. He was of the opinion that West German politicians and the West German broadcast media employed the uprising to taunt annually the GDR. For this reason he was not interested in accessing the programmes.

Significantly, the West German broadcast media programmes provoked recollection and discussion of 17 June 1953 amongst East German citizens and maintained the matter of 17 June 1953 in their consciousness. Heinz Kurtsiefer (born 1945) claimed:

> The uprising was only a topic of conversation if relatives had been involved. Otherwise it would have only come up because it was a holiday in the West and one registered that the TV schedules were out of the ordinary [*komisch*] on the day.

This suggests that without the West German broadcasts on the anniversaries of the uprising, many citizens of the GDR simply would not have discussed 17 June 1953 at all. Katrin Heidinger (born 1957) echoed Herr Kurtsiefer's sentiments when recalling why she had questioned her father about his experiences of the uprising:

> We only ever watched or listened to the West at home. And on Western television they always said 'Today is 17 June, the anniversary of the uprising of the poor citizens of the GDR', and one heard again and again at home, 'oh, yes, today is 17 June'.

Similarly, Doris Ritter (born 1956) said: 'We only spoke about the uprising when it was on the television.' And Christel Schlachter (born 1957) commented that, although the subject was rarely talked about in her family, 'when it was 17 June and it was on the television, then it automatically came up in conversation'. Werner Prauss (born 1958) remembered that he had questioned his father about his experiences of the uprising after seeing it mentioned in a West German television news bulletin. He also recalled that he asked an older work colleague about what he had experienced on 17 June 1953 in Magdeburg. Herr Prauss had been prompted to ask this question after he had seen a programme on West German television about the uprising the night before. Dorothea Freichel (born 1953) also remembered that West German television programmes always triggered discussions with older colleagues in her workplace about how they had experienced the unrest in Magdeburg.

Though few interviewees could offer specific details about programmes they had accessed, Katja Müller's (born 1962) recollection was particularly vivid. It suggests that these programmes and their promotion of 17 June 1953 inspired some East German citizens in their oppositional stance toward the SED:

> I can see myself. On one 17 June the radio programme was so good that I listened to it for the entire night through to 18 June or it could have been early morning on 17 June. It was 1976 or '77 and I sat in front of the window looking out, listening to the radio and I didn't sleep at all, because the radio programme on RIAS was so good. Because it was exactly what I wanted to listen to... Wolf Biermann and other GDR singer-songwriters. But then they spoke about the texts, then there were reports or interviews... It was probably 1977 after Wolf Biermann had been exiled... the broadcast interviews with other artists who had then been exiled. And on the one hand they were remembering the uprising, but on the other hand the topic was German unity, the 'Day of German Unity'. And I can still remember it well, how I listened to the radio for the entire night.

Frau Müller's parents had raised her as a non-conformist in the GDR. For example, they had shown her at an early age that the SED regime was corrupt. Frau Müller remembered that as a six-year-old child in 1968 her parents told her that they had voted against the GDR's new constitution in the referendum of 1968. They then showed her a copy of the local newspaper proclaiming that 100 per cent of voters in their borough had voted for the new constitution, demonstrating to her that the election results had been falsified. As a result of this influence Frau Müller grew up feeling 'a bit like the opposition. I actually felt I was a bit like something, a bit like an elite.' For someone who felt in opposition to the

SED, Frau Müller drew encouragement from hearing about the greatest show of opposition to the Party in the GDR's history, as well as other voices critical of the regime.

These broadcasts also made such an impression on Frau Müller because she did not always find it easy to carry on with her oppositional stance to the regime. Her parents had forbidden her to join the FDJ so that she did not become a part of the system. As a result her application to do her *Abitur*, the qualification required to attend university in the GDR, was rejected. By Frau Müller's account, this made life for her difficult. She stated several times that she was most unhappy with the career options that her life choices (or those made for her by her parents) had left her. After leaving school Frau Müller worked in low-paid jobs in the Church. Frau Müller stated that, looking back, she would have joined the FDJ if it had meant that her *Abitur* application would have been successful (in reality, as Frau Müller found out in the 1990s and contrary to what she had believed, her parents had not even submitted an application for her to do the *Abitur*). On 17 June 1976/1977 Frau Müller was at an age when her friends at school were going on to do their *Abitur* and leaving her behind. She stated that at these times she drew encouragement from listening to music that was critical of the GDR. One of her friends acquired records by Wolf Biermann from the West, as well as recordings by Bettina Wegner and Barbara Tahlheim. Frau Müller found the texts exciting: 'Some criticism against the politics of the GDR. Also, such encouraging songs when one didn't agree with everything.' This explains Frau Müller's comment that the RIAS programme she listened to was 'exactly what I wanted to listen to'. The RIAS broadcasts made such an impression on Frau Müller because she did not support the SED system at all, but also felt unhappy about the path on which this political stance had taken her. The programmes not only reassured her in her oppositional stance to the SED but also gave her encouragement to carry on when she found this difficult.

4.5 Conclusion

The West German media broadcasts aired to commemorate 17 June 1953 on the occasion of the 'Day of German Unity' presented East German citizens with accounts of the uprising that were far more comprehensive than what was available to them from official sources in their own country. The programmes informed viewers and listeners in the GDR in detail of the course and termination of the uprising. And although analyses of the nature of the uprising often varied between 'people's uprising' and 'workers' rebellion', the conclusions and evaluations drawn were in stark contrast to the SED regime's claims about a 'fascist-counterrevolutionary putsch'. However, by their own account, this was of little consequence to interviewees who had lived through the events of June 1953. They claimed that they did not learn much more than what they thought they had already learned about the uprising from their own experiences, as well as from what they had heard in the weeks immediately following the unrest. Moreover, conscious that the broadcasts might constitute Western propaganda, they also tended to view the programmes suspiciously. By contrast, many interviewees born after 1953 declared that they learned much more about the events of 17 June from the West German broadcast media than they had from official sources in the GDR. They also did not view the programmes with a similarly mistrustful eye. In fact, several stated that watching these programmes led them to question what they had learned at school about the uprising. Moreover, Karl Schirra suggested that citizens tuned into these broadcasts because they perceived a dearth of information about the unrest of 1953 officially available to them. He echoed the comments of several FDGB letter writers who indicated that this perceived lack of official information led citizens to conclude that the subject must be a taboo. Significantly, Katja Müller found comfort, reassurance and inspiration from these programmes and their accounts of 17 June 1953 for her oppositional stance toward the regime.

The number of programmes mentioning 17 June 1953 aired on its anniversaries each year, as well as the widespread accessibility to the West German broadcast media in the GDR, was sufficient to ensure the possibility that citizens were annually reminded of or informed about the fact of the uprising. Interviewees born after 1953 were just as aware of these programmes as those who had experienced the unrest first hand, despite the dwindling number of such broadcasts in later decades. Significantly, both groups of interviewees stated that the annual broadcasts by the West German media provoked recollection and discussion of the uprising. Eyewitnesses said that they were reminded of their own experiences of the day. The majority of those born later recounted that they were prompted to ask members of their family, friends and work colleagues about what they had experienced on 17 June 1953. Thus the West German broadcast media's programmes informing about or commemorating 17 June 1953 maintained the presence of the uprising in the consciousness of East German citizens who had experienced the day and of those who had no memories of it.

5
Remembering and Discussing the Uprising of 17 June 1953

By the majority of my eyewitness interviewees' accounts, the SED failed in its attempts to shape their perceptions of the uprising. The recollections of only two of these interviewees indicated that the SED's account of the uprising affected how they interpreted their experiences. Significantly, conclusions on the nature of the uprising that the majority of the eyewitnesses claim to have drawn contradicted not only the regime's official memory of the events but also the West German external collective memory of the unrest. Eyewitness interviewees evaluated what they had experienced in light of their own personal and political experiences, rather than with regard to the propaganda to which they were subjected. Moreover, eyewitness memories of the uprising were rarely 'communicated' (Assmann and Assmann, 1994) to other citizens. In fact, the subject apparently hardly came up in conversation at all, even amongst family members and even when a father, mother or other close relative had directly experienced the unrest. Consequently, eyewitnesses passed little information on to others about what they had witnessed. This is apparently due to the fact that, when citizens did actually discuss the subject, their conversations focused on the competing Western and Eastern evaluations of the uprising and not on personal experiences of the unrest. Such conversations about the events were most often triggered by the West German broadcast media's programmes about 17 June 1953 on the occasions of the 'Day of German Unity'.

When asked why the matter of the uprising was so rarely discussed, even with family members, several interviewees claimed that this was simply because it had become a forgotten matter for the majority of ordinary citizens in the GDR. For these interviewees, it was simply not relevant to their everyday lives. However, a number of interviewees stated that they had perceived the uprising to be a taboo topic in the

GDR, despite having encountered mention of it in official sources, most often at school. The discreet and brief manner in which these sources presented the uprising led these interviewees to think that they should not talk about the matter further. Thus the official sources' handling of the uprising encouraged these interviewees to impose a taboo of the subject upon themselves.

5.1 Remembering 17 June 1953

Many eyewitness interviewees claimed that what they remembered about the protagonists of the uprising contradicted what was stated in the SED's official account of the uprising. The Party's version of events implied that no citizens of the GDR had been involved in the unrest. However, the majority of these interviewees stated that they witnessed male and female citizens of all ages and from all social and professional backgrounds taking part in the uprising in Magdeburg. Thus their experiences challenged the SED's claims. Yet they also contradicted the interpretation of the uprising propagated by the West German broadcast media in the that the unrest was little more than a 'workers' uprising'. Heinz Kurtsiefer (born 1945) saw workers from the SKET, but also recalled: 'Everything was confused. Everything. There were not only people from the Thälmann plant but other people as well, who perhaps had not been at work and came out of their homes. It was a mix.' Jakob Balzert (born 1941) also recounted: 'I saw people from all strata of society: children, adults, young and old.' Peter Momber (born 1938) stated that he saw: 'Blue collar and white collar workers, women, children, youths, men and women. There was a mass of people.'

By contrast, the experiences of most of the eyewitnesses of the Soviet intervention during the uprising corroborated the claims made in the SED's account that the Soviets had merely shown a presence on the day and had not instigated any violence. Only 5 of the 20 eyewitnesses questioned had seen Soviet tanks and troops firing shots into or above the heads of the crowds during the uprising. However, the majority of the eyewitnesses stated that, even though they had no experiences of the armed Soviet intervention, they had believed rumours that spread in the immediate aftermath of the events that some citizens had died as a result of Soviet action. They asserted that their perceptions of the Soviet troops as violent led them to believe these rumours. Many had either experienced or heard about the supposed brutality of Soviet troops, whether that was during the Second World War or in the years since.

Eyewitnesses' personal and political circumstances played a role in how they processed their experiences of the uprising and the conclusions that they drew with regard to the nature of the unrest. Heinrich Schmidt's (born 1926) limited experiences of the uprising on 17 June 1953, coupled with his own favourable personal circumstances, led him to conclude that the unrest had been caused by nothing more than dissatisfaction with working quotas. On 17 June 1953 the 27-year-old Herr Schmidt was working in the foundry of the SKET in Magdeburg. Herr Schmidt recalled: 'The workers went from one factory to the other and took all the people with them. They said to us, "Come with us!" They were furious about the working quotas increase.' Herr Schmidt said that he did not follow the demonstrating workers into the city centre because he had always fulfilled his quotas. As a result, he did not witness the demonstration transform into a political protest involving citizens from all walks of life. Thus Herr Schmidt recalled the uprising as a workers' protest. His experiences of life in the GDR supported this conclusion because he was unaware of general dissatisfaction amongst citizens. This ignorance was not due to any kind of blind political allegiance to the SED, but to the fact that his personal circumstances were simply better than those of others. He always had enough food to eat because he grew vegetables and also kept several pigs. Furthermore, working in a foundry, he and his colleagues earned the second highest wage that a worker in the GDR could earn, approximately 1,000 Marks per month. Herr Schmidt used the fact that he could afford to buy his own motorbike in 1954 as an example of the high standard of living he enjoyed in the GDR.

Wolfgang Scholl (born 1933) also perceived that the main cause of the demonstrations on 17 June 1953 was the working quotas issue. Herr Scholl worked in a private brewery in the small town of Burg bei Magdeburg. He only took a passing interest in politics at the time. He said that he was too young in 1953 to have taken any sort of active interest in political matters and stated that the desire to do so only comes after one turns 40. His parents also did not involve themselves in politics in 1953 and did not discuss such matters at home. On 17 June 1953 Herr Scholl was attending college in Magdeburg city centre. In the middle of the morning workers tore open the classroom door and demanded that everyone inside come out and join the strikes. Herr Scholl left the college building and made his way to the main station in order to return home to Burg. He recalled only seeing workers taking part in the demonstrations. He stated that he assumed that they were protesting about their wages, with which he had heard many were unhappy. But he stated that as the employee of an enterprise that was not owned by the state: 'That didn't interest us because we weren't in the labour market so to speak.' There was no labour market in the capitalist sense of the word in the GDR. Herr Scholl apparently used this term to indicate that he and his fellow workers were not in the employ of the state and not subjected to the SED pressure under which state-employed workers had been placed and which he believed had triggered the demonstrations.

Peter Momber (born 1938) and Karl Berg (1932) interpreted their experiences of the uprising in respect of what they had experienced of living conditions in the GDR. They concluded that the demonstrations had been caused by citizens' dissatisfaction with living standards. Both claimed that they did not possess any particular political interest or opinion in 1953 and that this meant that they did not perceive political causes behind the uprising, only material ones. Peter Momber was 15 years old in 1953. As a teenager he took no particular interest in politics and was neither for nor against the regime. However, he knew that there was a lot of dissatisfaction amongst ordinary citizens, his family included, with the standard of living in the GDR: 'Things were simply tight for us. We talked about our dissatisfaction amongst ourselves. We could only press our noses up against the shop windows and that, of course, increased our dissatisfaction.' Twenty years old in 1953, Karl Berg said that he only took note of political developments affecting his passion for competitive cycling, such as policies governing racing in the West. Like Peter Momber, Herr Berg had experienced food and goods supply shortages, as well as high prices. He stated that these had led to 'a general dissatisfaction amongst working, from the factories to the offices'. Despite the fact that both Herr Momber and Herr Berg had heard about the working quotas strikes in Berlin on 16 June 1953, they asserted that their experiences of life in the GDR prior to the uprising led them to conclude that the causes of the unrest were rooted in general dissatisfaction with living conditions. Karl Berg stated: 'It was about general dissatisfaction. A high level of performance was demanded, without earning the right money. There was general discontent amongst the working population – from the workers to the offices.' However, Herr Berg's account of the uprising in Magdeburg did correlate with that of the SED regime with regard to one detail: the actions of Ernst Jennrich. Herr Berg was Jennrich's neighbour and he recalled seeing him with a rifle in front of the police headquarters in Magdeburg. Herr Berg remembered seeing Jennrich fire at least shots two shots at policemen in the windows of the building, though Herr Berg not know if these shots had killed or injured anybody.

Other eyewitnesses drew conclusions on why the uprising had started based on their political experiences prior to 1953 in the GDR. Jakob Balzert (born 1941) stated that as a child his experiences taught him that the SED terrorised anyone who did not support the new political system and that this led him to conclude that what he had witnessed on 17 June 1953 had been caused by citizens' political anger with the Party. After the Second World War, Herr Balzert's parents continued to run their tailoring shop in Magdeburg city centre. Herr Balzert recalled that this made them capitalists in the eyes of the state and he soon recognised: 'Whoever didn't commit or give themselves to the system had a particularly tough time.' Herr Balzert's teacher ('a teacher who was red through and through') would bully him for being a 'child of capitalism'. He recalled that on one occasion before 1953 he took a toy soldier to school with him: 'My parents had to go to the school and there was a big fuss... "Of all people, you, as capitalists! Your son is playing with toy *Wehrmacht* soldiers!" At school I was often berated for being a capitalist.' Herr Balzert stated that he became politically aware at a very young age because his family was constantly afraid that they would be dispossessed or imprisoned, as many of his father's customers had been, by the new political leaders: 'My whole situation was characterised by fear. Fear at home that my father might be taken away.'

On 17 June 1953 Herr Balzert attended school as usual. About halfway through the morning several older boys entered the classroom and headed for the 'Peace Corner'. This was a display of flowers with pictures of Walter Ulbricht, Lenin and Marx. The boys proceeded to throw the display out of the window. Herr Balzert recalled: 'The teacher ran straight out... and then after a few minutes she came back and what I noticed immediately was that she wasn't wearing her Party badge anymore. That struck me immediately.' The fact that Herr Balzert immediately noticed this shows how politically sensitive his upbringing had made him. He stated that, upon witnessing these events, he immediately formulated ideas about the causes of what was happening. He recalled that, even as a 12-year-old, it was now clear to him that the uprising would remove the SED from power because he knew that it was so unpopular.

After this incident, Herr Balzert and the other children were sent home from school. On the way, he remembered seeing protesters throwing documents and pictures out of the windows of buildings housing state agencies:

> There was quite a big crowd of people. And they were jeering and cheering. The people were hugging each other. It was an immensely happy situation. That came across immediately, to me too, now it's an uprising, now things will turnaround...That was clear to me as a 12-year-old. Now, finally, now this government, which was so unpopular, will be brought down.

Herr Balzert had not heard about the strikes in Berlin. Nor did he know the reasons why the uprising was taking place or what the demonstrators hoped to achieve. Thus his recollection of what he thought was happening – the fall of the SED – does not indicate what he knew about the aims of the uprising, but rather what he hoped them to be.

As Herr Balzert made his way home, he met his father who had come to look for his son. They went home to their flat from where they could see the police headquarters at the end of the street. His father decided to go to the headquarters because a lot of the family's friends were in the prison behind the main building. Herr Balzert joined his father. He perceived no danger in doing so: '...it wasn't dangerous...there was actually an indescribably lovely atmosphere'. Herr Balzert and his father observed the crowds ransacking the police headquarters until Soviet tanks arrived at about midday. The tanks raised their cannons into the air and fired warning shots above the crowds, bringing down the overhead tramlines. They then advanced and scattered the crowds. It was now becoming dangerous for Herr Balzert and his father. A Russian tank forced them down a side street next to the police headquarters with a group of demonstrators and they only narrowly escaped being crushed. After this they ran home. From the balcony of their flat Herr Balzert's father could see bodies lying on the square in front of the police headquarters. He could not tell if they were alive or dead. Later that evening the Balzerts could hear shots being fired from within the prison at the end of the road. They assumed that the authorities were executing protesters.

By contrast, Herbert Binkert (born 1930) recounted that his prior experiences of politics, as well as his experiences of the uprising, led him to conclude that a revolution was not taking place and that demonstrators were simply protesting about poor living conditions in the GDR. In 1953 Herr Binkert was 23 years old. He supported certain aspects of the regime, but was critical of others. He believed in the socialist state's ideals of peace and a better life, but was critical of the way SED functionaries simply parroted what was prescribed to them. He also did not like the fact that the SED had admitted that the course it had been pursuing since the summer of 1952 had been a mistake, but that it would be remaining in power. On 17 June 1953 Herr Binkert was attending business school in Magdeburg. He left in the afternoon and, upon seeing the unrest, headed straight to catch the train to his home in Schönebeck. He did not take particular notice of what was happening around him. His only concern was that he did not do anything that might get him into trouble after the uprising had finished. When considering the nature of what was happening, Herr Binkert compared his experiences of the day with what he had learned about the course of revolutions in politics lessons at school and at college. He had learned that revolutions require long-term planning. As a result of this, and despite the fact that he could understand why citizens might be angry with the SED, Herr Binkert concluded: 'It was sporadic. No one was thinking of bringing down the government.'

Similarly, Erwin Strempel (born 1932) claimed that his prior political experiences affected how he processed his experiences of 17 June 1953 in Magdeburg. However, he drew contrasting conclusions to Herr Balzert and Herr Binkert regarding the nature of the uprising. Herr Strempel stated that his unwavering support for the SED in 1953 led him to believe that West German organisations had instigated the unrest. Herr Strempel was born in Magdeburg. His father ran an upholstery and decorating business and his mother was a housewife. As a child Herr Strempel was a keen supporter of Hitler, a 'courageous *Pimpf*' (a member of the youngest subsection of the Hitler Youth) and very angry that Germany had lost the Second World War. But in 1946 the SED's claim that peace was its main priority attracted him to the Party. He reasoned: 'So, what they now wanted to do nevertheless had to be a good thing.'

In 1953 Erwin Strempel was working as a chemist's assistant in the north of Magdeburg. Having worked the night shift on 16 June 1953, he knew nothing about the strikes in Berlin. On 17 June 1953 his first experiences of the uprising came when he left work to go home for lunch and found that the trams were not running. At the tram stop Herr Strempel saw angry commuters milling about. He was told by one of the protesters: 'We are striking against the working quotas and against the Party slogan "First work better, then live better".' Herr Strempel did not believe this. He claims to have wondered: 'Why are they striking, when they own the factories? They couldn't be striking against themselves.' He stated that he also saw men commandeering vehicles because they needed them to inform the large factories in Magdeburg of the strikes. This made him think: 'Who is serving where and who is serving whom?' He claimed that he later saw a blind man giving orders to youths about where they ought to cause trouble next. Herr Strempel commented: 'There were certain people who knew which places had to be occupied in order to seize power'. He employed the term 'ring leaders' (*Rädelsführer*) to describe these men and claimed that they were telling others: 'Now we decide things!' Making his way into the city centre, Herr Strempel witnessed the destruction of buildings housing state agencies and recalled that he was thinking:

> What is going on here then? Who was really leading the whole thing? And then the suspicion arose in me... it is being steered. And it was in part steered by those people – *Ostbüro* Berlin, RIAS Berlin and a few others who here... there weren't just supporters of socialism here... there were also people who were against the regime. They sensed an opportunity.

He also remembered seeing typewriters thrown out of windows until the *Rädelsführer* put a stop to this. He claimed that they told the demonstrators that typewriters would be needed for the new government in the GDR.

Moving south through the city, Herr Strempel came to the police headquarters and jail where protesters were violently attempting to free political prisoners. He saw some demonstrators with weapons:

> And then the first shots were fired. But not by the Russians, but from weapons, some of which the *Volkspolizei* had handed over and others... where they came from... to be honest – I don't know till this day where weapons suddenly came from. They all at once had rifles. And then the five [sic] Magdeburgers were killed.

Herr Strempel fled as soon as the shooting began. On his way home he visited the FDJ headquarters to see what was happening there. He found the FDJ secretaries all sitting around a table in full uniform. He advised them to remove their Party badges and FDJ uniforms or else risk being beaten to death. The FDJ leaders did this and then asked Herr Strempel to look after and keep safe the official FDJ stamps and seals. They feared that the demonstrators would either destroy these or use them for their own advantage. He agreed to do this and took them home.

Herr Strempel's account suggests that eyewitnesses' personal and political experiences prior to the uprising not only shaped their perceptions of it but also determined how susceptible they were to SED propaganda about the uprising. Those interviewees who claimed to have rejected the regime for personal or political reasons in 1953 also stated that they had rejected the Party's account of the events. Moreover, there was no evidence in their recollections to suggest that they had subconsciously imbibed any of its aspects. Erwin Strempel claimed to have fully supported the Party in 1953. Significantly, his recollection of the uprising exhibited details of the SED's account of what had happened. Herr Strempel employed the term *Rädelsführer* to describe some of the demonstrators. This was common in the official account of the events. He also stated that the SPD's *Ostbüro* had had a hand in instigating the unrest, though he had no evidence of this. This was another key part of the SED's version. Finally, he recalled that during the uprising: 'RIAS were laying down a 24-hour barrage. They smelled blood.' Yet Herr Strempel would not have had the chance to listen to the radio until the evening of 17 June 1953 because, by his own account, he was in the city centre for the entire day. He must have learned this from the SED's account which cited RIAS and its broadcasts as major contributors to the unrest in the GDR. These details now form part of his personal narrative of the uprising of 17 June 1953.

Like Erwin Stempel, Horst Klauck (born 1924) was a convinced supporter of the SED regime in 1953 and this played a role in how he processed his experiences of the uprising. He totally accepted the SED's account of the events as a 'fascist-counterrevolutionary putsch' instigated by the West. This meant that he did not have to question the policies of the Party in the light of what he had witnessed and that he could continue with his fervent support for the state. Born in 1921, Herr Klauck recalled being an enthusiastic member of the Hitler Youth before the Second World War and served in the *Wehrmacht* on the Eastern Front. However, after the war he became a fervent supporter of socialism and the SED. His wife (also present at the interview) stated that they followed whatever the SED told them to do. Herr Klauck was in Leipzig with his wife on 17 June 1953 attending an FDGB conference on occupational health and safety. After the meeting ended they made their way to Leipzig main station and saw crowds of construction workers demonstrating. His wife recalled:

At Leipzig station typewriters were flying out of the windows, papers, files, everything. I sat in the car with my eyes shut in case anything came through the window. We were lucky that the car had a red cross on it [Herr Klauck worked in occupational health and safety]. We were allowed through. Then the first tanks arrived. And we drove in the wake of the tanks until we were clear of it. The next city was Halle and it was going off there too. Everything was wildly out of control. And then on to Magdeburg.

They arrived in Magdeburg at about 8pm and saw tanks patrolling the streets. Despite experiences of the unrest in three of the GDR's cities, Herr Klauck completely believed the SED's account of what happened during the uprising and still does today. Both Herr Klauck and his wife constantly played down the uprising during their interview, at one point questioning the merit of researching the events at all. Echoing the SED's account of the events, Herr Klauck stated that there was a normal mood amongst the workers in the SKET on 18 June 1953. He said that he could not recall any worker ever being unhappy there. He remembered having seen only smiling faces in the May Day parade that year.

Heinz Kurtsiefer's (born 1945) account suggests that later political experiences shaped how some eyewitnesses who were relatively young in 1953 evaluated their experiences of what they had seen on 17 June. Herr Kurtsiefer said that he was too young in 1953 to have held any serious political opinions or to have decided whether he was for or against the regime. He recalled that politics was never discussed at home when he was a child. His father had disappeared after being taken away by the Soviet authorities before Herr Kurtsiefer's birth and his mother and stepfather preferred to keep out of politics completely. His brother, who was born in 1930, had been a supporter of the Nazis and, according to Herr Kurtsiefer, had never come to terms with their defeat. But he did not get on with his stepfather and rarely visited the family.

Leaving school early on the morning of the uprising, Herr Kurtsiefer followed protesters to the police headquarters. He saw citizens ransacking buildings housing state agencies and SED members being attacked. In front of the police headquarters he witnessed some shooting and saw bodies lying on the ground. He ran home as soon as the Soviet tanks arrived. When Herr Kurtsiefer arrived home he found his older brother telling his mother that he had taken part in the protests and that he had been everywhere in the city. His mother told him to flee to the West because she feared he would be arrested. But he refused to do so. A few days later Herr Kurtsiefer's brother was arrested. The police had identified him in photographs taken by employees of the *Magdeburger Volksstimme*. The photographs apparently showed him taking part in the beating of one of the newspaper's employees in front of the *Volksstimme* offices on 17 June 1953. He was sentenced to three years in prison, which was increased to four years after his wife dared to write to Minister for Justice Hilde Benjamin and appeal for leniency.

Herr Kurtsiefer recalled that as he grew up he adopted political views in support of the SED regime. He found its 'antifascist' stance most attractive. Herr Kurtsiefer stated that he developed this view as a reaction to the political persuasions of his uncles whom he described as 'black and brown' (the colours of Conservatism and Nazism in Germany). They had supported the Nazis during the Second World War and Herr Kurtsiefer did not like what he knew about their pasts. One uncle had been in the military police and was stationed near Auschwitz. After the war he returned home with a box of jewellery that he claimed to have found in a cellar in Prague. Herr Kurtsiefer did not believe this story. Another uncle was imprisoned in the GDR for protecting one of his colleagues in the police by not reporting that this man had been in the SS.

Herr Kurtsiefer asserted that it was his brother's behaviour when he was released from prison, as well as his brother's political opinions, that finally persuaded him to commit himself to the SED. While in prison his brother's inability to come to terms with the Nazis' defeat and the new Soviet system had manifested itself as hatred of the GDR regime. This hatred affected his behaviour after his release:

> At some time or somehow because of these events, my brother remained at a standstill, politically. He did not develop any further. He somehow remained in that atmosphere of 17 June – that he had been wronged – and then nothing more happened with him. In his head he only had his little flat and that's all – do nothing more. Do nothing for anyone else, go home from work every night, stay at home. Finished. A disinterest developed in him, which I personally did not like.

This angered Herr Kurtsiefer. He expected young men to do more with their lives. But Herr Kurtsiefer also stated that he always saw this anger with his brother leading back to political things. Now that he had developed his own political opinions, Herr Kurtsiefer came into conflict with his brother because he apparently shared the views of his uncles:

> We argued. On Western television there was a presenter. He was called Löwenthal [Richard Löwenthal, a West German political scientist and

media commentator]. For me he was such a filthy swine. He projected his fascist disposition in such a way that he couldn't be accused of being unconstitutional. But it was so clear. And my brother supported such people: 'Hear, hear! They are right!' I could not put up with people such as Löwenthal. And we argued about that.

When asked whether he thought 'fascists' had been involved on 17 June 1953, Herr Kurtsiefer replied: 'Yes... [it] was only eight years after the Nazi Reich. There were still so many Nazis in Germany... people who were Nazis in their heads... there absolutely was a connection.' Too young (by his own account) in 1953 to understand what was taking place, Herr Kurtsiefer formed this view of participants of the uprising later in his life and as a result of his experiences with his brother and his uncles.

The rather curious accounts of the uprising of two eyewitness interviewees – Konrad Schreiner (born 1926) and Barbara Grabias (born 1927) – support Lutz Niethammer's theory that East German citizens' experiences of the unrest were perhaps more complex than their accounts reveal. However, it became necessary for citizens to recast themselves as passive bystanders to the events because their memories clashed with the Party's official account. On the day of the uprising Herr Schreiner was working in the luggage office of Magdeburg main station. He saw demonstrators pass by and heard that they were chanting that they wanted the removal of the government. This was something that he also wanted to happen. Herr Schreiner claimed to have seen little difference between the political system under the Third Reich (of which he had been a passive opponent) and that which was installed by the Soviets. He did not feel free under either system and for this reason he did not support the SED: 'With both regimes it was the case that they made laws that made you feel guilty if you were against them. Basically, even though there was a different philosophy to repress the people, both systems were the same.' Herr Schreiner maintained that he adopted an oppositional stance toward the regime in the GDR. This comprised airing his negative views on the state in meetings with SED representatives in his workplace: 'I was notorious as someone who was not faithful, at least not faithful to the state or how can I put it? I was a person who they did not trust.' Yet despite his oppositional stance, Herr Schreiner did not take the opportunity on 17 June 1953 to join the demonstrations against the regime when they passed by his place of work. His explanation of his non-participation in the protests distanced him from the unrest. Herr Schreiner explained that he did not join the protesters because he did not want to leave his post in the luggage office. He did not want to give looters a chance to steal luggage from the station.

Like Herr Schreiner, Barbara Grabias cast herself as a passive bystander to the events. She constructed an observation post so far removed from the events that one wonders if she noticed at all what was going on around her. Frau Grabias stated that witnessing the effect that politics had had on her father discouraged her from active involvement in such things. At the end of the Second World War her father was a member of the SPD. The forced merger of the SPD and the German Communist Party to form the SED in 1946 troubled him greatly. Frau Grabias recalled that her father stated that he felt unreliable and untrustworthy because in his lifetime he had already sworn allegiance to the Kaiser, the Weimar Republic and Hitler. And now he was required to swear allegiance to yet another political order. These feelings actually resulted in her father having a nervous breakdown. Consequently, even though he remained a member of the SED, he never got involved in politics again. Likewise, Frau Grabias was a member of the SED, but apparently only for appearances' sake. On the day of the uprising Frau Grabias was collecting firewood with her father from the yard of a factory in Magdeburg. She depicted this activity in far more detail than anything else she witnessed that day. After leaving the wood in a cart outside the factory, they went to the telecommunications and central post office in Magdeburg where they worked. Working on one of the top floors of the building, Frau Grabias noticed a demonstration making its way up the street to the post office at about mid-morning time. The demonstrators stormed the post office building and Frau Grabias saw them ripping the SED badges from the lapels of the postal workers. Upon witnessing this Frau Grabias' thoughts immediately turned to the wood that she had collected that morning. She left the post office building and cycled with her father through the unrest to where they had left the cart containing the wood chippings. Fortunately, it was still there. Satisfied that their haul was safe, they cycled back through the crowds and home.

5.2 Discussing 17 June 1953

All of the interviewees recalled having discussed the subject of the uprising of 17 June 1953 with their family or friends during the GDR period. By the interviewees' own accounts, there were various reasons as to why the subject cropped up in conversation. Annual mention of the uprising by the West German broadcast media on the anniversary of the events most often triggered discussions about 17 June 1953 with their family and friends. Thus the SED's perception that its citizens accessed these programmes and that this led to discussions of the subject amongst them was not without foundation. Eyewitness Konrad Schreiner (born 1926) explained that the programmes prompted him to talk about the uprising with his friends: 'Of course, we always watched it again on these anniversaries and then we recalled 17 June.' Christel Schlachter (born 1957) explained: 'When it was 17 June and you saw it on television, then it actually automatically came up in conversation.' And Dorothea Freichel (born 1953) remembered that the only trigger of discussions about 17 June 1953 in her family and amongst her colleagues was 'the reports on Western television on the occasion of the anniversary. We talked about it. It was always Western television.' In fact, Albert Keck (born 1959) was of the opinion that the West German media broadcasts guaranteed that the uprising 'could not fade into obscurity'. However, several interviewees stated that, although the West German broadcast media maintained the fact of the uprising in the consciousness of East German citizens, the discussions of 17 June 1953 that it triggered were not carried out in any great depth of detail. Brigitte Schneider (born 1956) recalled: 'It was never properly discussed.' Katrin Heidinger (born 1957) and Susanne Dobrat (born 1965) remembered that the extent of the discussions of the uprising triggered by the Western programmes often ran to nothing more than a few words in recognition of what was being commemorated.

Several interviewees said that discussions of the uprising within their families were triggered when either the interviewee or their children learned about 17 June 1953 at school. Monika Klein (born 1948), who experienced the uprising as a child, recalled: 'After we spoke about it at school, then I spoke about it with my parents.' Peter Momber (born 1938) stated that he also discussed the uprising with his daughter after she had told him that she had learned about it at school. He proceeded to 'correct' what she had learned. One could explain these discussions by stating that children do often talk about what they have learned at school with their parents. However, there is evidence to support the hypothesis that discussions of the uprising were prompted by the perception on the part of some citizens that they had not learned enough at school about 17 June 1953 and wanted to know more. The SED's official account of the events of 17 June 1953 apparently did not satisfy the curiosity of all citizens. Thus the Party's limited and dismissive approach to the events provoked discussion of and questions about it amongst citizens of the GDR who wanted to know more. Karl Schirra (born 1958) explained that he asked his uncle about the uprising because: 'The subject was not broached at all in our history lessons. But there was always an open atmosphere in our family. And I asked every possible question that interested me.' Thus Herr Schirra discussed the uprising with his uncle because he was interested in it, but had not learned enough about the events at school to satisfy his curiosity. Similar attitudes were also reflected in several of the letters sent to the FDGB nominating novels for the organisation's literature prize.

Heinz Kurtsiefer (born 1945) stated that discussions of the uprising with his daughter were prompted by the negative consequences that his brother had suffered as a result of his participation in the unrest in Magdeburg. Herr Kurtsiefer also suggested that discussions of 17 June 1953 were more likely to take place in families if relatives had suffered negative consequences as a result of their involvement in the uprising. Herr Kurtsiefer's brother was working in the SKET on 17 June 1953 when the strikes began. When he came home that evening he told his family: 'We were everywhere!' He ignored their pleas to flee to the West to avoid arrest. Unfortunately for Herr Kurtsiefer's brother, he had been photographed taking part in scuffles in front of the *Magdeburger Volksstimme* building. The *Stasi* magnified the photographs, identified him and sentenced him to three and a half years in prison. He died of cancer in 1961, which the family claimed was caused by his stay in prison. Herr Kurtsiefer stated that discussions of the uprising with his daughter were prompted by this particular part of his family history to explain to her what had happened to her uncle.

There is no evidence to support the hypothesis that incidents that took place in the Eastern Bloc similar to the uprising of 17 June 1953 sparked discussions of it amongst the interviewees. Some interviewees stated that the uprising in Hungary in 1956, the Prague Spring in 1968 and the *Solidarność* movement in Poland in the early 1980s had recalled to them their experiences of the uprising in the GDR. But none stated that they had discussed 17 June 1953 with family or friends as a reaction to these other uprisings. Karl Berg (born 1932) recollected that any discussions amongst the workers in his factory that did take place in 1968 focused on the leader of the Czechoslovak reform movement Alexander Dubček. Heinz Kurtsiefer (born 1945) was in the riot police in 1968 and was on a high state of alert, but he recalled that the earlier uprising in the GDR was not mentioned by anyone at all. Erwin Strempel (born 1932) explained retrospectively that he would not have discussed 17 June 1953 in 1968 because he drew no comparisons with the Prague Spring. He felt that in 1968: 'There was more to it. It was about war and peace.'

By the interviewees' accounts, when they talked about the events of 17 June 1953 with their family and friends, the discussions most often focussed on the competing Western and Eastern official accounts of the uprising. Horst Thiel's (born 1958) recollection of what was said about the uprising in his family exemplified the kinds of stories that interviewees remembered being recounted when the subject of the uprising came up in conversation:

> There were stories about a concentration camp guard... Erna Dorn... who was freed from prison and led the demonstrations in Halle. Then there were stories that the working quotas stipulation had been repealed and that the protests were senseless. Then I heard that the demonstrators in Berlin were former German prisoners of war, and that it was them who had destroyed Warsaw and Stalingrad and they weren't really workers, they were Nazis. I also heard a story about the foundry at the 'Ernst Thälmann' plant and how the workers had blocked the door with molten iron so that the demonstrators couldn't get in and they were the 'good workers'.

Doris Ritter (born 1956) and Karl Schirra (born 1958) stated that whenever they discussed the events, the conversation often took the form of a discussion of the SED's official account of the events and why this was wrong. Given that the broadcasts made by the West German media about 17 June 1953 most often led to discussions about the subject, it is hardly surprising that these conversations focussed on the differences between the Eastern and Western versions of events. These programmes presented the interviewees with an account of the uprising that contradicted what many had learned from official sources within the GDR. Thus these contradictions in the accounts became the main topic for discussion.

However, several interviewees recalled that eyewitnesses amongst their family and friends did talk about personal experiences of the uprising. Karl-Heinz Prinz (born 1921) and Werner Prauss (born 1958) asked friends to recount their experiences of the unrest in order to learn more about what had happened. Herr Prinz was in prison in Magdeburg on 17 June 1953 and, while he could hear the demonstrations, he knew very little about what was going on outside. Herr Prauss remembered that, after seeing something on West German television about 17 June 1953, he questioned an older colleague about his experiences of the uprising in Magdeburg:

> He was an apprentice here in Magdeburg in 1953, and he told me that typewriters and documents were thrown out of the windows of

the Party offices and that he travelled by train and that a train from West Berlin arrived and the people were saying, 'everyone, there is one Germany again'. And on the next day there were tanks all over Magdeburg.

Herr Prauss stated that he learned more about the unrest in Magdeburg from this friend than he had done from any other source. He learned that the demonstrators had hoped for a reunification of Germany. He also stated that he had not known Soviet tanks had violently quelled the uprising in the city until he had spoken to this friend at work. Herbert Binkert (born 1930) recalled that a colleague told him that he had been imprisoned for six years for joining in with chanting against the state on 17 June 1953. Herr Binkert believes that this colleague confided in him because he was regarded as a kind of father or priest figure in his work place to whom anyone could talk about their problems. And Franz Immig (born 1941) recalled that he always used to speak to his friends about their experiences because, as 12-year-old boys in 1953, the sight of protests, tanks and shooting made a lasting impression upon them: 'That is a day that is so long ago, but one which I can still remember exactly.'

Significantly, other eyewitnesses employed their recollections of the uprising to attempt to influence their listeners politically. Katja Müller's (born 1962) grandfather recounted his experiences of 17 June 1953 to her in the mid-1980s. He explained that in the 'Karl Marx' plant in Magdeburg where he was working the whole factory downed tools. Frau Müller gained a positive view of the demonstrations from her grandfather and why he had participated:

> My grandfather proudly joined the demonstrators and was very happy that the people took to the streets and he had really hoped that the people's uprising would change things politically. He had hoped for a reunification of both German states.

When asked why her grandfather had recounted his experiences to her, Frau Müller replied that she and her siblings had expressly asked their grandparents about the past because:

> It was important for us as young adults to talk about it with our grandparents and to realise that they had shown civil courage and they wanted to communicate to us, that you don't always have to

co-operate with things that might appear good for your career and it's better to reflect on things and take a look around.

Horst Thiel's (born 1958) paternal grandfather apparently also hoped to influence his grandson politically by telling him of his experiences of 17 June 1953. The matter of the uprising came up in a heated political discussion between his paternal grandfather, a former anti-Nazi resister and social democrat, Herr Thiel's father, a committed supporter of the SED, his uncle from West Germany and his maternal grandfather, who had been a supporter of the Nazis. Herr Thiel recalled:

> My [paternal] grandfather told me, 'The people who were talking at the head of the protests here in Magdeburg, I knew some of them and I didn't trust them'. And he held back and only watched it. He said, the people here in Magdeburg who were at the front and were expressing their views, they didn't share his ideas. In his opinion it could have led to Nazism.

By telling his grandson that the uprising could have led to Nazism, Herr Thiel's paternal grandfather confirmed one aspect of the SED's account of the unrest. But he was apparently not seeking to persuade Herr Thiel to back the regime because he also showed his grandson 'evidence' of the violence committed by the regime against East German citizens on the day. This 'evidence' was bullet holes which he claimed were made by Soviet machine guns on 17 June 1953 in the statue of Eike von Repgow opposite the police headquarters in Magdeburg. Herr Thiel's paternal grandfather employed his experiences of the uprising in the hope that they would influence his grandson into adopting his own social democratic political viewpoint and not the viewpoints of the other men in the family.

Similarly, a colleague of Dorothea Freichel (born 1953) employed his experiences of the uprising in order to express his political viewpoint. He apparently intended to reveal what he perceived to be the 'true' nature of the SED regime to his colleagues. Frau Freichel recalled that she and her friends at work began to talk about the 1953 unrest after watching programmes about it the day before on West German television. She remembered that one of her friends who had witnessed the events first hand repeatedly condemned the Soviet intervention to disperse the protesters and the SED's claims that the troops had rescued the citizens of the GDR from a return to fascism: 'He said that what happened wasn't right. The tanks came and it had nothing to do with democracy, the fact that it was put down. It had nothing to do with freedom.' Frau Freichel felt that this man emphasised this detail of the unrest because he had suffered at the hands of the Soviets during the war and apparently held a personal grudge against them.

Despite these instances, the majority of interviewees recalled that friends or relatives who had experienced the unrest very rarely discussed their personal memories of it during the GDR period. Most striking is the fact that, of the 18 interviewees born after the uprising in the GDR, only Christina Heinemann (born 1953) knew exactly how both parents had experienced the unrest on 17 June 1953. Ten further interviewees knew something before 1989 about the experiences of one parent or relative. However, for the majority of this cohort what they learned about relatives' experiences of the uprising was limited to one or two isolated details. For some this was because their relatives had witnessed very little. For example, Brigitte Schneider's (born 1956) mother stayed at home on the day of the uprising. Consequently, she simply told her daughter about the state of emergency and that: 'The SED big wigs got their comeuppance.' Yet the relatives of other interviewees experienced much more, but passed on very little. Their responses indicate unwillingness on the part of contemporaries of 17 June 1953 to talk about their experiences of the day to any great extent. Christel Schlachter (born 1957) stated: 'I knew that my parents experienced 17 June...but they didn't talk about it in detail.' An interview with Frau Schlachter's father (Karl Berg, born 1932) revealed that he had been present in front of the police headquarters in Magdeburg and had witnessed exchanges of gunfire between demonstrators and the police. Alexandra Brendel's (born 1950) father was the director of a factory in which unrest occurred; yet he simply told her that he had had to go there in the middle of the night. Werner Prauss' (born 1958) father recalled to him that there was a strike where he was working in Bernburg. However, he did not talk about what he had done during the strike. He just told his son that the next day everything had returned to normal.

For memories of 17 June 1953 to be communicated from one generation to the next within families in the GDR eyewitnesses to the uprising and their offspring had to show an interest in taking part in the process. If this interest was not there on either part, then the process did not occur and nothing was passed on. Such was the case for seven of the 18 interviewees born after the events of June 1953 who did not know how any of their relatives had experienced the uprising. They claimed that their lack of interest in politics and/or history in general meant that they never asked their relatives' whether they had experienced the uprising or not. Similarly, Peter Momber (born 1938) recalled that his children were simply not curious about the past: 'They said, "oh, not that again! Always the same stories from back then. Don't you have anything different to say?!"' Yet several eyewitnesses stated that they, too, had no interest themselves in telling their children about what they had experienced. Nikolaus Biewer (born 1934) explained: 'It was simply no longer relevant.'

Yet even in the families of interviewees in which there was an interest in politics and family members were actively involved in some sort of political role, there was apparently little enthusiasm to talk about personal experiences of 1953. Horst Thiel's (born 1958) father was SED Party Secretary in a large chemical works in Magdeburg. Herr Thiel described his father as a 'deeply convinced Marxist-Leninist' who never criticised or questioned anything the SED did. Yet although the uprising was discussed in Herr Thiel's family home, he never found out what his father had done on the day. Similarly, Susanne Dobrat's (1965) parents were committed supporters of the SED, to the extent that they cut off all ties with relatives in the West and never accessed the West German broadcast media. Her father also held a post on the District Party Control Commission, the inner-party watchdog responsible for disciplining party members. Frau Dobrat stated, although the uprising was discussed at home, she did not know how her father had experienced 17 June 1953. Moreover, although her mother lived very near to one of the main centres of the uprising in Magdeburg, she only told Frau Dobrat about Russian soldiers sitting and smoking on a wall. Karl Schirra's (born 1958) father, whom he described as 'convinced by the system', also never told his son about what he had witnessed either, even though the subject of the uprising did come up in conversations.

Horst Klauck's (born 1924) responses suggest that supporters of the regime in the GDR did not talk about the uprising and communicate their personal experiences of the unrest because they believed the SED's account completely. For these citizens, having completely accepted the official account of the uprising, there was nothing to discuss. Throughout the GDR period Herr Klauck was an ardent supporter of the SED. He proudly explained that he and his wife both watched the GDR's weekly television propaganda show *Der schwarze Kanal* (*The Black Channel*) every week. On 17 June 1953 the 29-year-old Herr Klauck was caught up in the demonstrations in Leipzig while attending a health-and-safety-at-work conference. He later witnessed unrest in Halle and tanks in Magdeburg. Yet despite these first-hand experiences, throughout his interview Herr Klauck consistently played down the significance of what had occurred. It was clear from his responses that he had fully accepted the SED's account of 17 June 1953. He recalled that no worker in his workplace had been unhappy prior to the events, despite the fact that he worked in the SKET in Magdeburg where over 10,000 workers went on strike. Herr Klauck drew support from the SED's account to explain his own experiences. However, Herr Klauck was so convinced by the SED's underplaying of the seriousness and scale of the unrest that he never spoke about the subject with anyone (and even questioned why I was so interested in talking about it!). He was (and still is) convinced that nothing significant happened on 17 June 1953 in the GDR.

Similarly, Monika Klein (born 1948) and Susanne Dobrat (born 1965) by their own accounts saw no reason to discuss the events of 17 June 1953 in any great detail during the GDR period because they totally accepted the regime's account of what happened. Frau Dobrat and Frau Klein were brought up in strict socialist households. Their parents were committed members of the SED and forbade access to the West German broadcast media. Both interviewees were raised to share their parents' political convictions. As a result, they did not question the manner in which the uprising was taught or presented in the GDR, nor did they question the contents of the SED's official account. After all, neither had been allowed to watch Western television and therefore did not access the West's alternative account. For them, there was nothing to discuss.

Yet the results of Erwin Strempel's (born 1932) interview indicate that some supporters of the SED did not tell their children about their experiences of the uprising because they knew that they would disprove the SED's account and did not want their children made aware of this. He stated that he did not tell his daughter about his experiences of 17 June 1953 because he knew that doing so might influence her politically. Although he had firmly believed the SED's account of the events in 1953, Herr Strempel admitted that he had lost a lot (but not all) of his faith in the SED and, as a consequence, its version of 17 June 1953 by the time his daughter asked him about his experiences of it in the 1970s. He recalled that his support for the Party wavered after witnessing how its officials operated in his factory. Herr Strempel claimed to have once told a Party official: 'The socialism that we proclaim is a pure theory. But its practice makes fools of us every day. I was a completely honest comrade. I said, "You can't shit on the people like that."' When asked what he told his daughter about his experiences of the June uprising, Herr Strempel recalled:

> Actually, not very much at all. In her school they were told that it was a putsch, Day X, that the Americans were behind it. And she didn't ask me much about it. And I also didn't say that that was wrong. I would have influenced her to take the wrong path.

Herr Strempel's response suggests that there was a link between how citizens of the GDR brought up their children and whether or not they recounted their experiences of 17 June 1953 to them. Several interviewees confirmed this by stating that they had raised their children in a manner that they described as 'double tracked' (*zweigleisig*). Upon learning that their children had encountered the SED's version of the uprising at school, parents who taught their children to be *zweigleisig* would then 'correct' this version at home. In other words, they would tell their children about what they believed had really happened. This usually contradicted the SED's account. They would make sure that their children knew that what they had been told must remain strictly at home and that, if they spoke about the matter in public, they must talk about it in the terms they had learned in school. Herr Strempel did not bring his daughter up to be *zweigleisig*. Thus he did not tell her of his experiences of 17 June 1953 because he knew that they contradicted what she had learned about it at school. He stated that if she had learned that what was taught in school was wrong, it would have affected her academic success. But there were underlying political motives in Herr Strempel's actions, too. Given the fact that the Party determined what was taught in school history lessons, contradicting what his daughter had learned at school would also have meant showing to her that the SED was lying to its citizens.

By the accounts of other interviewees, traumatic experiences of the unrest played a role in the fact that personal memories of the uprising were not communicated by family members. Katrin Heidinger (born 1957) explained that her father's silence about what he had experienced was a result of the disappointment he experienced when the uprising failed. Frau Heidinger recalled that her parents 'both leaned to the right' and opposed the regime, but that the extent of their opposition went no further than frequent complaints about the SED expressed in discussions at home. Both of her parents were opticians in their own privately-owned business, which they successfully managed to save from nationalisation throughout the GDR period. Frau Heidinger stated that the subject of the uprising came up in her parents' house on each anniversary. Her parents would always exclaim: 'Oh, today is 17 June again!' Yet Frau Heidinger did not know what her mother or father had done on the day. When she asked her father about it, he avoided her questions. He would simply say that 'evil things' had occurred in Magdeburg in connection with the 'Russian pigs' and would not elaborate upon this. As private business owners, the Heidingers were 'on the outside' in the GDR and no doubt suffered pressure to conform. This may further explain the reason why, as Frau Heidinger recalled, her father spoke about the uprising with a lot of regret, as if he regarded it as a 'missed opportunity'.

A trauma related to experiences of the uprising of 17 June 1953 also meant that Barbara Grabias (born 1927) did not communicate her memories to others. However, in contrast to Frau Heidinger's father, Frau Grabias claimed that her experience was so traumatic that she completely repressed all of her memories of the unrest and its aftermath. On the morning of 17 June 1953 Frau Grabias was collecting waste wood from a factory in the north of Magdeburg to use for her fire at home. She left the wood in a cart outside the factory while she went to work at the main telecommunications office in the city centre. When demonstrators entered the building she left immediately to check that the wood she had collected was still where she had left it. The fact that Frau Grabias worked in an important communications point in the city and that she had left her post during the uprising led the *Stasi* to put her under surveillance. She later found out that they watched her for two years. In 1955 they brought her in for an interview. They explained that her behaviour on 17 June 1953 had brought her to their attention and questioned her about this event, as well as her trips to West Berlin, where she would buy clothes. The experience of the *Stasi* interview traumatised Frau Grabias. She stated that when she returned home to her parents she was an emotional wreck. Frau Grabias said that the only way she could recover from this trauma was to repress her memories of the interview, as well as her memories of how she had experienced 17 June 1953. After this initial interview with the *Stasi* Frau Grabias' father told her to write down everything that had happened. He then hid the document. It was only in 2005 while moving house that Frau Grabias found the record of her experiences and remembered what had happened. Reading the document she recalled that in the face of the threats made by the *Stasi* she had agreed to work as an informer for them. However, her *Stasi* file shows that they released her from this obligation after a short period because she kept telling her handler that she had poor hearing and could not eavesdrop very well on conversations.

Other interviewees stated that the subject of the uprising was rarely a topic of conversation with friends or family because they simply saw no reason to discuss it. This was particularly so for interviewees born after 1953. Several of these interviewees tried to explain why they now think that they hardly ever talked about the uprising with friends or family. Manfred Ebert (born 1965) and Anna Siedel (born 1967) said that they did not talk about the uprising with friends because they were simply not interested in any political subject during the GDR period. By contrast, Christina Heinemann (born 1953) was interested in politics during the GDR period, but stated: 'As a subject, the uprising was a footnote, it wasn't a subject that was a problem that you felt had to be thrashed out. Absolutely not.' For Frau Heinemann and her friends the uprising was a fact that had to be accepted and there was no point discussing it further. Alexandra Brendel (born 1953) claimed that the daily struggle of the economy of scarcity in the GDR left her with no time or energy to think about past events:

> You only busied yourself with the present day: children, kindergarten, building a house. Everyday life, not the past, took precedence. You had to look for a flat. That really was a big problem. And work. You had to concentrate on your family. Then you couldn't really worry about such things, do you understand? Sometimes it was a struggle.

Two interviewees born after 1953 asserted that they found the uprising insignificant because they perceived it as an event in the past that had had no direct effect upon their lives. They stated that for this reason it held no meaning for them. Brigitte Schneider (born 1956) knew from her mother that an uprising had taken place in the GDR in 1953. Although she learned little from her mother, Frau Schneider later learned from the West German broadcast media that the uprising was large in scale and had been terminated by the violent intervention of Soviet troops. But Frau Schneider regarded the uprising as nothing more than an historical event. She stated that this was because it had had no direct impact upon her life, nor had it affected her parents, who had not witnessed the events. Frau Schneider summed up her thoughts on the uprising as follows: 'It held absolutely no significance for us. The uprising happened three years before I was born and had no visible effect for us.' Christel Schlachter (born 1957) echoed Frau Schneider's comments.

Frau Schlachter had learned about the events at school in the GDR, as well as from the West German broadcast media. But she took little interest in what was said. She stated that she could not relate to the events of June 1953 in any way because it was simply too inconsequential for her and her family, and too long ago in the past for it to be any kind of factor in the way she lived her life: 'I wasn't yet born. You just can't identify with it. It is the past. It was before the time that I existed. It is history.'

The majority of the interviewees recalled that political issues other than the uprising of 17 June 1953 were discussed more often in their homes. These consisted of political issues or events that, in contrast to the 1953 uprising, continued to have a direct effect on interviewees' lives. Horst Thiel (born 1958) recalled that 'international confrontations' were more often discussed; for Doris Ritter (born 1956) it was the economy of scarcity in the GDR. However, the most commonly discussed continuing issue was the Berlin Wall. In contrast to the uprising of 17 June 1953, interviewees perceived the Berlin Wall as a continuous condition in the GDR that affected their lives for many years. The 1953 uprising had lasted only a few hours and had lasting effects on the lives of only a minority of citizens. Christel Schlachter (born 1957) stated that, in contrast to the uprising which only became a topic of conversation on its anniversaries: 'The Berlin Wall was always an issue.' Horst Thiel (born 1958) recalled that in his family this subject was always more important than 17 June 1953. For several interviewees this was the case because the Wall had split their families in two. Werner Prauss (born 1958) recalled:

> For me, the Wall was always an issue. It had always been an issue within our family because we had relatives over there. As a youngster I asked, why can my cousin visit me but I am not allowed to visit her? It is difficult to grasp.

Wolfgang Scholl (born 1933) explained that the Berlin Wall was always a topic of conversation because his brother and his wife's twin sister were in the West. For Nadine Weber (1960) the fact that she was refused permission to travel to the West to visit her favourite aunt was the most important issue in her life. She stated: 'That was very difficult for me. It caused me a lot of pain. Yes, the Wall was definitely an issue. It determined destinies.' Other interviewees talked about the Wall more than the uprising because they felt oppressed by it. Dorothea Freichel (born 1953) described the GDR as a prison because of the Wall. Anika

Rosenkranz (born 1963) was unhappy because it meant she could not buy Western clothes.

While experiences of 17 June 1953 remained a topic of conversation between interviewees and their friends who had experienced the uprising first hand, those interviewees born after 1953 more often discussed political events of which they had first-hand experience. They had lived through these events and for this reason they considered them more significant in their lives, perhaps more real, than an uprising that they had not experienced. Alexandra Brendel (born 1950) recalled that she discussed 17 June 1953 very little with her parents: 'What really came up in our discussions was the exile of Wolf Biermann. I just could not comprehend that. We young people, we were enraged by that. My parents were of a totally different opinion.' Likewise, Doris Ritter (born 1956) recounted that other, more current political events were talked about in her family, rather than the uprising of 17 June 1953: 'The Kennedy assassination: that was talked about. Yuri Gagarin, the first man in space: that was talked about.'

For several interviewees, other events that had made more of a personal impact than 17 June 1953 on their lives or the lives of their family were discussed. Werner Prauss' (born 1958) mother and father and their families had been expelled from their homes in the areas of Germany handed to Poland at the end of the Second World War. Their recollections of their former homes, as well as the injustices they believed they had suffered, frequently dominated family conversations in his house. For Karl-Heinz Prinz (born 1921) more extreme experiences in his life often formed the basis of conversations with his family, not what he had witnessed for a few brief hours one June afternoon. After the Second World War he spent five years in the Soviet detainment camps Torgau, Mühlberg and Buchenwald. Soon after his release he was arrested by the *Stasi* and sentenced to several further years in prison. Similarly, Herbert Binkert (born 1930) talked more about other events in his life with his family than the uprising of 1953. In the mid-1950s he was expelled from business college for allegedly making negative comments about the state: 'I have to say that my issue was my expulsion from school, and that I was just so helpless in this country, that I could simply do nothing about it, even if I had been treated unjustly.' Herr Binkert's feelings of injustice and helplessness at this are still evident today.

Interestingly, several interviewees linked the frequency with which 17 June 1953 came up in conversation with the standard of living in the GDR. They stated that few citizens spoke about the uprising in later years because living standards improved. They asserted that citizens would only have talked about the uprising if they had had something to complain about regarding the standard of living. This suggests that they perceived that the desire to express dissent evoked memories of 17 June 1953 and not vice versa. When asked how often he had talked about his experiences of the uprising with his friends, Theodor Puff (born 1949) stated:

> It was very rarely an issue. It was over and done with for us. You have to realise that afterwards things got better in the GDR. Without question. Because the lads [the SED] certainly took note of what had happened. It got better for us... things were on the up.

Heinz Kurtsiefer (born 1945) expressed a similar opinion in relation to discussions of 17 June 1953 at home: 'The subject actually faded away with the prosperity that followed in the GDR. Prosperity kills everything and actually caused this matter to fade away.'

5.3 17 June 1953 as taboo

As workers writing letters to the FDGB arts prize committee did, so interviewees often referred to 'the taboo of 17 June 1953' in the GDR. In describing the parameters of this taboo, interviewees differentiated between the public and the private sphere. None recalled that they had perceived that it had been a taboo to discuss the uprising in private with family or with trusted friends. However, the majority of interviewees claimed to have felt that it was taboo to discuss the uprising in public, that is, with (or within earshot of) citizens who were not friends or family.

Paradoxically, interviewees stated that they recalled the subject of the uprising being addressed in a public setting in the GDR (namely at school), yet they still believed that it was a taboo to talk about the subject in public. Significantly, they perceived that it was taboo to address the subject at all in public, even in the manner and terms employed by the official account. Christel Schlachter's (born 1957) comments exemplified this paradox: '17 June was always mentioned at school, but it was a taboo subject, I have to say.' When these interviewees recalled what they had learned about the subject in school, they emphasised the brevity with which teachers addressed the matter. Their responses suggest that the short, sharp, discussion-free manner in which the subject of the uprising was officially communicated to citizens of the GDR contributed to their perception that the matter was something that ought not to be discussed further. Albert Keck (born 1959) remembered: 'It was dealt with very briefly and then it was done with.' Werner Prauss (born 1958) described his experiences of the teaching of 17 June 1953 as follows: 'The history teacher simply told us that there had been an uprising and that reactionary people had crawled out of their holes. Other than that the subject was absolutely not spoken about.' Karl Schirra (born 1958) stated that it was the discussion-free manner with which the subject was dealt at school that led him to believe that there was an enforced taboo of the matter:

> It was discussed, but shortly and sharply. It wasn't discussed comprehensively. We knew that there could be possible sanctions. You would attract negative attention. We took note of that and then it was done with. Officially, it was a taboo.

The fact that his experience of the subject at school suggested to him that it was taboo made Herr Schirra curious about 17 June 1953. Curiosity about the subject was also evident in letters sent to the FDGB arts prize committee. Several letter writers expressed the desire to know more about what they had long perceived to be a 'taboo issue' in the GDR. In the case of Karl Schirra, this curiosity led him to access West German media broadcasts about the uprising. Doris Ritter (born 1956) shared Herr Schirra's fears of possible sanctions for mentioning the uprising. Yet her perception of the subject of the uprising as a public taboo is also paradoxical, given the fact that she worked as a history teacher in the GDR, who taught about the events of 1953 to her pupils. Not only did she know perhaps better than most citizens the 'correct' manner in which the uprising could be addressed in public, but she also communicated it to other citizens (her pupils) in a public setting herself. However, she still perceived that, outside of the classroom, all mention of the uprising was a public taboo. Frau Ritter explained that she perceived any mention of the subject in public as a taboo because she did not know who might be listening to her conversations in public places.

By the accounts of interviewees who had experienced the unrest first hand, the regime's version of the events also led them to impose a taboo of the subject upon themselves in public. These eyewitnesses stated that this perception was encouraged by the fact that the official account of 17 June 1953 so drastically contrasted their and their family and friends' own experiences of the unrest. Franz Immig (born 1941) stated: 'It was always presented as an attempted fascist putsch, and everyone knew that that wasn't true. Because of that, we did not talk about it in public.'

Peter Momber (born 1938) also recalled: 'We were told, that it was organised by the West, but no one believed that. And because of that reason we simply didn't mention it.' These comments echo those of FDGB letter writers from 1979 who, in also claiming that the subject was taboo, stated that it was about time that subjects like the uprising of 17 June 1953 were 'addressed more often and honestly' in the GDR.[1] Thus citizens' disappointment with the official version in terms of its detail and of its credibility led them to believe that the subject was officially taboo in the GDR.

However, several interviewees stated that perceptions of 17 June 1953 as a public taboo ultimately depended on what people wanted to say about the subject in public. Heinz Kurtsiefer (born 1945) stated:

> I wouldn't say that it was a taboo. To mention the uprising itself was not dangerous. The words you used to evaluate it, they were dangerous. So, if you said 'That's all nonsense. It wasn't an uprising organised by the West, it was caused by our own politics', I think you would have been interviewed for that.

Katrin Heidinger (born 1957), as well as Kurt Clemens (born 1934), Karl-Heinz Prinz (born 1921) and Konrad Schreiner (born 1926) were all of a similar opinion. They believed that the only taboo regarding 17 June 1953 was discussion of the uprising outside the boundaries of the official account. This echoes Annette Leo's findings that workers in the steelworks in Hennigsdorf who had experienced the uprising only passed on details that were acceptable within the parameters of the SED's official account to younger colleagues (Leo, 1999, pp. 58–72).

5.4 Conclusion

The SED failed to shape eyewitnesses perceptions and memories of what they had experienced on 17 June 1953 in the GDR. Rather, the manner in which eyewitnesses interpreted their experiences of the uprising was affected by their contemporary political beliefs and their personal circumstances. The conclusions they drew about the nature of the uprising based on their interpretations often contradicted details in the West German and East German accounts of 17 June 1953. Significantly, the accounts of eyewitnesses Konrad Schreiner and Barbara Grabias echoed the results of similar interviews with East German citizens conducted by Lutz Niethammer. He found that many of his interviewees cast themselves as passive witnesses to the events. Niethammer concluded that their memories 'must have been far more complex than the particular perspective on which observers settled and which they established in the niche of their memory' (Niethammer, 2008, pp. 52–4). But the failure of the uprising made it necessary for citizens to distance themselves from what had occurred. Thus citizens' memories of the uprising became reports of what others had done.

The interviews indicate that East German citizens rarely discussed the uprising or personal experiences of it. Some were simply not interested in bringing up the subject of 17 June 1953 with friends or family. But in the majority of cases discussion of other subjects took precedence over discussion of the events of 1953. Some of these subjects were more politically and personally important to the interviewees than the uprising. Other issues, such as the Berlin Wall, were continuing conditions in the GDR, that is, they continued to influence the lives of the interviewees over the course of the GDR period. The uprising's nature as a single event meant that it did not continue to have any direct influence on their lives. It was something that many had experienced for, at the very least, one afternoon, at the most a day or two, but which had no discernible effects on the lives of the interviewees after this period. Thus interviewees perceived it as an irrelevant subject in their lives. Even when there was sufficient interest, many eyewitnesses still did not talk very much about their experiences. When 17 June 1953 was discussed in interviewees' families, the various and competing interpretations of it were talked about instead of family members' personal experiences. That this was the case can be attributed to the fact that programmes about the events aired by the West German broadcast media most often triggered conversations about 17 June 1953 amongst interviewees' families and friends. These programmes presented accounts of the uprising that contradicted the official account of which most interviewees were aware. Thus the contradictions between the two accounts became the main topic of conversation, not relatives' experiences of 17 June 1953. Yet the fact that interviewees rarely discussed the subject of the uprising suggests that they did not watch such West German broadcasts very often.

Several interviewees claimed that there was a public taboo of the subject of the uprising of 17 June 1953 in the GDR. They explained that this perception had led them to avoid mentioning the uprising in public, or discussing it with citizens whom they did not trust. Paradoxically, interviewees perceived the matter of the uprising as a public taboo, despite the fact that they had often encountered mention of it in a public setting, most commonly at school. By the interviewees' accounts, the content of the SED's official version of events, as well as the manner of its communication, led them to impose a taboo of the subject upon themselves. For interviewees who had witnessed the events, the simple fact that the SED's account of the unrest contradicted so drastically what they had experienced led them to draw the conclusion that they ought not to talk about what they had experienced themselves. Other interviewees stated that the brief, discussion-free manner in which official sources communicated the matter of the June uprising led them to believe that there would be sanctions against discussing the matter further. Thus they too imposed a taboo of the subject upon themselves.

6
17 June 1953: A Symbolic Talisman of Opposition in the GDR?

The ghost of the uprising of 17 June 1953 and the possibility that it might one day happen again haunted the SED regime until its demise in 1989. The fear of a repetition of the June uprising led the Party to monitor closely the mood of its citizens and take the necessary action to crush discontent. This is exemplified by the much less often quoted reply that Minister for State Security Erich Mielke received from his officers in 1989 when he asked about a possible repetition of 17 June 1953: 'That won't happen tomorrow. That's why we are here' (Eisenfeld, 2005, p. 359). The state's monitoring of citizens took many forms, from reports on discussions in factories made by FDGB officials, to the covert bugging of the homes of suspected 'provocateurs' by the *Stasi*. The regime took particular note of any reference to the 1953 uprising made by its citizens. It perceived that memories or awareness of the events might inspire further unrest. The Party and its organs were particularly vigilant to this around the anniversaries of the uprising each year. Accordingly, the state security services and armed forces annually undertook massive operations on and around 17 June in order to nip any potential unrest in the bud.

The reports filed by the SED and mass organisations in Magdeburg, as well as the *Volkspolizei* and the *Stasi*, show that these state agencies often recorded East German citizens making reference to the uprising in public. Examination of the frequency of these incidents indicates a correlation between the temporal proximity to the uprising and the regularity with which ordinary citizens made reference to it in public. Such incidents, while not disappearing altogether, decreased steadily from highs in the 1950s and 1960s to much fewer instances in the 1970s and 1980s. However, the extent to which the East German security forces prepared for the anniversaries of the uprising did not similarly diminish.

In fact, the evidence suggests that the extent of their preparations (and thus their perception of the potential of memories and awareness of the uprising to inspire unrest) was actually influenced by the extent to which West Germany commemorated the anniversaries of the uprising.

Significantly, the reports indicate that citizens most often evoked memories or awareness of 17 June 1953 when expressing dissent against the regime. This occurred not only in verbal references to the uprising but also in the form of non-verbal references, such as graffiti. Yet, while many citizens often threatened their local Party or trade union official with 'a second 17 June', it is clear from the references that citizens were simply venting their frustration with the current state of affairs. The vast majority of citizens recorded in the files are simply grumbling about living conditions and the state of society in the GDR and referencing 17 June 1953 in the process.[1] Ultimately, as the accounts of two interviewees in particular also show, the uprising of 17 June 1953 took on a symbolic character for East German citizens. They evoked its memory to express their opposition to the regime, but threats about a 'second 17 June' were empty.

6.1 1950s

In anticipation of the first anniversary of the uprising, in the GDR, the State Secretariat for State Security initiated 'Aktion Bollwerk' ('Operation Bulwark') on 28 May 1954. Orders dispatched to the various arms of the security forces across the GDR indicated that the SED regime was most concerned about West German 'provocations':

> According to current reports the enemy is preparing new provocations and attempts at sabotage with the intention of sparking unrest on 17 June 1954. This is being planned by the same people behind the attempted fascist putsch. All enemy measures are being steered by Bonn... the SPD's *Ostbüro* is also preparing provocations on 17 June 1954.
>
> (Schulz, 2006, p. 73)

Three days before this first anniversary of the uprising the *Stasi* formed task forces across the GDR (Wolle, 1996, p. 112). The GDR's security forces were put on a state of increased alert and units were readied to mobilise at a moment's notice. Regional security chiefs were to report the slightest signs of unrest and *Stasi* informers were ordered to be especially vigilant. According to the files possible 'provocations' might include 'negative' discussions, wage demands, the spread of rumours, threats of strikes or unusually high absenteeism in factories. Sites such as water and gas works, as well as airports and other transport routes, were all especially observed. Any kind of organised activities scheduled for 17 June, such as staff excursions, were prohibited. Certain groups of citizens, such as former SPD members or those arrested on 17 June 1953 and since released, were also subjected to keener observation (Eisenfeld et al., 2004, pp. 179–83).

Similar steps were taken on each anniversary in the 1950s. In 1955, for example, the chief of police in Magdeburg received orders from his superiors in Berlin detailing the measures to be put into place to guard against attacks by the 'enemy' on the anniversary of 17 June. The extent of the precautions to be taken reveals the extent to which the Party feared a repeat of the 1953 unrest in this period:

> All essential factories and installations, such as electricity power stations, long distance communication and telegraph offices, gas works, explosives and poison stores, as well as Soviet memorials and cemeteries, important VEB, MTS, VEG, LPG, penal institutions, detention centres, prison hospitals, young offender institutes and prison work camps are to be covered by patrol and guard duties, reinforced with voluntary police helpers... Particular attention is to be paid to rumours about carrying out a minute's silence, strikes, questions about working quotas, questions about the material supply of the workers etc. This also includes current discussions about difficulties in the supply of butter, margarine and oil.

Policemen were further ordered to report immediately any such discussions of the issues listed above.[2]

The regime's fears about further unrest inspired by the anniversaries of the uprising were not unfounded. Representatives of the state and its various institutions often observed citizens making threatening references about the uprising. For example, in early June 1954 conversations about 17 June 1953 amongst citizens in Magdeburg were recorded:

> 17.6 is being mentioned more and more in Magdeburg. It is reported that in the HO and KG [both types of state-run shops] customers are saying: soon it's the anniversary of 17.6, which is a day of remembrance in West Germany, and that it won't be much longer before a new 17.6... One colleague... reported that his co-workers were

saying: 'if 17.6 last year was the wedding rehearsal, this year it will be the wedding'.[3]

Such reports of references to the uprising show that the *Volkspolizei* was correct in identifying a link between citizens' dissatisfaction with the supply of basic foodstuffs in this period and memories of 17 June 1953.

Discontent with this aspect of their lives frequently triggered mention of the uprising from citizens in the 1950s. They made verbal references to 17 June 1953 when grumbling about the poor quality or lack of food. On 5 May 1955 it was reported in the weekly report of the SED district leadership that the poor food supply in the area was provoking from citizens: 'such utterances... for example, "on 17.6 we surrendered, when it happens a second time, we won't do the same"... two workers said, that they won't be surprised, if 17.6 comes a bit earlier this time'.[4] In the same month, it was similarly reported to the district leadership:

> In Magdeburg and other boroughs of the district there were large crowds of people where margarine was on sale... heated discussions often arose... individual elements used these as an opportunity to declare that 'a 17.6. must come again soon'... It has been established that such discussions about 17.6 took place in various locations.[5]

In the same week FDGB representatives reported in connection with intensive discussions about the food supply amongst workers: 'A few colleagues declared: for you lot it will take another 17 June 1953... then everything will be available again.'[6] The following week the district leadership's weekly report stated that in the queues of citizens waiting for margarine: 'frequently such opinions surfaced such as there has to be a new 17.6'.[7] In September 1955 the FDGB again reported that consumers had expressed such things as: 'If they take the HO margarine away from us again, then we will see where that will lead them. This time 17 June will turn out differently.'[8] The FDGB reports from the following year show that similar complaints about the food supply again provoked mention of the date amongst ordinary citizens: '[there] are... discussions about a second 17 June if the supply situation doesn't change as quickly as possible.'[9]

Many instances of such grumbling suggest that citizens' memories and awareness of the uprising did not comply with the SED's official account of what happened. In June 1955 an FDGB-led discussion took place about the threat of 'imperialist attacks' on the GDR. The trade union representative noted, 'great uncertainties still persist about the character of 17 June 1953. For example, someone asked where the proof was that agents instigated 17 June.'[10] In January 1956 the question of the construction of a national army in the GDR raised concerns in the Karl Liebknecht plant in Magdeburg: 'the question was posed: Aren't the government making a mistake like the one they made on 17.6.1953?'[11] In May of the same year the FDGB in Magdeburg reported that there was a degree of disquiet in factories concerning working quotas: 'for example, a youth said, "Are you starting your working quota nonsense again? You scrapped them in 1953 because they led to 17 June and now that stuff is going to start all over again".'[12] In July 1957, amidst discussions by workers in the SKET of Nikita Khrushchev's ousting of several internal opponents in Moscow, it was reported: 'People are trying to allude to 17.6.1953 along the lines of: our government made big mistakes back then, without carrying out any reorganisation here.'[13] The grumbling of citizens also shows that citizens remembered the role of East German citizens in the uprising differently to what the SED claimed. The Party maintained that the majority of East Germans stood with the regime against the provocateurs. Yet in October 1955 a report on discussions amongst ordinary citizens about GDR–USSR relations stated: 'two colleagues... openly led anti-working class discussions.... On the subject of the events of 17.6.1953 they declared, that this showed the real mood of the masses.'[14]

Interestingly, some citizens apparently recalled the uprising as having achieved positive results for them. In 1958 workers in the Hornberger lime works mentioned the uprising in a discussion about a recently introduced new passport law which, so these workers believed, was intended to increase the difficulty of successfully leaving the GDR. They stated: 'the implementation of the passport law [is] a governmental method of pressure... and it would be changed, if the general public make a stand against it. This was linked to 17.6 and the New Course.'[15] This comment suggests that these workers believed that the uprising had forced the SED to introduce the New Course of relaxation of repression in the GDR. Thus they believed it had had at least one positive result. In reality, the New Course was introduced before 17 June 1953.

The files also indicate that the Party was aware that citizens were accessing coverage of the West German commemorations of the uprising. In June 1956 it was reported to the SED city leadership in Magdeburg that citizens in the city had been questioning why free pan-German elections were not taking place. The report noted: 'The manner of the discussion indicates that people... are strongly influenced by Western broadcasters and leaflets, which, on the occasion of the anniversary of the fascist putsch on 17.6, want to provoke these arguments amongst the population.'[16] The fact that its citizens accessed the Western broadcasts was made clear to the Party by a worker from the SKET in June 1959: '[he] turned to different negative and fickle colleagues and demanded that they listen to [Mayor of West Berlin Willy] Brandt's speech on Western stations on the occasion of the return of 17.6.'[17] But some citizens in the 1950s apparently did not need to be encouraged to commemorate the anniversary by the West German broadcast media. In March 1955 a worker (under the influence of alcohol at the time) declared: '1 May [is] null and void for the workers... the workers will, however, celebrate their national holiday on 17.6. He himself will be getting hammered on 17.6.'[18]

One significant aspect of these recorded references to the uprising is the age of the citizens who made them. In several reports the citizens expressing comments about 17 June 1953 were described as 'juveniles' (*Jugendliche*). For example, in 1957 it was recorded by the SED city leadership in a report on 'enemy activity' in the city: 'the juvenile W. openly railed against the Party and the government... [and] said, that on a second 17 June the factory trade union chairman and the political officer would be the first to be hanged.'[19] In the 1950s any East German citizen between the ages of 14 and 18 was a 'juvenile' in the eyes of the law. Some of these 'juveniles' may indeed have experienced the uprising as children in Magdeburg. However, it is possible that some were too young to have been actively involved or too young to be able to recall the uprising. This would suggest that younger generations of citizens were aware of the uprising. Given that the subject was only introduced in schools in the 1960s, it would also indicate that these youths learned about 17 June 1953 from another source. One such source was identified in a comment reported in 1956: 'A juvenile said: 17.6.53 was correct. It will happen again soon, my father was at the forefront. But this time it will be better.'[20]

Amongst the many incidents in the 1950s of citizens evoking the memory of 17 June 1953 while grumbling, a more serious expression of dissent linked to the uprising occurred in Magdeburg in 1956. A resident of the city, Herr Abraham G., received a letter from an organisation calling itself the NTS. The letter made reference to the events of 17 June 1953 with the express intention of encouraging opposition to the SED. The NTS or Narodnyi Trudovoy Soyuz (National Labour Council) was a Russian émigré group founded in Belgrade in July 1930. Its anti-Marxist philosophy attracted many who wanted to see the restoration of the

Tsarist Empire. After the Second World War and with backing from MI6, the CIA and the West German secret service, the group undertook intelligence operations in the Soviet Union and set up the Possev publishing house in Munich. Millions of leaflets were printed here for use in propaganda operations within the USSR (Dorrill, 2000, pp. 404–25). The NTS wrote to Herr G. requesting his support and asking him to pass on a second letter (apparently in Russian and unfortunately missing from the file) to any Russian acquaintances he might have. During the Second World War the NTS had targeted known dissidents in the Red Army in the hope of encouraging a mutiny. It is possible that the content of the missing half of the letter was of a similar nature.

The NTS addressed the uprising of 17 June 1953 in the very first line of the letter: 'There are surely no Germans who do not think of 17 June 1953 with justifiable pride and quiet sorrow!' The NTS then stated: 'This day has become a symbol of German resistance against a system, which does not know life in peace and freedom'.[21] Thus, the NTS perceived that that the uprising of 17 June 1953 had already become a reference point for acts of resistance against the regime in the GDR.

6.2 Strikes in Magdeburg in 1956

1956 was a year of crisis in the Eastern Bloc. Nikita Khrushchev's denunciation of Stalin left communist party members in the Soviet Union and its satellites in disarray. Citizens reacted angrily when their respective communist parties followed suit in denouncing Stalin and his policies of the past years, under which many had suffered. Dissatisfaction with political leaders began to simmer and was a contributing factor to unrest in Poland in late June 1956 and the uprising in Hungary in mid-October of the same year. Soviet tanks crushed the protests in both countries (see Wolle, 2006a).

The uprising in Hungary in 1956 appears to have prompted citizens to recall 17 June 1953. Several interviewees stated that this was also the case for them, but in contrast to those citizens recorded in the files, they stated that they did not verbalise their recollections. The recorded references indicate that citizens were comparing what they recalled about the unrest in their country with what was happening in Hungary. For example, in late October 1956 one citizen, a member of the SED in fact, stated in a Party meeting: 'the putsch in Hungary came from within exactly like it did with us on 17.6.53'.[22] It was also reported that workers were making 'comparisons with the events of 17.6.1953... and arguing that the governments of the peoples' democracies only had a minority of like-minded people behind them and were thus forced to support their power with foreign bayonets'.²³ Another SED report lamented that workers apparently did not understand that the uprising in Hungary constituted an attack on the entire socialist camp: 'the events [are being] compared with 17 June and interpreted thus: that the provocations were possible because workers in Hungary and Poland are unhappy.'²⁴ The events in Hungary were also accompanied by a wave of graffiti in Magdeburg, including 'Strike like the Hungarians', 'We follow Hungary' and 'SED – SO ENDET DEUTSCHLAND [Thus ends Germany]'.²⁵

Unrest in the GDR provoked by the events in Hungary was not limited to verbal or written expressions of discontent. Strikes occurred across the country in October 1956, with Magdeburg at the centre (Wolle, 2006b). Unrest in the factories of Magdeburg had actually started in early September with workers in the steel cleaning and foundry sections of the Karl Marx plant. The *Stasi* reported disgruntlement and discussions amongst these workers about new collective wage agreements, new working quotas and general living conditions.²⁶ Such discontent continued and spread to the SKET and Georgi Dimitroff plant. By early October 1956 workers in sections of all three factories were regularly downing tools in protest, demanding that things change.²⁷ Each time, the SED managed to appease the strikers with concessions, but strikes continued sporadically and discontent simmered away well into December 1956.

Workers referenced 17 June 1953 when threatening to strike, indicating that their memories of the uprising in the GDR played a role in their protests. One worker in the SKET commented:

We were the first ones there on 17.6.53 when it went off. There are about 70 of us who will immediately come together if it should go off here. They ought to take note of us. We are always ready to fight against the current circumstances.²⁸

The demands made by striking workers also suggest that they were drawing on their experiences of the June uprising during these strikes in 1956. In the SKET workers demanded that the working quota system be abolished in favour of steady, hourly wages, and that the Soviet armed forces withdraw immediately from the GDR. Perhaps to cover themselves against the accusations levelled at workers on 17 June 1953, those on strike in the SKET in 1956 also demanded that fascism and militarism never be reinstalled in a united Germany.²⁹

Considering the SED's paranoia about a second uprising in the GDR, it is small wonder that the events of 17 June 1953 were also on the minds of the Party leadership in Magdeburg in the autumn of 1956. In a meeting to discuss what should be reported to the Politburo, the local SED leadership criticised the Party's reaction to the unrest in 1953 and implicitly stated that this reaction had made the situation worse: 'If we act like they did on 17.6.53, simply trying to regulate the situation by changing the working quotas, then that will create difficulties for us.' In the same meeting, one committee member made a rather striking admission that indicates that not even SED members believed the Party's account of the June uprising. Complaining about the fact that the city leadership was arguing about whether to report the incidents to the Politburo as a 'downing of tools' or a 'strike', he stated: 'There is nothing to discuss in talking about whether it is a downing of tools or a strike. After 17.6.53 we tried to prove something that could not be proved.' Furthermore, reports of the strikes in the Western press were making the Magdeburg SED even more nervous about a repeat of 17 June 1953. The West Berlin newspaper *Der Tag* had run an article on 18 October 1956 claiming that strikes in the Karl Marx plant had taken place and that armed units of the *Volkspolizei* and the *Stasi* had been needed to put an end to the unrest (*MVS*, 1956, p. 1). The Magdeburg SED leadership regarded these reports as a blatant attempt by the West German media to provoke a new uprising in the GDR: 'They are talking about a new 17 June. That is a process that develops. They are trying to provoke confusion. For this reason we must strengthen our vigilance and the provocateurs must be confronted.' Soon after these reports appeared the SED launched a propaganda campaign to refute the 'lies' in the Western press. They even invited journalists from the West German newspapers and magazines *Frankfurter Rundschau, Westdeutsche Allgemeine Zeitung, Frankfurter Allgemeine Zeitung* and *Der Spiegel* to tour the Karl Marx plant and see for themselves that no strikes were taking place. This move backfired. After returning from Magdeburg the journalists claimed that they had seen: '1. Dissatisfaction and protests amongst the workers; 2. Downing of tools; 3. Military protection of the factories'. Needless to say, the Magdeburg Party leadership was furious.[30]

6.3 1960s

Though the *Volkspolizei* in Magdeburg continued to receive orders from Berlin about how to prepare for and prevent 'provocations' on the anniversaries of the uprising throughout the 1960s, there was an important development in its operations. On 18 June 1961 the information division of the BDVP Magdeburg produced a 'Special Report' (*Sonderbericht*) of the anniversary that year. This report detailed occurrences and incidents specifically related to the anniversary of the uprising. Similar special reports were now produced annually. The 1961 document included information on West German commemorations of the uprising along the stretch of the inner-German border adjacent to Magdeburg and the surrounding district. The report included information on demonstrations and memorial bonfires, how many West Germans attended, and the details of any speeches made. It also noted that West Germans in Magdeburg on 17 June 1961 had not caused any trouble, suggesting that they had been under surveillance.[31] It was not unknown for visiting West Germans to mention 17 June 1953. In October 1954 a member of a West German delegation visiting a factory in Magdeburg had reportedly told the workers there: 'It's better for us over there [in the West]. You could have had it exactly the same, if you had really given it a go on 17 June 1953.'[32]

Orders issued in preparation for 17 June 1962 indicate that the security forces in the GDR were now most concerned that any disturbances that might occur would be influenced by West German commemorations of the uprising:

> The Bonn Ultras, revanchists and militarists use 17 June annually in order to celebrate their failed attempted putsch in the GDR in 1953 and to carry out agitation, provocations and subversive activities.... Subsequently, the armed forces in Magdeburg are to increase their vigilance and stand by for action, in order to guarantee security and order in the district and prevent disturbances. Focus is to be directed on the Autobahn, district capital and border regions.[33]

The fact that the majority of East German citizens could only have learned of these commemorations through accessing the West German broadcast media further demonstrates the regime's preoccupation with the perceived impact of these programmes on its citizens. The report on activities relating to the anniversary of 17 June 1953 produced by the *Volkspolizei* in the wake of the 1962 anniversary again included information on West German commemorations of the uprising along the border. Also included were details of leaflets found that had apparently been transported from West to East via balloon: 'The content of all of the leaflets related in a rabble-rousing manner to 17.6. Therein stood the demand to ring all bells during the night of 16–17.6.'[34] On the same anniversary the *Stasi* in Magdeburg discovered what they described as a Western newspaper titled '17 June' while checking a car travelling through the area.[35]

In June 1964 the BDVP Magdeburg began to produce reports specifically about the commemorations taking place on the western side of the inner-German border. The report from this year stated that on the night of 16 June 1964 an 'agitation rally' (*Hetzkundgebung*) of approximately 150 people took place near Radenbeck. A bonfire was then lit. Moreover, at 9 p.m. in Offleben 2,000 people gathered and in Büddenstadt a torchlight-procession took place.[36] The following day at 3 p.m. there was a demonstration near Wernigerode and at 4 p.m. 200 people protested for German reunification near Eckertal.[37] Such reports specifically about the Western commemorations on the border continued over the next few years. It was noted on 15 June 1965 that, as well as there being an increase in leafleting actions from the West, a bonfire was being built near Benneckenstein[38]; 300 youths aged between 15 and 18 years of age took part in a torchlight procession in Lengde on 16 June 1966[39]; and on 17 June 1967, 880 people gathered in Oebisfeld to hear an address by the Federal Minister for Expellees and Refugees Kai-Uwe von Hassel.[40]

Further evidence for the hypothesis that the regime's fear of potential unrest on 17 June was directly linked to the extent to which West Germany commemorated the uprising can be found in the BDVP Magdeburg files from the late 1960s. As the West German broadcast media's commemoration of the uprising began to dwindle in 1968, so did the GDR's security forces' concerns about unrest on the anniversaries each year. In the year that the West German broadcast media all but ceased to air any kind of commemorations of the uprising, the BDVP Magdeburg ceased producing special reports of crimes committed or activities taking place related to the anniversary of 17 June 1953. The *Volkspolizei* in Magdeburg also ceased producing its reports on West German events at the border in 1968. From 1968 any occurrences related to the anniversary of the uprising were simply recorded in the daily reports along with other crimes committed on the day. Such incidents apparently no longer warranted their own special report.

Despite the regime's intensification of measures to prevent 'provocations' on 17 June throughout the 1960s, the state authorities in Magdeburg actually recorded fewer mentions of the uprising amongst citizens in the city. However, the daily reports of the *Volkspolizei* from the 1960s indicate that the anniversary of the uprising each year triggered increases in crimes referencing 17 June 1953 and general cases of slandering of the state (*Staatsverleumdung*) or anti-state agitation (*staatsgefährdende Hetze*). Such expressions of dissent referencing 17 June 1953 continued to be provoked by citizens' dissatisfaction with the standard of consumption in the GDR. For example, on 17 June 1961 two national flags of the GDR were torn down from outside the HO restaurant 'Fortschritt'.[41] The following day three more flags were removed from outside the same establishment.[42] On 16 June 1964 three 'agitation notes' (*Hetzzettel*) titled '17 June' were found stuck to the windows of nearby HO shops.[43] By targeting state-owned HO establishments, the people behind these incidents were no doubt expressing their anger with the consumption opportunities available to them, and referencing 17 June 1953 in the process.

Interestingly, as was the case in the 1950s some citizens again expressed positive views about the outcome of the uprising. Their comments indicate that they felt that the unrest had achieved something. For example, one worker in the SKET stated, 'on 17.6.1953... the workers downed their tools because they wanted to live better. They achieved this to an extent.'[44] Moreover, while grumbling about SED policy, one worker in the SKET in 1960 told his FDGB representative: 'You should remember 17 June 1953, after which came a significant relaxation in interzonal traffic on the part of our government... you should relax travel restrictions to West Germany.'[45] This comment suggests that the fact that citizens felt that the uprising had actually brought them some positive results apparently led them to adopt an optimistic attitude to the possibility that they had the power to change things in the GDR.

The files also show that citizens too young to have experienced the uprising continued to make reference to it in the 1960s. In 1961 workers in the Fahlberg-List factory were discussing the latest travel restrictions to the West. The issue of the right to strike somehow came up in these talks: 'A younger colleague stated that at a strike the people would be quickly shot at by tanks, as was the case on 17 June 1953.'[46] As in several instances in the 1950s, the person making reference to 17 June 1953 is described in the report as a young person. Once again it is impossible to know how old this young woman was. However, the fact that her comment was recorded eight years after the uprising took place would suggest that she might indeed have been too young to have personally experienced the uprising. The *Stasi* was apparently aware that 17 June 1953 held some significance for younger citizens in the 1960s. On 17 June 1963 it particularly noted how school pupils had behaved: 'The operative informants reportedly that no discussions about 17 June occurred and no one spoke about it. Likewise, nothing occurred in the schools. The pupils attended class in their [FDJ] blue shirts, like every other day.'[47]

Two further reports suggest that 17 June 1953 held some meaning for younger generations of East German citizens. On 18 June 1968 a man was arrested for being drunk and disorderly. He swore at the policemen and stated: 'You red big shots, you really have forgotten 17 June... when it happens again, I will kill you.' This man was born on 12 May 1950.[48] Thus he was only three years old on 17 June 1953. Yet he still made reference to the uprising in his expression of dissent. Moreover, on 17 June 1965 two boys in a children's home had swastikas tattooed on their forearms. After this they got drunk and gave the Hitler salute.[49] The fact that both were resident in such an institution 12 years after the uprising took place indicates that they would have been very young, if alive at all, in 1953. Although it is impossible to conclude from the file whether the boys wanted to show real political opposition with their swastika tattoos, it is possible to imagine that the date of their misdemeanour was no coincidence. Moreover, such incidents only served to heighten the Party's paranoia about the anniversary of the uprising.

Several reports from the 1960s indicate that the annual West German commemorations of the uprising held some significance for East German citizens, too. A 28-year-old man (14 years old in 1953) was arrested after expressing the following to a member of the National People's Army (NVA): '[he] said... that he will celebrate the "Day of German Unity" on 17.06.67.' He then told the NVA soldier that if a second uprising came about: 'then we will hang you.'[50] The file did not state what happened to him after his arrest. It is interesting to note that citizens recorded making reference to a second 17 June often also threatened to hang representatives of the state on such an occasion. Yet on 17 June 1953 no such hangings occurred in Magdeburg. The three members of the security forces who died were killed by gunfire. References to hanging possibly emanated from memories of such occurrences during and immediately after the Second World War. Alternatively, some citizens may have drawn on what they knew of hangings during the uprising in Hungary in 1956.

Whereas there was evidence that the uprising in Hungary in 1956 prompted citizens to recall 17 June 1953, there is no such evidence that the events of the Prague Spring in Czechoslovakia in 1968 caused citizens to do the same. This indicates that as the uprising moved further into the past it played a smaller role in citizens' expressions of dissent against the regime. Despite the fact that in August 1968 the *Volkspolizei* recorded high levels of anti-state graffiti, none referenced 17 June 1953. Their content focused on supporting Dubček or calling for more freedom in general.

6.4 1970s

In comparison to earlier decades, the security forces in the GDR in the 1970s scaled back their preparations to nip in the bud repeats of the 1953 unrest on its anniversaries. This development occurred at a time when the West German broadcast media had massively reduced the amount of coverage it was dedicating to commemorating the events. Once again, this shows that the SED regime's level of concern about memories or awareness of 17 June 1953 inspiring a repeat performance was linked to the extent to which West German television and radio stations broadcast programmes about it.

In accordance with the regime's modified perception of the potential for unrest on or around 17 June throughout the 1970s the security forces in Magdeburg cut back the extent of their preparations for trouble. However, they did not cease altogether their preventative measures. Moreover, the precautions that they took included one significant development. The *Volkspolizei* and *Stasi* now turned their attention from activities on the Western side of the inner-German border to possible troublemakers within the borders of the GDR itself. This further demonstrates that the SED regime's perception of a threat from the West was altered by the lack of West German media commemorations. Accordingly, individuals and/or organisations in the GDR identified as 'right-leaning', 'revanchist' or 'neo-fascist' were now of particular concern (Eisenfeld et al., 2004, p. 189). However, West German groups occasionally provoked concerns. For example, in 1975 preparations made by the *Stasi* in Magdeburg for the anniversary of 17 June concentrated on the activities of the West Berlin branch of the *Junge Nationaldemokraten*, the youth organisation of the West German extreme right wing National Democratic Party of Germany (NPD). This group was travelling through the GDR to Bonn. The author of the report also voiced concerns about the trouble-making potential of the *Junge Union*, the youth organisation of the CDU.[51]

Despite this overall scaling back, security preparations were stepped up in anticipation of 17 June 1977. Over the period around the anniversary this year meetings between Eastern and Western powers were due to take place in Belgrade in order to discuss future co-operation. The *Stasi* was concerned that this occasion might be used as an opportunity to trigger debates about human rights in the GDR (Eisenfeld et al., 2004, p. 191). On 10 June 1977 the head of the *Stasi* in Magdeburg received a 17-page document detailing the measures to be taken, in accordance with orders issued by Minister for State Security Erich Mielke. Once again, the *Stasi* was most concerned about 'enemy forces' in the FRG and West Berlin. The *Junge Union* was also mentioned in this context. Moreover, citizens expected to cause trouble, including those known to have been active in the uprising of 17 June 1953, were to be more intensively observed. The churches in Magdeburg, as well as the university and medical academy, were also identified as places from which unrest might emanate.[52]

The head of the BDVP Magdeburg also received more extensive orders than usual detailing the preparations to be made for potential demonstrations this anniversary. Identified as places of potential unrest were the border with West Germany, transport hubs and politically, militarily or economically important buildings. The *Volkspolizei* in Magdeburg were to ensure that there was complete observation of all individuals from non-socialist countries in the city. No security personnel were to be allowed to take holidays from 16 to 20 June 1977; prisoners were not to be allowed out of their cells; and the *Volkspolizei* stations responsible for the border area were to be reinforced with border guard regiments. All suspicious incidents were to be immediately reported to the *Stasi*.[53]

Records of East German citizens making reference to the uprising of 17 June 1953 in public in the 1970s suggest that, as the events moved further into the past, they played a smaller role in citizens' expressions of dissent. The lack of Western coverage of the anniversaries, which provided an annual reminded of the uprising to citizens, no doubt contributed to this. In this decade the SED's district leadership only recorded one citizen making reference to the uprising. In November 1979 the SED was investigating complaints amongst citizens regarding the food supply, increasing prices and the value of GDR currency. In one such discussion with editors of a factory newspaper, the question 'Do we simply need a new 17 June?' was posed.[54] There was also a decrease in the number of crimes committed in the period around the anniversaries of the uprising in the 1970s, though some incidents did still occur. On the night of 17 June 1970 a school in Magdeburg was broken into and the picture of Lenin from classroom 17 was stolen.[55] The period around the anniversary of the uprising in 1974 saw a comparable incident in which the tyres on 17 cars in Magdeburg city centre were slashed.[56] On 17 June 1973 graffito appeared that read: 'Remember the dead of 1953.'[57]

On 27 June 1975 a crime was reported that once again linked 'fascism' with the anniversary of 17 June 1953. Graffiti were discovered scrawled across the emblem of the Society for German–Soviet Friendship on its headquarters in the south of Magdeburg. These consisted of 'fascist' symbols such as swastikas and SS runes, as well as the date

'17.6.1953'.[58] It is again difficult to establish whether the perpetrators of this crime had any serious political agenda, or whether they simply did it because they knew that drawing such symbols represented dissent against the SED. During the periods around the anniversaries of the uprising in the following two years, no relevant incidents were reported. And there were no particular increases in cases of slandering of the state. On 17 June 1978 two incidents occurred that could possibly be linked to the fact that it was the 25th anniversary of the uprising. Fifty-five anti-state leaflets were found in Magdeburg city centre. Unfortunately, the files contain no information regarding the content of these leaflets.[59] In the period around the final anniversary of the decade, no comparable incidents were recorded.

The security forces in Magdeburg apparently perceived that the potential for unrest inspired by memories or awareness of 17 June 1953 was waning. In 1978 the *Volkspolizei* in Magdeburg was put on a higher than usual state of alert in preparation for the 25th anniversary of the uprising, yet they were apparently no longer as anxious about potential unrest as they had been in the 1950s and 1960s. The evidence also indicates that they were also not as anxious about the role that the West German broadcast media might play in this. From 17 to 18 June 1978 the twenty-fourth press festival organised by the *Magdeburger Volksstimme* newspaper took place in the city. This was unusual because public events, works' outings, club meetings and even private parties were rarely permitted to take place on the anniversaries of the uprising. The authorities feared that these might provide the perfect opportunity for 'provocations'. Moreover, because this was a significant anniversary, the West German broadcast media aired more hours of commemorative programmes in this year than they had done throughout the 1970s. This perhaps did influence the higher than unusual state of alert in the GDR on the day. Yet the security forces in Magdeburg still allowed the *Volksstimme* press event to take place, despite the increased Western media coverage.[60]

6.5 1980s

In the 1980s West German politicians and the West German broadcast media showed renewed interest in commemorating the uprising of 17 June 1953. At the same time, West German commemorations of the uprising along the inner-German border once again became the focus of the Magdeburg security forces' activities. In preparation for 17 June 1985 the *Stasi* in Magdeburg recorded details of demonstrations and other similar events due to take place at the inner-German border. Such reports about activities at the border had not been compiled in the 1970s. The main *Stasi* HQ in Magdeburg advised its regional branches in the rest of the Magdeburg district: 'You must operatively observe meetings that have not been made known to us and, in co-operation with other security organs, contribute to keeping enemy activities under control.'[61]

By 1989 *Stasi* reports on West German commemorations had become most extensive. With opposition growing in the GDR, the state apparently perceived an increase in the likelihood that such commemorations would spark unrest. Extensive details of 23 separate West German events scheduled to take place between 13 and 17 June 1989 were reported. For example, at 9.15 a.m. on 17 June 1989 there would be a wreath laying at the memorial to Peter Fechter (who was killed trying to get over the Berlin Wall in 1962) in Charlottenstraße by Heinrich Lummer of the CDU. At 9.30 a.m. on the same day, there would be a similar ceremony organised by the KUD at the memorial in West Berlin dedicated to those killed in the uprising of 17 June 1953. It was noted that attempts were being made to have the president of the West Berlin House of Representatives, Jürgen Wohlrabe, speak at this event. And near the West German town of Bad Harzburg, close to the border with the *Bezirk* of Magdeburg, there would be an '[a]gitation meeting at the "Cross of the German East" memorial on the Uhlenklippe rock, organised by the "The Committee of the Day of Germany Unity" on 17 June 1989; it is planned that former President of the *Bundestag* Jenninger will be the key-note speaker.'[62]

The uprising of 17 June 1953 was barely referenced in citizens' expressions of dissent in the 1980s. In fact, the information on the mood of citizens in Magdeburg compiled by the SED in this decade reported no mentions of 17 June 1953. And in the first three years of the 1980s the *Volkspolizei* reported no particular incidents relating to 17 June 1953. Moreover, in contrast to previous decades the *Volkspolizei* recorded very few cases of slandering of the state in the periods around the anniversary each year. However, on the 30th anniversary of the uprising in 1983 there was an overall increase in such cases. Handwritten notes attacking the SED and the *Volkspolizei* were found on a park bench. An anonymous caller threatened to blow up the borough council building in Stendal, and 92 anti-Soviet and anti-GDR leaflets were found in Magdeburg.[63]

On the next two anniversaries of the uprising, graffiti of a 'fascist' nature once again appeared in Magdeburg. The content of these did not directly reference the uprising. However, the fact that they appeared on its anniversary must not be ignored. On 17 June 1984 'fascist' symbols and slogans were found on two public benches.[64] On 17 June 1985 the *Volkspolizei* reported three fascist symbols and nine slogans on a tram shelter on Boleslav-Bierut-Platz in central Magdeburg.[65] The culprits were not apprehended, making it once again impossible to establish their motives.

Despite the relative dearth of recorded expressions of dissent referencing 17 June 1953 during the 1980s, one particular incident on 17 June 1988 drew the attention of the *Stasi* in Magdeburg. On this day its mail surveillance section intercepted an envelope addressed to Erich Honecker. The envelope had been posted in Magdeburg city centre between 3 p.m. and 7 p.m. The *Stasi* reported that the 16 A4 pages found in the envelope contained 'hostile-negative remarks against the leading role of the SED... and... unconstitutional attacks against the socialist principles of the GDR'.[66] These 16 pages were divided into four separate documents: 'Covering letter to the General Secretary of the SED, demand for his resignation on the occasion of the "Day of German Unity" for freedom'; 'Explanation of the situation in the GDR'; 'National reunification: the legitimate right of the German nation'; and 'Proclamation for peace, for unity, justice and freedom!' All of these items were signed by the Committee for Peace, for Unity, Justice and Freedom (*Das Komitee für Frieden, für Einigkeit und Recht und Freiheit*, KFERF).

Though the medium through which this dissent was expressed differed to the majority of those previously examined, the nature of the dissent was effectively the same: the KFERF grumbled about the current state of affairs in the GDR. In their letter to Erich Honecker, the author(s) proclaimed: 'Actually existing socialism in the GDR has failed!' The author(s) based this claim on the various supply problems in the GDR: 'This state is not in the position to sufficiently and satisfactorily supply the citizens of this country!' They stated that the GDR was becoming an economically backward country and pointed to the GDR's work productivity, technology, per-head income, medical provision and supply of industrial goods. Above all, however, the author(s) identified the poor supply of food and basic clothing as the most pressing problem in the GDR. They asserted that at the root of these problems were 'the Party and government's politics which are hostile to the people'. They also claimed that the government's policies had led to a scarcity of goods, increasing prices and the poor quality of what was actually available.[67]

The author(s) complained not only about the supply situation in the GDR but also the extent to which the SED regime limited East German citizens' freedom. They wrote that free political parties, organisations and trade unions did not exist in the GDR because all were subordinated to the Party. They also claimed that there was no free press, free speech, freedom of assembly or freedom of religion in the GDR. They explained that those citizens who had applied to leave the GDR

> are searching for a country in which they can live freely!...a country in which there are free, secret, equal and direct elections!...a country in which there is freedom of belief, of religion, of free expression of opinion, of a free press...a country in which people have representatives in a free parliament![68]

The author(s) employed numerous terms to express their view of the GDR as a totalitarian state. Explicitly labelling the SED regime a dictatorship, they referred to the 'state regulation, tutelage and stultification' that they believed made life impossible for many citizens in the GDR.[69] The authors then stated that a state of 'total surveillance by the organs of the State Security Service' existed in the GDR. They claimed that the GDR possessed one of the largest intelligence organisations in the world in order to suppress human rights. In this context the author(s) once again blamed the SED for the fact that so many citizens were unhappy: 'These people are seeking escape from totalitarian surveillance and repression by the Party!' The author(s) also criticised the high number of security force personnel in the GDR and condemned the cost in terms of material, time, personnel, money and human rights created by the Berlin Wall ('the biggest prison fence in history').[70]

Although the KFERF chose the anniversary of the uprising to send these documents to Erich Honecker, it is clear that the uprising itself held little significance for them. Throughout the 16 pages of detailed analysis and scrutiny of the apparent failings of GDR society and the SED regime, the KFERF only actually referred to the events of 17 June 1953 once. This was done only in passing and after the committee had stated that the current political and economic circumstances in the GDR were forcing the SED to make certain concessions. The author(s) claimed that this was due to the fact that '17 June 1953 is still in your memories!'[71]

6.6 Interviewees

No interviewees claimed that memories or awareness of the uprising of 17 June 1953 inspired them to commit acts of open and direct dissent against the regime. Moreover, only two interviewees – eyewitness

Jakob Balzert (born 1941) and Katja Müller (born 1962) – stated that their memories and awareness of 17 June 1953 played a role in their oppositional stances toward the regime. For the other interviewees the uprising held little significance.

Herr Balzert recounted that his experiences of 17 June 1953 led to the first (and only) tangible manifestation of his oppositional stance toward the regime. This came in the form of a greeting that referenced the uprising. The fact that Herr Balzert practised this greeting for many years after the uprising had taken place further suggests that his memories of the uprising continued to inspire in some part his oppositional stance toward the SED regime. The greeting took the form of a hand gesture invented by him and his friends shortly after the uprising had been put down: 'You stretch out two fingers and clap them onto the palm of the other hand. That means: the second time it will succeed.' Herr Balzert stated that he and his trusted friends made this gesture in secret every time they met.

Katja Müller (born 1962) stated that she drew encouragement from her grandfather's communicated memories of the unrest in the GDR to continue on the non-conformist path that her life had taken. She recalled that in the mid-1980s she and her siblings spoke to their grandparents about the life choices that they had made. Her grandparents had trodden a similar path. They had not supported the Third Reich and had been members of the 'Bekennende Kirche', a Church-based opposition group to the Nazis. They had not done a great deal against the Nazis, but they 'had their eyes open for injustices and them tried to support people who were having a bad time'. When the Second World War came to an end neither grandparent joined the SED. However, her grandfather did not just draw on his experiences under the Third Reich to reassure his grandchildren. He also spoke about his experiences of the uprising of 17 June 1953 in Magdeburg. He told Frau Müller that he was very proud to have protested with his fellow workers. Frau Müller drew encouragement from these memories when the pressure of continuing with her oppositional stance and the disappointing options with which this had left her grew hard to bear.

6.7 Conclusion

The state authorities and security forces in the GDR were aware that memories and awareness of the uprising of 17 June 1953 existed amongst citizens. The regime perceived that these held the potential to inspire further unrest and possibly a repeat of the uprising. Moreover, the Party saw a direct correlation between the extent to which the West German broadcast media commemorated the events and the extent of the potential for trouble. This indicates that the authorities in the GDR were aware that citizens were accessing such programmes. However, as the uprising moved further into the past, the regime's anxiety about a repeat apparently receded. The extent of the measures taken to nip any unrest around the anniversaries of the uprising in the bud was at its highest level in the 1950s and 1960s and did not reach similar heights in later decades. The recollections of Heinz Kurtsiefer (born 1945), who worked for the *Volkspolizei*, confirm this. Herr Kurtsiefer joined the riot police in 1964 and served for 25 years. He recalled that in the 1960s the police were always prepared to undertake major operations on the anniversaries of the uprising. Emergency staffs were formed, extra provisions were made available and leave was cancelled. Particular attention was to be paid to what citizens in the street were saying in case a demonstration was being planned. Officers also had to watch for graffiti referencing 17 June 1953 and check if state flags had been hung out as usual. However, Herr Kurtsiefer remembered that, although emergency measures were always in place in the 1980s, the extent of the preparations was in no way comparable to that of the 1960s.

Citizens most often made reference to the uprising of 17 June 1953 when expressing dissent against the regime. It is fair to assume that memories or awareness of the events of 1953 inspired such acts committed over the period of the uprising's anniversary each year. However, references to the uprising made in complaints about living conditions, as well as those made at times of the year other than the period of the anniversary, suggest that the need to express dissent apparently evoked memories or awareness of the uprising and not vice versa. Temporal proximity to the uprising affected how often ordinary citizens made reference to it in their expressions of dissent. Recorded occurrences of such dissent decreased from highs in the 1960s to much fewer instances in the 1980s. Moreover, while the uprising in Hungary in 1956 evoked memories of the June uprising amongst citizens in Magdeburg, this was not the case 12 years later during the Prague Spring. Thus memories or awareness of the uprising played an ever-decreasing role in citizens' expressions of dissent over the period of the GDR's existence.

There is no evidence to suggest that there were serious political agendas behind the majority of these expressions of dissent. In most cases of general slandering of the state found in the security forces' files, the citizens involved were drunk. The context of many of the references also makes clear that citizens were simply letting off steam about their frustration with living conditions in the GDR. The fact that the Committee for Peace, for Unity, Justice and Freedom only gave the uprising a fleeting mention in its lengthy condemnation of the state of GDR society and the SED, yet nevertheless posted its message on the anniversary of the uprising, shows that 17 June 1953 held no more than symbolic significance for the author(s) of the text. Unhappy, grumbling citizens knew that any kind of threatening mention of or reference to the events was a sure-fire way to strike fear into the hearts of those propping up the regime and to attract their attention. As Mary Fulbrook has concluded, 17 June 1953 served as a 'symbolic talisman' of opposition to the SED, even if citizens did not carry out their threats to instigate 'a second 17 June' (1995, p. 178). However, that is not to say that memories or awareness of 17 June 1953 played no role in citizens' opposition to the regime. Though Jakob Balzert's experiences of the unrest did not alter his already negative attitude toward the state, they did encourage him to exercise a small act of passive resistance in the form of the invention of a greeting amongst his friends that recalled the events of 1953. Communicated memories and awareness of the uprising also reassured and encouraged Katja Müller to continue passively to defy the SED regime and its tenets.

7
Remembering 17 June 1953 in 1989

In the autumn of 1989, hundreds of thousands of East German citizens protested for the removal of the SED and for a better form of socialism in towns and cities across the GDR. These demonstrations, which ultimately culminated in the fall of the Berlin Wall and the fall of the SED regime, evoked memories and thoughts of the uprising of 17 June 1953 in the minds of state functionaries, such as Erich Mielke. But were citizens also thinking of the events of 1953? Although the files of the state authorities show that no public mention of 17 June 1953 was recorded during the demonstrations that took place in Magdeburg in the autumn of 1989, one might expect interviewees (eyewitnesses of the June uprising in particular) to recollect that their thoughts turned to the events of 1953. One might also expect that this was the one point in the history of the GDR in which memories or awareness of the June uprising were most likely to affect the behaviour of citizens. This was certainly the case for eyewitnesses of the earlier uprising in the GDR with whom I spoke. By their accounts, the most prominent memories of 1953 that resurfaced in their minds in 1989 were those of acts of violence that they had experienced first-hand during the June uprising. Such memories provoked feelings of fear in them and deterred many from taking part in demonstrations in 1989. By contrast, the majority of interviewees born after 1953 claimed that thoughts of the earlier uprising did not cross their minds in 1989 and therefore played no role in the decisions that they made or the manner in which they behaved. They stated that intense fears, emotions and worries about the day-to-day events of the autumn of 1989 eclipsed any thoughts about the past. Thus for many, action influenced memory and not vice versa.

7.1 The successful revolution of 1989 in Magdeburg

Over the course of the 1980s the state of the East German economy steadily worsened due to economic mismanagement and the increasing indebtedness of the regime. These problems were compounded by the fact that, due to its own economic plight, the Soviet Union could no longer subsidise the economies of its satellite states. The increasingly poor health of the GDR's economy led to a deterioration in living conditions for its citizens. The state simply could no longer qualitatively nor quantitatively satisfy the needs of its citizens. Throughout the decade more and more citizens made applications to leave the country (though few were permitted) as it slipped further into economic crisis. These developments were accompanied by the formation of various protest movements in the 1980s, beginning with peace and environmental groups in the early years of the decade (see Dale, 2005, pp. 98–120; Neubert, 1997, pp. 825–905). Such groups held their meetings in churches in the GDR because it was here that citizens enjoyed a degree of freedom of political expression. In return for permitting this to happen, the SED expected the Church to ensure that dissenting voices within its midst did not become too loud. Thus the SED effectively allowed churches to become places where citizens might legally let off some steam. The Party reasoned that this was better than unhappy citizens taking to the streets and demonstrating as they had done on 17 June 1953 (see Fulbrook, 1995, pp. 87–123). However, by the end of the decade social and political protest groups had formed and were moving out of the churches.

Since 1983 prayers had been offered in Magdeburg cathedral every Thursday evening for those citizens wishing to leave the GDR. But in 1989 the clergy of Magdeburg cathedral became more and more concerned that they were not doing enough for those citizens who wanted to remain in the country and who hoped to change society for the better. On 14 September 1989 the heads of the cathedral met and decided:

> Praying for those who want to leave is indeed important. Because for many of them it is an offer of help and strength, it should not in any case be cancelled. But what is now necessary is prayer for societal renewal in our country.
>
> (Beratergruppe Dom, 1991, p. 14)

These prayers for 'societal renewal' would take place every Monday evening in Magdeburg cathedral. An important component of this activity was the time allocated for the exchange of ideas and political discussions after the prayers had been offered. During this time the opposition groups forming in the GDR in the autumn of 1989 could also present their agendas to those in attendance (Münchow, 2007, pp. 62–3).

The first Monday prayer meeting, advertised simply by a notice pinned to the cathedral door, took place on 18 September 1989 and attracted 130 citizens. In the form of prayers citizens expressed their worries and hopes for the future, as well as their complaints about life in the GDR. In the following discussion, others spoke boldly about problems with society, the economy and their determination to change and 'renew' the GDR. The following Monday prayer meetings would follow a similar pattern. News of these meetings soon spread by word of mouth and attracted more and more citizens to the cathedral every Monday night. On 25 September 1989, 450 attended; on 2 October 1989, there were 1,300 present.

Despite the state's special relationship with the Church, it did not shy away from intimidating citizens attending the meetings in Magdeburg cathedral. On Thursday 5 October 1989 the prayer service for citizens in Magdeburg hoping to leave the GDR took place as usual. When the service was over the 300 citizens in the cathedral filed out and were joined in the street outside by groups of youths, some of them skinheads, who had been attracted by rumours that a demonstration and fights with police were going to take place. There were now about 500 people outside the cathedral. As the crowds began to move away from the cathedral, police in full riot gear surrounded them. Several fights broke out and numerous arrests were made. On Saturday 7 October 1989 there were more incidents involving the security forces and ordinary citizens. This day was the 40th anniversary of the founding of the GDR and the security forces were on alert for any signs of unrest in relation to the date. That evening police surrounded groups of youths who had been sitting outside and singing songs in Magdeburg city centre. Passersby were also forced into the kettle. The police punched and beat with truncheons anyone who got in their way and made further arrests.

On the day of the next Monday prayer meeting, 9 October 1989, the SED organised a campaign of agitation to prevent citizens from attending. SED secretaries in factories, offices, schools and universities warned their colleagues not to attend the meeting. In one factory it was announced:

> Tonight blood will flow. The cathedral preachers will be arrested. Today we will get the better of them. The most reactionary forces of

the evangelical church are in the cathedral. Everyone ought to give the cathedral a wide berth as of this afternoon!

Moreover, primary school teachers told their pupils that they would be taken into care if their parents attended the service that night (Beratergruppe Dom, 1991, pp. 16–21). The violent events of the last week in Magdeburg, coupled with these threats of further violence, were meant to deter citizens from attending this service and any future meeting at the cathedral. The presence of over 2,000 members of the security forces in Magdeburg on this day only served to increase tension. Some could not help but recall images they had seen in June that year of the Tiananmen Square massacre, especially since Erich Honecker's second-in-command, Egon Krenz, had publicly condoned the action taken by the Chinese authorities. But many others would not be deterred. Despite the threats of violence, 4,500 people attended the prayer meeting on Monday, 9 October 1989. The security forces gathered in the city did not intervene (Münchow, 2007, pp. 72–8). This date can be considered a turning point in the events of the autumn of 1989 in Magdeburg. Not only had citizens conquered their fears and attended the service in the face of threats of violence but also the state had shown that it was not prepared to follow through with its threats.

About 7,000 citizens attended the following week's Monday prayer service on 16 October 1989. Two days later, and with hundreds of thousands of people demonstrating across the GDR, Egon Krenz replaced Erich Honecker as general secretary of the SED's Central Committee becoming the de facto ruler of the GDR. But for many citizens this move did not constitute 'societal renewal'. They felt that they had to do more to achieve this goal. The members of the clergy in Magdeburg cathedral decided to organise a demonstration in Magdeburg on Monday, 23 October 1989. This would take the form of a silent march with candles through the city centre. The organisers from Magdeburg cathedral stressed repeatedly that this demonstration ought to be a sensible and non-violent protest (Beratergruppe Dom, 1991, p. 27). On the evening of 23 October 1989, 10,000 people attended the prayer meeting and took part in the march that followed. They carried placards with slogans such as 'Democracy instead of Dictatorship', 'Free Speech for Free Citizens', 'All Power to the People' and 'Stop Censorship of the Press and Culture'. This date proved to be a watershed in the autumn revolution of 1989 in Magdeburg. It was the first of many public demonstrations against the SED in the city. On 30 October 1989, 15,000 people gathered in front of the cathedral. On 4 November 1989, 50,000 were present. Up to 80,000 attended on 6 November 1989 (Münchow, 2007, pp. 83–97).

Three days later the Berlin Wall was opened as the SED steadily lost its grip on power. Very soon, calls for 'societal renewal' would be drowned out by shouts for the reunification of Germany.

7.2 Eyewitness interviewees

Somewhat surprisingly, only 12 of the 20 interviewees who had witnessed 17 June 1953 first hand stated that the events of 1989 provoked recollection of their experiences of the earlier uprising in the GDR. For the majority of these 12 the memories of the violence that they had witnessed 36 years previous were most prominent and deterred them from participating in any protests in 1989. Jakob Balzert (born 1941) recalled that the violence committed by Soviet troops he witnessed during the earlier uprising in Magdeburg deterred him from taking part in the demonstrations that took place in October 1989. On 17 June 1953 the 12-year-old Herr Balzert narrowly escaped being crushed by a Soviet tank. He then witnessed tanks firing their cannons into the air and recalled seeing bodies lying in the streets. In October 1989 Herr Balzert stated that he feared a repetition of this violence. On the evening of Monday, 9 October 1989, he was in Leipzig on a business trip. Rumours had been flying around the city all day that the SED intended to crush the demonstration due to take place that evening. Employees were told by their bosses to stay out of the city centre lest they be caught up in the expected violence. The fact that there was a noticeable military presence in the city on that day and that local hospitals had been alerted to expect many casualties only increased citizens' anxiety (Childs, 2001, pp. 71–2). Herr Balzert recalled that, because of his experiences of the Soviet suppression of the 1953 unrest, he decided to stay in his hotel on this evening. He was too scared to go out into the city centre. It was only in December 1989 that Herr Balzert joined a demonstration in front of the *Stasi* prison on Moritzplatz in Magdeburg because he perceived that there was little threat of a repetition of the violence he had witnessed in June 1953. At this point the momentum lay with the protesters and the dissolution of the *Stasi* had also begun (Münchow, 2007, pp. 114–26). Herr Balzert stood with fellow demonstrators in front of the prison and chanted 'Stasi out!' He also recalled that all the political prisoners had been released and that the only occupants of the prison at this point were the *Stasi* guards.

Herbert Binkert (born 1930) also stated that his memories of his experiences of the violence of 17 June 1953 deterred him from participating in demonstrations in 1989. But comparison of his remembered experiences of the uprising with his later fears of violence indicate that he feared a repetition of acts of violence of which he had no first-hand experience. Nevertheless, he spoke as if he had actually witnessed such acts of violence. This suggests not only that he incorporated what he later learned about the violence of 17 June 1953 from other sources into his personal narrative of the day but also that reports of the violence of the uprising in 1953 were enough to deter citizens from participating in the later autumn revolution. Herr Binkert stated that he was not a supporter of the SED. However, he said that after being offered no support from various state authorities to fight his 1954 expulsion from college for making a negative comment about the regime, he realised that he simply had to adapt to the system. Nevertheless, he did not join the SED, even though doing so would have meant further promotion in the factory where he worked as a section manager. On 17 June 1953 the 23-year-old Herr Binkert attended college as usual. In the middle of the morning lessons were cut short and the students were told to go home. Herr Binkert made straight for the station to catch a train to his home in Schönebeck. He did not want to get involved in the unrest, fearing that if he did, his actions would come back to haunt him at a later date. At the station he saw a policeman being dragged from a prison carriage by demonstrators. They tore his epaulettes off and took his truncheon and his pistol. Herr Binkert then witnessed another policeman being hit over the head. He particularly remembered that he was horrified by the sight of the blood streaming from this policeman's head. Soon after this Herr Binkert caught the train home. Yet when explaining that he had not attended protests in 1989 because he feared a repetition of the violence he had witnessed on 17 June 1953, he stated that he had experienced certain acts of violence that he had actually not witnessed at all: 'I was afraid because of my experiences...of the shooting and deaths and such...once bitten, twice shy'. By his own account, Herr Binkert had witnessed no shooting and no deaths. No such things took place at Magdeburg station on 17 June 1953. Such acts only occurred in front of the police headquarters in Magdeburg on the day, an area of the city that Herr Binkert did not visit on the day.

Similarly, Konrad Schreiner (born 1926) and his wife (born 1934) explicitly stated that it was other eyewitnesses' communicated memories of the violence of 17 June 1953 that served as a deterrent to participation in 1989. Neither Herr Schreiner nor his wife had witnessed violence on the day of the uprising. Thus communicated memories of the uprising played a larger role than their own memories of it in their behaviour during the successful revolution of 1989 in the GDR.

Herr Schreiner and his wife both claimed to have been passive opponents of the SED regime. They both said that they saw no difference between the repression practiced by the Nazis and that carried out by the SED regime. Moreover, during the 1970s they suffered at the hands of the *Stasi*. Elisabeth Schreiner complained several times to the police about rowdy parties taking place in the pub below the flat in which they lived. These parties were organised by and for local *Stasi* officers in Magdeburg who did not take kindly to the complaints. The *Stasi* placed the Schreiners under indiscreet surveillance bordering on direct intimidation for several years.

On 17 June 1953 Herr Schreiner stayed at his post as a baggage clerk in the main station in Magdeburg for the entire day of 17 June 1953. Although he saw the demonstrations pass by and witnessed a couple of protesters tearing the Party badge from the coat of a member of the SED, this was the extent of his experience. His wife was working the night shift on 17 June 1953 in the ticket office of Schönebeck station. Elisabeth Schreiner's experience of the uprising was limited to having a Russian sentry posted in the office with her. Neither had any direct experiences of the violence committed during the uprising. Herr and Elisabeth Schreiner stated that in 1989 they chose not to attend the demonstrations in Magdeburg because of what they had heard from others about the violence of the earlier uprising:

> [that was] a scary day, even when you think back to it...because no one can do anything against tanks. That's what the Russians did back then. They rigorously took action against everyone who demonstrated...some people were shot dead.

When asked how they knew about this, given that neither had first-hand experience of such action, Elisabeth Schreiner replied: 'That wasn't announced in the newspapers at all. Nothing. You heard about everything only through hearsay.'

Significantly, whereas several eyewitness interviewees were deterred from attending demonstrations in 1989 by their fears of a repetition of the violent acts committed by representatives of the state authorities that they had witnessed on 17 June 1953, memories of violence committed by demonstrators during the uprising in Magdeburg were more prominent in the minds of others. Kurt Clemens (born 1934) remembered that on 17 June 1953 protesters instigated violence that then provoked a violent response from the Soviet troops. Such memories deterred him from attending protests during the autumn revolution because he feared that the demonstrators would once again turn violent. Herr Clemens said that he took little active interest in politics in the GDR and was neither a supporter nor an opponent of the regime. He stated that he recognised that some things that the Party did were good and some things were bad. But he simply adapted to the system and focused on his work in the SKET in Magdeburg. He did, however, join the SED in the mid-1950s. This was apparently because several workers in his factory were due to be made redundant and he reasoned that joining the Party would give him a better chance of avoiding this.

Herr Clemens' first encounter with violent protesters on 17 June 1953 came at work. He was working in the foundry of the SKET. Workers from other factories on the SKET complex entered the foundry and demanded that the foundry workers join the strike. But hardly any of those working in the foundry wanted to participate. The workers in the foundry earned one of the highest wages in the complex. Herr Clemens recalled that the foundry workers were put under a lot of pressure and threatened by the other workers to stop their work. After downing tools he followed the demonstrators as they marched into Magdeburg city centre. The first thing Herr Clemens noticed was the vandalism being committed by the protesters. He did not like what he was witnessing: 'They threw typewriters out of the windows and I thought that was completely stupid. Why do such valuable things have to be destroyed if you want different circumstances? It's complete rubbish. It all has to be bought again.' Moving to the police headquarters Herr Clemens saw a group of demonstrators beat a policeman to the floor and overturn his car. Reflecting on this incident he stated: 'That's how it got more and more out of control.' Up to this point Herr Clemens had witnessed no violence committed by Soviet troops or the GDR's security forces. Moreover, he recalled that when the Russians came they were peaceful until a tank commander was hit on the head by a stone thrown by a demonstrator. It was only after this incident that the troops opened fire on the crowd. Herr Clemens said that his experiences of the unrest in Magdeburg on 17 June 1953 ultimately taught him: 'If someone throws a stone, then it is over. Then they will come with their weapons.'

In contrast to the interviewees above, Peter Momber (born 1938) stated that he actually drew encouragement from his memories of the violence of 17 June 1953 that the revolution in 1989 would be successful. The 15-year-old Herr Momber was attending school in Magdeburg on 17 June 1953. He could not remember the exact reason why, but the school was closed early and the pupils were told to go straight home. Leaving the school building Herr Momber saw the demonstrators vandalising buildings and symbols of the regime and he noted that there was a mood of destructiveness amongst them. He joined the protests out of a youthful sense of adventure and followed them to the police headquarters in central Magdeburg. He recalled that at about 2 p.m. a state of emergency was declared and the demonstrators in front of the police headquarters were notified of this via loudspeakers. When they did not disperse, Soviet tanks rolled forwards into the crowd. Herr Momber stated that this was the threat that ended his participation in the uprising. He ran straight home. When he arrived, he found that the Soviets had installed an anti-tank cannon at the bottom of his street.

Herr Momber claimed that he knew from his experiences that the Soviet intervention was the only reason the earlier uprising failed. He said that the fact that he knew that Mikhail Gorbachev had announced in 1988 that Soviet troops would no longer intervene in the affairs of the satellite states encouraged him to protest without fear because there would be no repetition of the Soviet intervention of 1953: '[in 1989] there was a different quality. It would not have worked if Gorbachev had not been there. Then it probably would have ended as it had done on 17 June, tanks and shooting.' Reassured by this, he attended several services and demonstrations in Magdeburg cathedral in the autumn of 1989.

The memories of the violence he had witnessed on 17 June 1953 also reassured Heinz Kurtsiefer (born 1945) that he would come to no harm during the protests in 1989. However, in contrast to Herr Momber, Herr Kurtsiefer found himself on the other side of the barricades – in 1989 he was an officer in the *Volkspolizei* in Magdeburg. He stated that he had experienced how powerless the crowds were against armed might on 17 June 1953 and, now that he was a part of this armed might, he felt safe in the knowledge that he would be able to defend himself if the demonstrations of 1989 turned violent. As an eight-year-old boy in 1953, Herr Kurtsiefer had witnessed the destruction of state buildings and symbols during the unrest. In front of the police headquarters, he had seen the crowd pelt Soviet tanks with stones. Upon this the tanks moved forwards into the mass of demonstrators. This scared Herr Kurtsiefer so much that he ran away. While making his escape he saw bodies lying on the ground. He assumed these citizens had been shot and killed by the Russians. In the autumn of 1989 Herr Kurtsiefer worked in the same police headquarters in Magdeburg in front of which he had been so scared 36 years before. He recalled that a number of his colleagues who had experienced 17 June 1953 in the building were very agitated:

The older ones were remembering back... At some time in November young people came from the direction of the city centre one evening. And young people are loud, they make a racket and a din. It was on a Monday when something was happening in front of the cathedral. And in the police headquarters building there was an officer in charge of building security in case someone tried to get in, and he was so agitated. [He was shouting] 'They are coming, they are coming, they want to get in!'

Yet Herr Kurtsiefer stated that he did not share his colleague's fear because he knew that the building was better protected than it had been in 1953: 'In 1953 there were no bars on the windows of the BDVP... and in the meantime weapons had become better, communication technology was different, in the building.' From his own experiences of the earlier uprising, Herr Kurtsiefer knew the storming of the police headquarters in 1953 would not be repeated in 1989.

Franz Immig (born 1941) also stated that his experiences of violence on 17 June 1953 were prominent in his thoughts in 1989. However, he claimed that such memories played no role in his decision not to attend demonstrations in 1989 and did not affect his behaviour in any way. By Herr Immig's account he did not participate in protests in 1989 because he worked long hours and because the protests clashed with an English language night school course that he was taking. Yet Herr Immig's recollections indicate that it was actually his memories of the violence he witnessed on 17 June 1953 that deterred him from participating in the protests in Magdeburg in 1989. Herr Immig stated that he held bourgeois-conservative political views throughout the GDR period. He was not a supporter of the regime, particularly after his mother's private butchers shop was nationalised in 1957. He stated that he and his family, however, adapted to the political system and did nothing to draw attention to themselves. He even joined the SED in order to fit in better. Herr Immig was 12 years old in 1953 and attended school as usual on the day of the uprising. In the middle of the morning the teachers allowed the pupils to leave early on the day of the uprising and ordered them to go straight home. On his way home Herr Immig saw demonstrators beating up a member of the SED and witnessed a lot of vandalism to buildings occupied by state agencies. He recalled Soviet tanks driving up the Breiter Weg in central Magdeburg and scattering the protesters as they did so. He also remembered hearing small arms fire in the side streets off the Breiter Weg. When asked for the main reason why he had not attended demonstrations in 1989, Herr Immig stated: 'Lots of things contributed to it. I worked long hours. I was learning English. There was always something to be done.' But he recalled later in the interview:

> Actually, into the early months of 1990 I was always afraid that there would be a counter putsch. I could not have imagined that the Russians, the GDR regime... that they would give up without a fight in such a way... part of me was also afraid that there could be shooting.

This suggests that, although Herr Immig cast himself as someone too busy to take part in the demonstrations in 1989, his memories of the violence of 17 June 1953 actually played a larger role in his non-participation than the version of events upon which he has settled indicates.

Despite the above cases, there were several eyewitness interviewees who stated that memories of their experiences of 17 June 1953 did not cross their minds at all in the autumn of 1989. These interviewees asserted that they did not recall their memories of the June uprising in 1989 because they had dismissed their experiences of the uprising as insignificant to such an extent that not even the occurrence of events broadly similar to those of 1953 could evoke these memories. For example, on 17 June 1953 Heinrich Schmidt (born 1926) was working in the foundry of the SKET in Magdeburg. But he did not join the protests because he had always surpassed his working quotas. Herr Schmidt was also unaware of general dissatisfaction amongst citizens because, in comparison to many others, he was financially and materially well off. Thus Herr Schmidt could not sympathise with the protagonists of the uprising. The events of 17 June 1953 effectively passed him by. He gave the impression throughout his interview that he regarded his experiences of the uprising as irrelevant, so much so that he did not even recall them when a similar event occurred in the GDR in 1989. Similarly, Horst Klauck (born 1924) claimed that he had dismissed his experiences of 17 June 1953 to the extent that they did not cross his mind during the events of 1989. In contrast to Heinrich Schmidt, Herr Klauck had experienced the unrest first hand. On a business trip to Leipzig, he had driven through crowds ransacking the main station. Moreover, he had traversed the demonstrations in Halle on his way back home to Magdeburg, where he arrived at 8pm to be confronted by a Soviet tank. Yet as a convinced supporter of the SED since the Party's founding in 1946 Herr Klauck fully accepted the SED's account of the events. Thus he did not perceive the events to be all that significant in the history of the GDR, let alone in his own life history and not even the events of 1989 reminded him of what he had witnessed. Interestingly, Herr Klauck actually claimed that no demonstrations whatsoever had taken place in Magdeburg in 1989, so nothing occurred that might have triggered his memories of 17 June 1953 anyway. It is possible that Herr Klauck was ignorant of the demonstrations in 1989. But considering his opinion of 17 June 1953 one might conclude that his political conviction as a convinced supporter of the regime meant that he did not want to accept what was happening in 1989.

7.3 Interviewees born after 1953

Six of the 18 interviewees born after the uprising of 1953 stated that they recalled thinking of the events of 17 June during the successful revolution of 1989 in the GDR. Four of these interviewees claimed that such thoughts had affected their behaviour in 1989. As was the case for many of the eyewitness interviewees, Horst Thiel (born 1953) said that what he knew of the violence of the June uprising played a role in his decision not to attend demonstrations in 1989. He had learned of the events from the external collective memory of the events presented by the West German broadcast media, as well as from his grandfather's communicated memories of the uprising. Yet when questioned about why he had not attended the protests in 1989, Herr Thiel first stated that this was because they were run by the Church. This clashed with his own beliefs: 'That was not my scene. I am an atheist through and through.' It was only when asked whether he was thinking about 17 June 1953 in 1989 that Herr Thiel then stated that his awareness of the violence of the earlier uprising had also deterred him from participating in the later revolution. In contrast to eyewitness interviewee Peter Momber, Herr Thiel stated that he did not believe that, just because the Soviets were refusing to intervene, there was no threat of violence:

> I was always afraid in the back of my mind that some sort of armed incident could happen...I really was scared that something would go off...the GDR military, which was closely involved in the Warsaw Pact...who would also get involved in such action...I was really scared of this military presence.

Herr Thiel knew that extreme violence had occurred on the streets of Magdeburg during the earlier uprising. His grandfather had shown him bullet holes opposite the police headquarters in Magdeburg that he claimed had been made by Soviet machine guns on the day. Herr Thiel had also learned of the bloody end to the uprising from West German television programmes. However, there was a further factor that contributed to his non-participation in 1989. He stated that previous negative experiences with the state's security forces also encouraged him to stay at home during the autumn revolution:

> I could not size up the army. I was in the army for three months in 1986 and met so many idiots in it. I thought if no one is controlling them then there will be chaos. And I also had limited trust in the police.

Although Herr Thiel did not say so, this comment about his limited trust in the *Volkspolizei* suggests that some sort of negative experience with them might also have caused him to fear violence in 1989.

The external collective memory of the events of 1953 presented by the West German broadcast media, as well as communicated memories of the uprising, also discouraged Dorothea Freichel (born in 1953) from participating in protest marches in 1989. She recalled that her awareness of the violence of the earlier events made her afraid that the autumn revolution would come to a similar end. This fear led her to stop attending demonstrations in 1989. Frau Freichel stated that in the autumn of 1989 she was considering what she had learned from West German television, as well as what she had heard from eyewitnesses, about the violence of 17 June 1953. She had learned from West German television programmes that about 50 or 60 citizens had been killed during the Soviet intervention in 1953. Moreover, a colleague at her workplace had recounted to her how he had witnessed Russian tanks roll into Magdeburg and put an end to the uprising. Frau Freichel stated that she had managed to suppress such thoughts and the resulting fear in order to attend several protests in Magdeburg in 1989, but that after a certain point (which, however, she did not make clear) she could no longer overcome her fear:

> I had always thought, it will turn out exactly like it did in 1953... At some point the factory militia will come... and at some point the army will step in and crush everything... I thought, here comes the army to shoot everyone dead.... I was afraid for my child.... I thought, something will happen and you can't do it. Perhaps I made the decision for myself.

Frau Freichel attended no more demonstrations after having these thoughts.

Brigitte Schneider (born 1956) also stated that thoughts of 17 June 1953 crossed her mind in 1989. She said that her awareness of the earlier uprising and the comparisons she made with the events of 1989 actually encouraged her to attend demonstrations during the autumn revolution. Frau Schneider recalled that she was comparing what she knew of the two uprisings and reasoned that the autumn revolution had a greater chance of success:

> I also had the uprising of 1953 in the GDR in my memory... I knew that it was put down... And I thought that that uprising had had little chance of success. But it was a different story in 1989, with the opening of the border in Hungary, with the cutting of the border fence with Austria [in May 1989] that things were changing for the first time across Europe. The situation that prevailed in Europe, in Germany and in the GDR, there had never been such a situation until that point, that for the first time the Iron Curtain had been opened.

Frau Schneider came from a middle-class family and, working as a doctor in the GDR, had achieved a high level of education in the GDR. Moreover, she was married to a historian. Thus she was educated and informed enough to consider and assess the situation in this way. In contrast to Dorothea Freichel and Horst Thiel, Frau Schneider stated that her awareness of the June uprising came exclusively from the external collective memory of the events presented by the West German broadcast media. She said that she had learned from these programmes that unrest had occurred in the GDR and that Soviet tanks and troops had bloodily put it down. By contrast, she learned nothing from the communicated memories of eyewitnesses. Her mother simply told her that on 17 June 1953 'the SED bigwigs had finally got their comeuppance', and her father did not speak of his experiences of the events at all. Significantly, Frau Schneider stated that the demonstrations in 1989 led her to assess her awareness of the events of June 1953 in detail for the first time in her life. Before this time she had not given the uprising much thought at all because 'before there was not such a similar situation... a mood of upheaval... such that perhaps... associations and connections were made'.

Katrin Heidinger (born 1957) also claimed that in 1989 she was comparing her awareness of the June uprising with the contemporary situation in the GDR. In contrast to what she knew about the uprising of June 1953, Frau Heidinger stated that she saw that the events of 1989 were being carried by the majority of citizens who were protesting on a broad range of issues fundamental to daily life in the GDR. As was the case for Frau Schneider, Frau Heidinger's awareness of 17 June 1953 came exclusively from the external collective memory of the events broadcast by the West German broadcast media. She learned almost nothing from eyewitnesses to the uprising. Her father would only tell her that 'evil things' had been committed by the 'Russian pigs', before changing the subject and avoiding further questions. Her mother never spoke of the events. Frau Heidinger stated that the main thing that she learned from the West German broadcast media was that the 1953 uprising was a localised 'workers' uprising' involving mostly workers unhappy with their working quotas. She compared this account of the events as a small and limited affair to what she perceived was happening in the GDR in 1989. As a result, she claimed that she concluded that the 1989 uprising would succeed where the 1953 one had failed and joined the demonstrations.

By contrast, Katja Müller (born 1962) recounted that communicated memories of 17 June 1953 encouraged her to attend demonstrations in Magdeburg in 1989. She claimed that her grandfather's stories of how he experienced the June uprising inspired her to participate, even though she had witnessed first-hand state violence at protests in October 1989. Frau Müller, 27 years old in 1989, experienced the events of autumn 1989 in Magdeburg intensely. Her husband was working as a verger in Magdeburg cathedral. The couple lived directly behind the cathedral with their two children. They had witnessed the growing popularity of the cathedral as a place for citizens to talk freely about their troubles. From mid-September 1989 Frau Müller had attended the Monday night prayer meetings at which calls for a 'societal renewal' of the GDR were made. Her most intense experience came on 7 October 1989. She stated that on this day she witnessed 'civil war' on the streets of Magdeburg. Frau Müller witnessed one arrest herself:

> A man ran out of the line of policemen and ran toward us. He grabbed a young woman. He ran back through the line of policemen to a van whose engine was running, threw the young girl into the back of this army van and it drove away very quickly.

Witnessing this incident did not deter her from attending the following Monday's prayer meeting on 9 October 1989. Frau Müller explained that her grandfather's communicated memories of 17 June 1953 gave her the civil courage to participate.

Nadine Weber (born 1960) stated that her desire to bring about change in the GDR outweighed her fear of a repeat of the violence of 1953 and meant that it did not deter her from participating in the autumn revolution. Frau Weber remembered that the earlier uprising in the GDR was in her thoughts in 1989 because the demonstrations taking place triggered conversations about the earlier uprising with her mother. Frau Weber recalled that her mother had already told her about her experiences of the uprising before 1989, but was not sure when. The content of her mother's communicated memories constituted Frau Weber's entire awareness of the subject. Frau Weber did not learn anything about it at school and could not remember learning anything from the West German broadcast media either. Her mother told her that there had been demonstrations in Magdeburg and that Soviet tanks had put the uprising down. Frau Weber felt that her mother had been traumatised by what she had seen of the Soviet intervention on the day, even though her mother had not mentioned any specific incidents of violence. Although limited in content, this communicated memory of 17 June 1953 nevertheless provoked the fear in Frau Weber that the protests in 1989 would end in a similar fashion. Yet she did not let this prevent her from attending the demonstrations in Magdeburg in the autumn of 1989. And even when her fears were augmented by her suspicion that the cathedral was full of *Stasi* officers, judging by the number of those present she saw who were not singing or clapping, she continued to attend. When asked how she overcame these fears and attended the demonstrations, Frau Weber replied, 'It was somehow... I think it tipped the scales that we felt locked in.' The restriction on foreign travel had played an important role in Nadine Weber's life. She had an aunt in West Germany. Her aunt visited her many times in the GDR. But when Frau Weber had applied to visit her, the application had been rejected. Upon this her aunt decided that she would not visit the GDR anymore. This upset Frau Weber immensely and led to her decision while on holiday near the Czechoslovak border in 1989 that, if the opportunity to flee to the West through Czechoslovakia presented itself, she would take it. In 1989 Frau Weber's anger at not being allowed to travel prevailed over her fears of a second 17 June and compelled her to attend the demonstrations in Magdeburg. She had simply had enough of feeling restricted in the GDR.

Despite these cases, the majority of interviewees born after 1953 stated that thoughts of 17 June 1953 were not in their minds during the autumn revolution. The results of the interviews indicate that the extent of the awareness of the earlier uprising on the part of these interviewees, whether great or small, did not play a role in whether or not they thought about the earlier uprising during in 1989. The subject did not cross the minds of some of those who knew a fair amount about the 1953 unrest. For example, Susanne Dobrat (born 1965) had worked on an FDJ project in 1988 researching the lives and deaths of the policemen killed in Magdeburg on 17 June 1953. Doris Ritter (born 1956) had taught the subject to pupils in class ten since 1980. Anika Rosenkranz (born 1963) had learned from various sources that there had been an uprising in 1953 involving workers and white-collar employees. She knew that it had been triggered by the state's demands that its citizens ought to work more. Moreover, Frau Rosenkranz was aware that there had been also a lot of dissatisfaction amongst citizens of the GDR about what was available to buy in the shops in 1953. She also knew that citizens had died during the uprising. Yet, none of these women recalled making any mental connections with the earlier uprising in 1989.

Several interviewees stated that the revolution of 1989 was such an exciting experience for them that contemporary events occupied their minds completely and took precedence over any thoughts about the past. Thus for many of them awareness of the events did not affect their everyday action, as might usually be the case, but was rather supplanted by it. Brigitte Schneider (born 1956) recalled that 17 June 1953 was not in her thoughts while she attended demonstrations in Magdeburg because the emotions she experienced during these demonstrations occupied her mind completely: 'The demonstrations captivated me so emotionally, that I was completely focussed on the present, that I did not think about the past at all. It really moved me – everything.' Similarly, Doris Ritter (born 1956) stated that she was caught up in the excitement of the events. However, for her this feeling was not confined to the autumn of 1989. She said that the excitement of events that took place throughout 1989 occupied her completely and meant that she did not give any thought to 17 June 1953: 'You can say that from January or February... starting with the [anti-state demonstrations on the] anniversary of the death of Rosa Luxemburg in Berlin... you somehow noticed that there would be changes.' Christina Heinemann (born 1953) recalled that excitement at events on a smaller, but no less important, scale meant that she did not consider the earlier uprising in the GDR in 1989. She and her husband were trying to wrest control of the factory, where they were divisional managers, from the SED-controlled management. Their main aim was to prevent the destruction of files.

Frau Heinemann explained that 17 June 1953 did not cross her mind at this time because

> [w]e took each day as it came. It was all so exciting. Every day there was new excitement, a new high point, a new story that we had to investigate. We looked in the files to shed light on everything. Every day these was new excitement in the factory.

The stress of Frau Heinemann's efforts and a dirty tricks campaign led by the SED management against her and her husband led to her suffering an attack of neuritis in December 1989.

Others recounted that it was not feelings of excitement in 1989, but fear of the unknown and the revolution's consequences for their personal circumstances that took precedence over any thoughts of 17 June 1953. None were members of the SED and claimed that they were not sorry to see the demise of the regime. They were simply worried about what was going to come next. Many were concerned about how the unfolding events would affect their career and job prospects. Thus for them, too, everyday action affected how they interacted with their awareness of the 1953 uprising and not vice versa. When asked whether 17 June 1953 had crossed his mind, Werner Prauss (born 1958) stated, 'No, absolutely not. You just said, where will this lead? People were running away. How can the state continue to exist?' Manfred Ebert (born 1965) also said that he was not thinking about 17 June 1953 in 1989 because

> [a]t the time the question for me was: what is coming now? How will it continue? I was in the middle of my degree. Because part of it was politics, the question of course was: will it continue? Will it be recognised [in the West]? Such a degree.

Similarly, Albert Keck (born 1959) recalled that he had not thought once about 1953 in 1989 because 'there were new problems in 1989. No one was thinking of 17 June'.

7.4 Conclusion

Not all of the interviewees thought about, considered or drew comparisons with the earlier uprising of 17 June 1953 in the GDR during the successful revolution of 1989. Understandably, memories and awareness of the unrest of 1953 most affected the behaviour in 1989 of those interviewees who had experienced first-hand the events 36 years before. The majority of these interviewees stated that memories of the violence that they had witnessed on 17 June 1953 in Magdeburg were most prominent in their minds. Significantly, in 1989 they were not only recalling violent acts committed by Soviet troops during the earlier uprising but also those committed by demonstrators, too. Such memories provoked feelings of fear in them in 1989 and deterred them from taking part in the successful revolution. However, Peter Momber (born 1938) claimed that his memories of the violent Soviet intervention actually encouraged him to participate in 1989. He had witnessed the Soviet military's show of force and believed that this was the only reason why the 1953 uprising had failed. With no threat of a Soviet intervention, he saw no reason why the autumn revolution might fail. By contrast, several eyewitness interviewees said that they were not recalling their memories of 17 June 1953 at all in 1989. For these interviewees, their experiences of the earlier uprising had played no role in their thoughts or behaviour since the day that it had occurred because they deemed that it had not affected their lives in any significant way. Consequently, not even the events of 1989 in the GDR succeeded in provoking recollections of their past experiences of similar occurrences.

The majority of interviewees born after 1953 asserted that they were not thinking of 17 June 1953 at all in 1989. This was despite the fact that all but one of them had known that an uprising had taken place before in their country and knew at least a few details of what had happened. The extent of knowledge of the events of 1953 on the part of these interviewees apparently played no role in whether they were thinking about them in 1989. This suggests that even for those who knew relatively a lot about the earlier uprising, it held little significance for generations of East German citizens born afterwards. For many of these interviewees, the emotions and feelings that they experienced during the events of 1989 took precedence over any thoughts of 1953. The 'crisis' nature of current events in the GDR in the autumn of 1989, as well as the great uncertainty of how it would end and what would follow, meant that their minds and thoughts were completely focused on the present time. Events through which they were actually living took precedence in their thoughts over those that had occurred in their country before they were born.

Nevertheless, several interviewees born after the earlier uprising did claim that thoughts of 1953 surfaced in their minds in 1989. By their accounts, this was the first time that the events of 1953 gained any significance for them and the first time that their awareness of the events played any role in their behaviour. For the first time, too, they assessed and analysed in detail what they had learned about it from the West German broadcast media and eyewitnesses' communicated memories and compared this with what was occurring in the GDR in 1989. For some, considerations of the violent end to the earlier uprising deterred them from attending demonstrations in 1989. However, although thoughts of the violence of 1953 occurred to Nadine Weber, she did not let these deter her from attending protests in 1989. Her experiences of the restrictions of life and the feeling that she was 'locked in' in the GDR led her to adopt a 'now or never' attitude in 1989. Only in the case of Katja Müller (born 1962) did awareness of the events of 17 June 1953 inspire an interviewee from this group to attend demonstrations in 1989. In 1989 she was inspired by the communicated memories of her grandfather to emulate his example of civil courage on 17 June 1953.

8
Conclusion

8.1 Aftermath

Although isolated strikes continued into July 1953, the uprising in the GDR was effectively over as soon as Soviet tanks arrived to restore order in the late afternoon of 17 June 1953. By the evening, approximately 90 people lay dead. Approximately 80 of these died while taking part in the protests or were simply passing by the wrong place at the wrong time. Up to 15 of those killed were members of the various state security forces (Kowalczuk, 2003, p. 104). A further 18 people were executed by the Soviet military authorities between 18 and 22 June 1953 for the role that they had allegedly played in the unrest. In fact, on the morning of 17 June 1953 the Soviet leadership had ordered that 18 people be executed to deter further unrest (Kowalczuk, 2003, p. 245). In the two weeks that followed the uprising approximately 10,000 people were arrested. However, many of these were released shortly afterwards. And apart from two death sentences and three life sentences, the 1,800 people tried and convicted of crimes relating to the uprising received relatively mild sentences. Perhaps in fear of popular reaction, Erich Mielke, then deputy head of the *Stasi*, had ordered on 23 June 1953: 'Mass reprisals are prohibited' (Kowalczuk, 2003, p. 251).

On 21 June 1953 the Central Committee of the SED convened for the first time since the events of a few days earlier. At this crisis meeting, leader of the SED, Walter Ulbricht, declared that the Party was to go onto the offensive (Kowalczuk, 2003, p. 261). In the following weeks, SED ministers and functionaries visited factories across the GDR to speak to workers. They hoped to regain the support of the workers by convincing them that what had happened had constituted an attempted 'fascist-counterrevolutionary putsch' against the SED that had been steered by the West in the hope of triggering a Third World War on German soil. Most of these meetings ended in acrimony and confrontation with workers. According to one *Stasi* report, Politburo member Fred Oelßner's meeting with 600 workers in the Buna-Werk in Schkopau descended into chaos. This was triggered by an announcement read out by the factory's Party secretary (presumably for the benefit of Oelßner) in which the workers apparently distanced themselves from the 'provocateurs' of 17 June 1953. Those workers present made clear that they strongly rejected this claim (Mitter and Wolle, 1993, p. 112). Many of the meetings had to be cancelled because the attendant workers vacated the room as soon as anyone from the SED began to speak (Kowalczuk, 2003, p. 261). Even Walter Ulbricht himself was confronted by angry workers as he visited the factory that bore his name, the VEB Leuna-Werke Walter Ulbricht in Halle on the Saale, on 24 June 1953. Workers there demanded freedom of speech, the release of political prisoners and the separation of the trade union and the Party (Mitter and Wolle, 1993, pp. 111–2). In some cases SED ministers did not help their own cause. Fritz Selbmann, who had confronted the protesters outside of the House of Ministries in Berlin on 16 June 1953 and thus was the only senior SED minister to address in person protesters during the uprising, apparently asked the workers in the factory he visited: 'Why aren't you pigs working?' (Kowalczuk, 2003, p. 261).

While there was no doubt that the SED would remain in power after the uprising, Walter Ulbricht was in a very precarious position. Not only had demonstrators more or less universally called for his resignation, there was also growing opposition to Ulbricht within the Politburo. In early July the Politburo's Organisation Committee proposed the formation of a Central Committee Presidium to replace the Secretariat of the Central Committee (Ostermann, 2001, p. 168). The Secretariat was responsible for implementing the decisions made by the Politburo. Ulbricht used his commanding position in the Secretariat to edit and amend the Politburo's decisions to his liking, often only informing the Politburo of the changes made when it was too late for any discussion of the matter (Görldt, 2002, p. 228). At a Politburo meeting on 8 July 1953 discussions turned to Ulbricht stepping down. All members of the Politburo except Erich Honecker and Party Control Commission Chairman Hermann Matern expressed their desire for Ulbricht to resign the Party leadership. Confronted with this challenge to his leadership, Ulbricht employed a delaying tactic by announcing that he would make a statement on his position at the fifteenth plenary session of the Central Committee on 24 July 1953 (Ostermann, 2001, p. 168).

On 10 July 1953 Ulbricht and the prime minister of the GDR, Otto Grotewohl, flew to Moscow after being summoned by the Soviet leadership (Knabe, 2003, p. 389). There they learned that the power struggle that had been raging in Moscow since Stalin's death on 5 March 1953 was over. The troika of Nikita Khrushchev, Vyacheslav Molotov and Georgi Malenkov had succeeded in thwarting the apparent attempts of Lavrenti Beria to take control of the Soviet Union. Beria was arrested and later executed. Against the background of this turmoil, the new leaders of the Soviet Union had decided that the best course of action to take concerning the leadership of the GDR was to maintain the status quo. Though they were aware that Ulbricht was unpopular with East Germans, they also viewed him as an experienced and reliable hand who could steady the ship (Ostermann, 2001, p. 179). Thus Ulbricht returned to East Germany to face the Central Committee at the 15th plenary on 24 July 1953 safe in the knowledge that, no matter how many people opposed his rule, he had the backing of the Soviet leadership and would remain in power.

Ulbricht used this knowledge to his advantage and executed a piece of expert political manoeuvring that allowed him to eliminate those who had opposed him in the Politburo, as well as other 'opponents' in the Party, thereby further consolidating his position and strengthening his grip on power in the GDR. At the 15th plenary, Ulbricht accused Politburo member and chief editor of *Neues Deutschland*, Rudolf Herrnstadt, as well as Politburo member and Minister for State Security, Wilhelm Zaisser, of building a 'faction' against him. Both Herrnstadt and Zaisser had been the most prominent critics of Ulbricht before and after the uprising of 17 June 1953. For example, it was Zaisser who had suggested liquidating Ulbricht's Secretariat. Herrnstadt had supported this move and also suggested that the Central Committee Presidium that would replace the Secretariat should consist of Politburo members except Ulbricht, effectively calling on him to step down (Müller-Enbergs, 1991, pp. 223–4). In his speech at the plenary, Ulbricht accused the pair of plotting against the leadership of the Party and, by implication, the SED regime. Moreover, he claimed that they were partly responsible for triggering the uprising of 17 June 1953 through their promotion of 'liberal' politics. Finally, he announced that both had been in league with Lavrenti Beria (Kowalczuk, 2003, pp. 263–5).

One by one the speakers who followed Ulbricht at the plenary, recognising what was occurring and no doubt hoping to save their own necks, also attacked Herrnstadt and Zaisser for their 'plotting' against the Party (Müller-Enbergs, 1991, pp. 296–8). Rudolf Herrnstadt and Wilhelm

Zaisser were later removed from their positions and faded into obscurity. After the plenary Ulbricht further secured his position by cleansing the SED, other parties and mass organisations, such as the FDGB, of 'opponents', that is, people who had criticised his leadership before, during or after 17 June 1953. Functionaries at all levels launched investigations into who had been where and when during the uprising. All Party members were asked about their own conduct during the unrest. Their careers depended on the answers they gave (Eisenfeld et al., 2004, p. 205).

A further significant consequence of the uprising of 17 June 1953 was the regime's reform and expansion of its security forces. The uprising had made clear to the SED that there were serious deficiencies in its security apparatus (Diedrich, 2003, p. 33). The *Volkspolizei* had proven during the unrest that it did not have the numbers or the mobility to react quickly to extraordinary situations. To rectify this situation 14,000 new officers were recruited (Diedrich, 2003, pp. 35–6). The SED accused in particular the armoured branch of the *Volkspolizei*, the *Kasernierte Volkspolizei* (Garrisoned People's Police, KVP), of having failed in its duties. In the absence of an army (created only in 1956), the KVP had been geared to respond to threats from abroad. In the wake of the uprising the force was restructured to enable it to deal also with threats from within. Twenty-four new units, comprising 180 men each and armed with machine guns and armoured cars, were created and stationed across the GDR (Eisenfeld et al., 2004, pp. 168–73).

In addition to these reforms to existing services, the regime created in late 1953 armed workers' militia groups (*Kampfgruppen der Arbeiterklasse*). These were formed in factories across the GDR and consisted of workers from those factories. Their main task was to respond immediately to strikes or demonstrations and put a stop to them before they had the chance to spread (Eisenfeld et al., 2004, p. 159). Finally, on 24 January 1954 the SED created a central security commission comprising Walter Ulbricht and other key members of the Politburo. This commission would instigate and co-ordinate the security forces in the event of a repeat of 17 June 1953. Regional security committees were also created to co-ordinate the security forces at a local level (Diedrich, 2003, p. 37).

The SED also extensively reformed the *Stasi*. There were two reasons for this. First, the service had completely failed to fulfil its main task of recognising the early signs of discontent amongst East German citizens and taking appropriate and decisive action. Second, the experience of the uprising traumatised the SED and made it consistently afraid of a second uprising. In his novel *Das Impressum* (1972), Hermann Kant describes this trauma when recounting the effect of the uprising on the character Fritz Andermann who, as an SED minister, had confronted the crowds on 17 June 1953 and been assaulted by them:

> Attention, Fritz Andermann, watch out. Be alert, stay vigilant, don't be gullible... the fight is not over, we aren't at that stage yet, we can't allow that yet... appearances can be deceptive, take another look, check again, expect something again, if this means: never giving the enemy an inch again, and never giving that day in June another chance.
>
> (1972, p. 280)

The SED perceived that only through massive expansion of the *Stasi* could it hope to nip possible opposition in the bud and thereby prevent a repetition of the unrest of 1953. By 1956 the number of *Stasi* employees increased from 1953 levels by 3,000 to 16,000, and its budget more than doubled from 428 million to 882 million marks. The *Stasi* also increased the size of its network of 'unofficial employees' (*inoffizielle Mitarbeiter*) or informers. In 1953 there had been approximately 20,000 *Stasi* informers. Three years later there were 30,000 (Eisenfeld et al., 2004, pp. 175–6). The *Stasi* continued to expand during the rest of the regime's existence. By October 1989, the ranks of the *Stasi* had swollen to over 90,000 full-time employees (Gieseke, 2000, pp. 552–7), aided by 173,081 informers (Müller-Enbergs, 2008, p. 36). But it was not just the size of the *Stasi* that changed after 1953. Its role also altered. It was no longer to be a 'jack of all trades' as far as security matters were concerned. On 11 November 1953 Politburo member Hermann Matern directed leading *Stasi* officials to draw the correct conclusions from the uprising:

> There must be no liberalism against the enemies of the Republic in the ranks of the State Security Service. There is no place in our ranks for weak-kneed pacifists or dreamers. Comrade Walter Ulbricht once said at a Central Committee meeting: We must turn the German Democratic Republic into a hell for enemy agents.
>
> (Mitter and Wolle, 1993, pp. 153–4)

Thus after the uprising the *Stasi* was tasked with the mass surveillance of East German society in order to ensure that all potential opposition was also eliminated. Effectively, the State Security Service was now to work toward the prevention of a repetition of the uprising of 17 June 1953.

However, the SED did not react to the uprising by simply increasing the means with which it could control and infiltrate Eats German society. The Party implemented short-term measures designed to improve living and working conditions. Shortages in foodstuffs such as meat, butter and cheese were tackled and overcome (Eisenfeld et al., 2004, p. 212). The Party increased wages, while at the same time decreasing the prices of thousands of items in shops (Dale, 2005, p. 36). Increased investment in the energy supply industry ensured that the number of power cuts diminished (Kowalczuk, 2003, p. 267). Similar investment in the consumer goods industry also led to an overall improvement in living standards. Moreover, many citizens imprisoned under the measures taken to build socialism in 1952 were released. Many of the farmers amongst them, imprisoned during the collectivisation campaign, received their land back (Hagen, 1992, p. 203). These policies were not designed to win back the trust of the population; East German citizens had not trusted the Party before 17 June 1953. Moreover, the uprising had conclusively demonstrated to citizens that the SED's position of power rested not on popular support, but on the presence of Soviet bayonets (Mitter and Wolle, 1993, p. 162). The measures taken in the aftermath of the uprising were designed to temporarily appease workers and citizens in order to calm the situation in the GDR and allow the Party to regain control (Eisenfeld et al., 2004, p. 212).

8.2 History, memory and the uprising of 17 June 1953

Oral history is often dismissed as a technique of historical investigation by historians who favour written contemporary testimony, such as an authentic diary entry, over oral testimony recorded years after an event has taken place (Grele, 1998, p. 41). One oft-cited reason for this is the issue of the accuracy of interviewees' memories and accounts of historic events, periods, their thoughts and feelings. The simple fact is that memories fail. When questioned, several of my interviewees stated that they could not remember a great deal of what they had seen on 17 June 1953 or heard about it later on. They could not recall how they had reacted to major personal or political events. They had forgotten how they had felt in specific situations or episodes in their lives. They could only suggest what they now thought their past selves would have been feeling or thinking. However helpful these suggestions were, there is danger in accepting them at face value. Such accounts of the past are often coloured by an individuals' current circumstances, knowledge, prejudices and opinions.

It must also be borne in mind that the accuracy of individuals' accounts of the past is affected by the conscious or subconscious transformation of their autobiographies according to a variety of motives, often to argue a certain point of view (Fulbrook, 2011b, pp. 94–100). These motives affect not only the details that an interviewee recalls (or chooses to recall) to others but also the emphasis that the interviewee places on certain aspects of an account of his or her own life or role in historic events. The majority of my interviewees considered themselves to have been either victims of the SED regime or opponents of it. Both groups consistently attempted to direct their interview toward recounting their personal experiences of victimisation or opposition. Those who considered themselves victims focused on recounting details and events that demonstrated how they had been treated unfairly or suffered during the GDR period. Interviewees' who claimed to have been opponents of the regime often cast themselves as the 'hero' in their own narratives, emphasising the occasions on which they felt they had scored victories over the regime.

The accuracy of individuals' accounts of what they experienced may also be affected by past and current frames of remembering historical events. In some cases, this can occur to the extent that an individual incorporates details from these frames into their recollections. These details then form part of what the individual believes was their lived experience. For example, eyewitness interviewee Erwin Strempel recounted that RIAS broadcasts were stirring unrest in the GDR throughout the day of 17 June 1953, a claim that was prominent in the SED's official version of events. However, by Herr Strempel's own account, he was in Magdeburg city centre before and during the unrest with no access to a radio set to be able to hear RIAS' broadcasts. Nevertheless, Herr Strempel recounted this as part of his lived experiences of the day. In other cases, frames of remembering not only affect specific details of personal accounts but also shape the manner in which an individual recounts their agency in historical events. The accounts of eyewitnesses Konrad Schreiner and Barbara Grabias support Lutz Niethammer's conclusion that, due to the failure of the uprising and the SED's account of 'fascists' and Western agents, it became necessary for citizens to distance themselves from what had occurred. Herr Schreiner's and Frau Grabias's accounts of the uprising consisted of memories of what they had seen other people do and included very little detail of what they themselves had actually done, thought or felt. Thus, they recast themselves as passive bystanders to the unrest going on around them.

One might assume that the effect that past and current frames of remembering have on individuals' accounts of their experiences is a subconscious one. However, this may not always be the case. Individuals consciously distort accounts of their experiences to ensure that they adhere to currently accepted frames of remembering historical events. The majority of my interviewees condemned the SED's official account of the uprising of 17 June 1953 as nonsense and claimed that they had always completely rejected every aspect of it. This may have been the case given that the majority of the interviewees cast themselves as opponents or victims of the regime in the GDR. But it may also be the case that few would have been prepared to state that they had believed an account that has been completely debunked and which was promoted by a regime that has been so thoroughly condemned since its fall. Of course, this can work both ways. Eyewitness interviewee Horst Klauck was a committed supporter of the SED during the GDR period and completely accepted the regime's version of the events of June 1953. Despite the current academic and political frameworks of remembering the uprising, Herr Klauck consistently downplayed the significance of the events of 17 June 1953 (as the SED had done) throughout his interview.

If memories can be unreliable, coloured by contemporary perspectives and shaped (consciously or subconsciously) by frames of remembering the past, can they be of any use to historians? As Grele argues, 'the usefulness of any source depends upon the information one is looking for, or the questions one seeks to answer' (1998, p. 41). Analysis of oral testimony (with appropriate consideration of the issues outlined above) was essential to investigating the questions central to my study. Archive documents and written testimony were only partially sufficient. Consider, for example, the report on the mood of citizens written by an SED functionary in Magdeburg in 1956 who overheard the following: 'A youth said: 17.6.53 was correct. It will happen again soon. My father was right at the forefront of it. But next time it will go better.'[1] This report tells us that this young man was aware of the uprising and that he regarded verbal reference to it as a form of dissent against the regime. But the file does not explicitly indicate what provoked this comment. Moreover, it does not tell us why this young man felt the uprising was correct; what he knew about what had happened; what his father had told him of his experiences of the unrest; or what he hoped to achieve by making such a comment. It does not even tell us exactly how old the young worker was in 1956, so that we may calculate his age in 1953 and ponder the possible extent of his experiences of the unrest. Consider, also, the fact that analysis of history textbooks and teaching guides shows that the subject of the uprising of 17 June 1953 was on the history curriculum in the GDR. Moreover, these texts suggest that school pupils were encouraged to discuss the matter critically and that a number of sources were available for teachers to use in order to engage their students. However, my interviews revealed that the subject, if addressed at all in school history lessons, was not taught in any great detail and that there was certainly no discussion of it.

Oral history interviews are also particularly insightful when investigating the ways in which the same historical event is remembered by people of differing ages, social and political backgrounds (Fulbrook, 2011b). My interviews revealed a significant difference between the nature of eyewitnesses' memories of the uprising and the nature of the awareness of the events on the part of East German citizens born after 1953. Although all of the eyewitnesses interviewed had experienced the uprising of 17 June 1953 in Magdeburg, their memories can best be described as 'collected' since there were few commonalities between their recollections of the uprising and how they evaluated their experiences. Their memories were often more variegating than unifying due to the fact that the majority had evaluated their experiences of the unrest in light of their individual social and political experiences in the GDR prior to the day. By contrast, the majority of interviewees born after 1953 stated that during the GDR period, they had evaluated the events of 17 June 1953 as a people's uprising for democratic values. The shared nature of their awareness of the events was no doubt encouraged by the West German broadcast media, which many cited as their main source of information about the uprising. This confirms the apparent perception on the part of the SED that the West German external collective memory of the events was contributing to the construction of a collective awareness amongst younger East German citizens. Conversely, eyewitness interviewees claimed that they had dismissed these programmes either as propaganda or because they had experienced the events themselves. Thus the programmes had no such effect on their evaluations of the unrest.

Significantly, while analysis of oral testimony can reveal much about the extent to which individuals' memories adhere to, clash with or are shaped by past frames of remembering an historical event, it can also expose challenges to current narratives. Although my eyewitness interviewees' accounts support the conclusion that citizens from all sectors of society (not just industrial workers) were involved in the uprising of 17 June 1953, no eyewitnesses mentioned hearing calls for a reunification of Germany during the unrest. That is not to say that such demands were not made. But my eyewitness interviewees remembered the uprising as one which primarily sought to bring down the SED regime. They concluded this from witnessing many instances of the destruction of visible symbols of the regime such as flags, placards and typewriters, as well as the assaults of badge-wearing members of the Party. As Jakob Balzert recalled, 'It was clear to me as a 12-year-old. Now, finally, now this government, which was so unpopular, will be brought down.'

Furthermore, the accounts of my interviewees challenge the narrative of the uprising of 17 June 1953 promoted by the political establishment in Germany. Though Federal Chancellor Merkel has described the events as a significant 'landmark' in German history, few interviewees regarded the uprising with similar reverence. By the accounts of my eyewitness interviewees, the uprising was an extraordinary event that they had experienced for a few hours one afternoon, but which had had no direct bearing on their lives at the time or in the years that followed. For interviewees born after the uprising took place, the events of June 1953 held even smaller significance. In fact, it was difficult to persuade many interviewees born after 1953 to take part in interviews because they claimed that the uprising of 17 June 1953 played such a small role in their lives during and after the GDR period that they had nothing to say on the matter. Some could not relate to an event that had happened before their birth and which had no perceivable effect on their everyday lives. Other subjects, ranging from the building of the Berlin Wall and the subsequent travel restrictions, to matters such as not being able to find their own home, took precedence over any thoughts about 17 June 1953. Katrin Heidinger echoed the comments of the majority of interviewees born after 1953 when she recalled that the only time that she gave the 1953 uprising any more than a cursory thought was when it was commemorated by the West German broadcast media. Even on such occasions her reflections on the subject were often limited to a simple verbal acknowledgement of the date: 'on Western television they always said "Today is 17 June, the anniversary of the uprising of the poor citizens of the GDR", and one heard again and again at home, "oh, yes, today is 17 June".' The majority of eyewitness interviewees stated that their memories of 17 June 1953 only acquired significance for them in the autumn of 1989. The sight of the demonstrations during the successful revolution in the GDR led them to recall their memories of 1953 and particularly the violence they had witnessed. Fearing a repetition of this violence, many chose not to participate in the protests of 1989.

By contrast, despite the fact that 17 of the 18 interviewees born after 1953 stated that they had been aware of the uprising during the GDR period, very few asserted that thoughts of it crossed their minds in 1989. The majority explained that such thoughts did not enter their heads in 1989 because the crisis nature and ensuing fears and emotions of the autumn revolution occupied their minds completely.

The statements of my interviewees also challenge political attempts to cast the events as part of a broader historical narrative of German political resistance. Jakob Balzert was the only eyewitness interviewee who was inspired by what he had experienced on 17 June 1953 to commit an act of dissent against the SED regime. Yet the extent of this only extended to the invention of a hand gesture amongst his friends. Only one interviewee born after 1953 – Katja Müller – explicitly stated that she drew encouragement from her awareness of what had happened in 1953 to continue to defy passively the SED regime and its tenets. Analysis of documented instances of dissent referencing the uprising of 17 June 1953 also demonstrates that the few cases in which memories or awareness of the uprising apparently played a role rarely constituted serious acts of opposition against the regime. Threatening references made to the events of 1953 in expressions of disgruntlement with living conditions in the GDR were common. However, the context of many of these references makes clear that citizens were simply letting off steam about their frustration with the prevailing circumstances. Thus this frustration led them to invoke the memory of 17 June 1953 and not vice versa. Common, too, were graffiti, usually daubed around the anniversary of the unrest each year, in which some reference was made to the uprising and an imminent repetition thereof. However, such threats were empty. For dissenters in the GDR the uprising of 17 June 1953 served as nothing more than a 'symbolic talisman' for and a means of expressing their opposition against the regime (Fulbrook, 1995, p. 178).

Study of individual life stories not only tells us much about how specific historical events and incidents were experienced, processed and interpreted by ordinary East German citizens but also helps us to identify and illuminate the gap between the SED regime's central policy and what actually happened 'on the ground' in GDR society. As such, they are highly revealing with regard to how citizens reacted to and interacted with state power in the GDR. Despite the differences in the manner in which both groups of interviewees interacted with their memories or awareness of the events, the majority of eyewitness interviewees and interviewees born after 1953 asserted that they believed that an official taboo of the subject of 17 June 1953 had existed in the GDR. This was despite the fact that the SED had not censored all reference to the date. Workers who had written letters to the FDGB literature and arts prize committee expressed similar views. They welcomed the fact that the works were addressing what they perceived as a taboo subject for the first time in the literature of the GDR. However, the texts praised were not the first published in the GDR to address the subject. Several citizens also indicated that they felt the texts were breaking not just a literary taboo, but also a social taboo, surrounding the subject. Interviewees' accounts of their belief in the taboo nature of the subject suggest that the taboo was a self-imposed one, albeit one induced by the content and construction of the Party's official memory of the uprising. Eyewitness interviewees stated that they gained the impression that the subject was taboo because the official memory clashed with their own experiences of the events. Interviewees born after 1953 cited the brevity and lack of detail in the official account as the reason why they perceived that the subject ought not to be discussed further. These accounts support Melani Schröter's conclusion that a subject can be perceived as officially suppressed when one's expectations of what will be officially said about that subject are disappointed (Schröter, 2008, p. 117). For eyewitness interviewees the Party's account did not correspond with their own experiences. For other interviewees the SED's official memory did not correspond in terms of detail, information or conclusions with what they had learned about the uprising from the West German broadcast media. Thus the expectations of both groups were disappointed, leading them to perceive that the subject was officially suppressed.

The fact that the SED's official memory of 17 June 1953 led East German citizens to impose a taboo of the subject upon themselves demonstrates that, although the state did not enjoy total control over its citizens, its public exercise of power indirectly influenced citizens to limit, monitor and 'control' themselves to the extent desired by the Party. Few spoke about the subject with people other than their close family, and even this was rare. Consequently, the uprising of 17 June 1953 held little significance for the majority of East German citizens and became more or less a forgotten matter amongst them, particularly for those who had no direct experience of it. This lack of significance meant that few were inspired to practice further opposition against the regime by their memories or awareness of the uprising in the GDR. Thus, paradoxically, although East German citizens internalised accounts of the uprising that contrasted the SED's official memory, this did not destabilise the regime. It is nevertheless ironic that the Party succeeded in neutralising the significance of the earlier unrest in the minds of East German citizens to the extent that the generation of 40-somethings who carried the protest movement in 1989 were not deterred from demonstrating by what they knew about the uprising of 17 June 1953.

Appendix A: Interviewees

Interviewees

The following list of interviewees shows their years of birth, as well as their membership of political parties in the GDR. All names have been changed.

Eyewitness interviewees

Jakob Balzert, b.1941, LDPD
Karl Berg, b.1932, SED
Nikolaus Biewer, b.1934, SED
Herbert Binkert, b.1930
Kurt Clemens, b.1934, SED
Karola Fritzen, b.1921
Barbara Grabias, b.1927, SED
Franz Immig, b.1941, SED
Horst Klauck, b.1924, SED
Monika Klein, b.1948, SED
Heinz Kurtsiefer, b.1945, SED
Peter Momber, b.1938
Werner Otto, b.1942
Karl-Heinz Prinz, b.1921
Theodor Puff, b.1949
Heinrich Schmidt, b.1926
Wolfgang Scholl, b.1933, NDPD
Elisabeth Schreiner, b.1934
Konrad Schreiner, b.1926
Erwin Strempel, b.1932, SED

Interviewees born after 17 June 1953

Alexandra Brendel, b.1953, SED
Susanne Dobrat, b.1965, SED
Manfred Ebert, b.1965
Dorothea Freichel, b.1953
Katrin Heidinger, b.1957
Christina Heinemann, b.1953
Albert Keck, b.1959
Katja Müller, b.1962
Werner Prauss, b.1958
Doris Ritter, b.1956
Anika Rosenkranz, b.1963

Karl Schirra, b.1958, SED
Christel Schlachter, b.1957, SED
Christel Schlachter, b.1957, SED
Brigitte Schneider, b.1956
Anna Siedel, b.1967
Gerhard Siedel, b.1966
Horst Thiel, b.1958, SED
Nadine Weber, b.1960

Appendix B: Publishing Figures of the Novels Featuring Scenes of 17 June 1953

The information relating to the publishing figures of these novels was found in the files containing the *Druckgenehmigungen* (publication permits) of the respective publishing houses in the Bundesarchiv Berlin. Information relating to further editions of the novels was obtained from correspondence with the still-existing publishing houses.

Bastian, H. (1974). *Gewalt und Zärtlichkeit: Erster Roman* (Berlin: Verlag Neues Leben).
First print run: 20,000. Thirteen further editions before 1989.
Claudius, E. (1957). *Von der Liebe soll man nicht nur sprechen* (Berlin: Volk und Welt).
First print run: 20,000.
Heiduczek, W. (1977). *Tod am Meer: Roman* (Halle/Saale: Mitteldeutscher Verlag).
First print run: 15,000.
Hein, C. (1982). *Der fremde Freund* (Berlin: Aufbau Verlag).
First print run: 15,000. A further 60,000 published before 1988.
Hermlin, S. (1966). *Erzählungen* (Berlin: Aufbau Verlag).
First print run: 5,000. Four further editions before 1980.
Jakobs, K.-H. (1961). *Beschreibung eines Sommers* (Berlin: Verlag Neues Leben).
First print run: 15,000. A further 50,000 published in 1962 and 15 further editions before 1979.
Joho, W. (1972). *Die Kastanie* (Berlin: Aufbau Verlag).
First print run: 50,000.
Kampling, H. (1981). *Der Mann aus der Siedlung* (Halle/Saale: Mitteldeutscher Verlag).
First print run: 10,000.
Kant, H. (1972). *Das Impressum* (Berlin: Rütten und Loening).
Before 1989, 335,000 copies published.
Neutsch, E. (1973). *Auf der Suche nach Gatt* (Halle/Saale: Mitteldeutscher Verlag).
First print run: 20,000. A further 200,000 copies in 12 editions before 1987.
Neutsch, E. (1978). *Der Friede im Osten. Zweites Buch: Frühling mit Gewalt* (Halle/Saale: Mitteldeutscher Verlag). First print run: 40,000. A further 70,000 in 11 editions before 1983.
Reinowski, W. (1956). *Die Versuchung* (Halle/Saale: Mitteldeutscher Verlag).
Two further editions before 1959, approximately 20,000 copies.
Scholz, R. (1981). *Mein lieber alter Lukowski* (Halle/Saale: Mitteldeutscher Verlag).
First print run: 15,000.
Seeger, B. (1981). *Der Harmonikaspieler* (Halle/Saale: Mitteldeutscher Verlag).
First print run: 30,000. A second edition of 10,000 copies in 1982.

Seghers, A. (1968). *Das Vertrauen: Roman* (Berlin: Aufbau Verlag).
First print run: 70,000. A further 120,000 copies published before 1989.
Selbmann, F. (1966). *Die Söhne der Wölfe* (Halle/Saale: Mitteldeutscher Verlag).
First print run: 20,000. A further six editions before 1982.
von Wangenheim, I. (1957). *Am Morgen ist der Tag ein Kind* (Berlin: Verlag Tribüne).
First print run: 10,000. A further 10,000 copies in 1958.

Audience Figures of the Films Featuring Scenes of 17 June 1953

By 1985, 4,035,337 people in the GDR had seen the film *Schlösser und Katen*.[1] In the period from 9 June to 30 September 1967, there were in the district of Magdeburg 552 screenings of the film *Geschichten jener Nacht* attended by 58,700 people (figures provided by Dr Sean Allan of the University of Warwick through personal correspondence, 2010). Before 1985, 1,291,544 people had seen the film in the cinemas of the GDR.[2]

Notes

1 Introduction

1. 'Diskussionen in der Bürositzung am 19.10.1956 über den Bericht vor dem Politbüro', *LHSA-Ma Rep* P 13 IV/2/3/74, n.p.

2 Day X: Fascists, Spies and Thugs

1. 'Zusammenarbeit des Sekretariats der Gesellschaft für Deutsch-Sowjetische Freundschaft mit dem Verlag Kultur und Fortschritt', *SAPMO-BArch DY* 32/6100, n.p.
2. FDGB 'Aufträge, Belege. 1953–55', *SAPMO-BArch DY* 78/9439, n.p.
3. ' "Geschichte der Stadt Magdeburg" – Korrekturabzug', *SAM Rep* 41/276, pp. 634–5.
4. 'Niederschrift über die 26. Sitzung des Rates der Stadt Magdeburg, am 23.6.1954', *SAM Rep 18/4 Ra* 34, n.p.
5. 'Niederschrift über die 27. Ratssitzung am 30.6.1953', *SAM Rep 18/4 Ra* 34, n.p.
6. 'Handhabung bei Straßenumbenennungen', *SAM Rep* 41/382, p. 57.
7. 'Analyse über den faschistischen Putsch am 17. und 18. Juni 1953 im Bezirk Magdeburg', *LHSA-Ma Rep M 24 Film Nr* 23, p. 66.
8. 'Niederschrift über die Sitzung der Stadtverordnetenversammlung der Stadt Magdeburg am 27.7.1954', *SAM Rep 18/4 St* 16, n.p.
9. 'Letter to VEB Magdeburger Schilderfabrik from Stellvertreter des OB für Inneres, 24 March 1975', *SAM Rep* 41/360, pp. 23–4.
10. 'Was Magdeburger Straßennamen erzählen 1984–1985: Band I', *SAM Rep* 41/491.
11. 'Erläuterung der in Magdeburg vorhandenen Straßennamen: Stadtbezirk Süd', *SAM Rep* 41/381, n.p.
12. 'Straßen, die nach Widerstandskämpfern bzw. Führern der Arbeiterbewegung benannt sind und gekennzeichnet werden müßten', *SAM Rep* 41/379, p. 377.
13. 'Wolfgang Stave – Gliederung zur Belegarbeit', *BStU MfS BV Magdeburg Abteilung* IX–13, pp. 131–77.

3 Tales of That Day

1. '*Der Mann aus der Siedlung* – Verlagsgutachten', *SAPMO-BArch DR* 1/2184, no pagination.
2. 'Büro Hager: Arbeit mit Schriftstellern', *SAPMO-BArch DY* 30/IV A 2/2.024/71, no pagination.
3. *SAPMO-BArch DY* 30/IV A 2/2.024/71, n.p.

4. 'SED ZK Abt. Kultur 1972–1980. Anlage 1 – Zum 17. Juni,' *SAPMO-BArch DY* 30/IV B 2/9.06/31, p. 128.
5. *SAPMO-BArch DY* 30/IV B 2/9.06/31, p. 131.
6. *SAPMO-BArch DY* 30/IV A 2/2.024/71, no pagination.
7. 'Bemerkungen zum "Impressum" von Hermann Kant, 24. Juli 1969', *BArch DY* 30/IV A 2/2.024/65, n.p.
8. '*Auf der Suche nach Gatt* – Verlagsgutachten', *SAPMO-BArch DR* 1/2176a, p. 197.
9. 'Letter to Minister for Culture Kurt Hager from Sektor Verlage Abt. Leiter Kempke', *SAPMO-BArch DY* 30/IV A 2/2.024/65, n.p.
10. *SAPMO-BArch DY* 30/IV B 2/9.06/31, n.p.
11. *SAPMO-BArch DY* 30/IV A 2/2.024/65, n.p.
12. *SAPMO-BArch DY* 30/IV A 2/2.024/65, n.p.
13. 'Letter from Graphische Werkstätte Leipzig, 11 December 1956', *SAPMO-BArch DY* 34/1725, no pagination.
14. 'Letter from Herbert Schilke to the Bücherei v. VEB Bau Berlin, 25 March 1957', *SAPMO-BArch DY* 34/1725, n.p.
15. 'Letter from Gewerkschaftsgruppe des Mathias-Thesen-Werft Wismar, 14 February 1979', *SAPMO-BArch DY* 34/11726, n.p.
16. 'Letter from Klubbücherei VEB Gerätewerk Karl-Marx-Stadt, 31 March 1958', *SAPMO-BArch DY* 34/6957, n.p.
17. 'Letter from Verband der Konsumgenossenschaften der DDR Berlin, 10 April 1979', *SAPMO-BArch DY* 34/11726, n.p.
18. 'Letter from VEB Automobilwerk Eisenach', undated, *SAPMO-BArch DY* 34/12445, n.p.
19. 'Letter from Bergbaubetriebes Schmirchau der SDAG Wismut, 21 May 1982', *SAPMO-BArch DY* 34/12445, n.p.
20. 'Letter from Bücherei v. VEB Bau, Berlin, 25 March 1957', *SAPMO-BArch DY* 34/10016, n.p.
21. 'Letter from VEB Automobilwerk Eisenach', undated, *SAPMO-BArch DY* 34/11727, n.p.
22. 'Letter from Ministerrat der DDR Staatliche Zentralverwaltung für Statistik to FDGB, 2 August 1979', *SAPMO-BArch DY* 34/11728, n.p.
23. 'Letter from VEB Waggonbau Ammendorf to FDGB, 27 May 1974', *SAPMO-BArch DY* 34/10016, n.p.
24. 'Letter from VEB Schwermaschinenbau Verlade- und Transportanlagen Leipzig, 10 April 1957', *SAPMO-BArch DY* 34/1725, n.p.
25. 'Letter from VEB Automobilwerk Eisenach, 3 September 1975', *SAPMO-BArch DY* 34/10932, n.p.
26. 'Letter from Gewerkschafts- und Patientenbibliothek Bezirkskrankenhaus Cottbus, 5 April 1979', *BArch DY* 34/11726, n.p.
27. 'Letter from Peter Gallasch, Schichtelektriker', undated, *SAPMO-BArch DY* 34/11725, n.p.
28. 'Letter from Gewerkschafts- und Patientenbibliothek Bezirkskrankenhaus Cottbus, 5 April 1979', *SAPMO-BArch DY* 34/11726, n.p.

4 Watching the West

1. 'Hörfunk- und Fernseh-Programmfahne, 17 June 1978', *DRA-F*.
2. 'Fernseh-Programmfahne, 17 June 1986', *DRA-F*.

3. 'Hörfunk- und Fernseh-Programmfahne, 17 June 1987–1989', *DRA-F*.
4. 'Fernseh-Programmfahne, 17 June 1985', *DRA-F*.

5 Remembering and Discussing the Uprising of 17 June 1953

1. 'Letter from Gewerkschafts- und Patientenbibliothek Bezirkskrankenhaus Cottbus, 5 April 1979', *SAPMO-BArch DY* 34/11726, n.p.

6 17 June 1953: A Symbolic Talisman of Opposition in the GDR?

1. Grumbling by citizens was not unusual. Indeed, the GDR is often depicted as a 'grumbling' society, in which citizens consistently made complaints, most often about the standard of living. They were even encouraged to make official complaints (and thus participate in society) through the submission of 'petitions' (*Eingaben*), which the regime promised to deal with within four weeks (see Fulbrook, 2005, pp. 269–88).
2. 'Befehl Nr 5/55 des Chefs der Volkspolizei im Bezirk Magdeburg zum Befehl 33/55 des Chefs der Deutschen Volkspolizei', *LHSA-Ma Rep M 24 Film Nr 1*, pp. 625–7.
3. 'Auszug aus dem Informationsbericht der Bezirksleitung v. 4.6.54 – Stimmung der Bevölkerung', *LHSA-Ma Rep P 13, IV/2/4/19*, n.p.
4. 'Wochenbericht, den 5.5.1955', *LHSA-Ma Rep P 13 IV/2/3/48/1*, p. 247.
5. 'Wochenbericht. den 26.5.1955', *LHSA-Ma Rep P 13 IV/2/3/50*, p. 46.
6. 'Diskussionen über Versorgungsfragen. Wochenbericht für die Zeit vom 23. – 28.5.1955', *LHSA-Ma Rep P 43 1276*, n.p.
7. 'Wochenbericht. den 2.6.1955', *LHSA-Ma Rep P 13 IV/2/3/50*, p. 177.
8. 'Wochenbericht. den 30.9.1955', *LHSA-Ma Rep P 43 Film Nr 114*, p. 97.
9. 'Informationsbericht, den 12.7.1956', *LHSA-Ma Rep P 43 1278*, p. 2.
10. 'Diskussion über den Entwurf der abgeänderten Satzung des FDGB, den 2.6.1955', *LHSA-Ma Rep P 43 1272*, n.p.
11. 'Stimmungen zur Bildung der Nationalen Volksarmee, den 19.1.1956', *LHSA-Ma Rep P 43 Film Nr 111*, p. 278.
12. 'Informationsbericht der 10. Sekretariatssitzung vom 23. Mai 1956 des Bezirksvorstand Magdeburg der IG Eisenbahn', *LHSA-Ma Rep P 43 1247*, p. 2.
13. 'Informationsbericht, den 5.7.57', *LHSA-Ma Rep P 16 IV/5/1/78 Film Nr 28*, p. 826.
14. 'Wochenbericht, den 14.10.1955', *LHSA-Ma Rep P 43 Film Nr 114*, p. 107.
15. 'Informationsbericht, den 5.11.1958', *LHSA-Ma Rep P 43 Film Nr 115*, p. 742.
16. 'Informationsbericht – Stimmung der Bevölkerung, den 26.6.1956', *LHSA-Ma Rep P 16 IV/5/1/69 Film Nr 25*, p. 14.
17. 'Analyse über die Einschätzung der Feindarbeit, den 30.12.1959', *LHSA-Ma Rep P 16 IV/5/1/140*, p. 32.
18. 'Ausschluß vom Arbeiter Walter Z., den 30.3.1955', *LHSA-Ma Rep P 16 IV/5/1/60 Film Nr 23*, p. 53.
19. 'Informationsbericht zum Punkt Feindarbeit, den 11.5.1957', *LHSA-Ma Rep P 16 IV/5/1/74 Film Nr 27*, p. 952.

20. 'Bericht über die Stimmung der Bevölkerung, den 1.11.1956', *LHSA-Ma Rep P* 13 IV/2/5/46, p. 59.
21. *BStU MfS BV KD Magdeburg* 16700, pp. 6–11.
22. 'Situationsbericht, den 7.11.1956', *LHSA-Ma Rep P* 16 IV/5/1/163 Film Nr 54, p. 300.
23. 'Informationsbericht, den 29.10.1956', *LHSA-Ma Rep P* 16 IV/5/1/163 Film Nr 54, p. 275.
24. 'Situationsbericht, den 25.10.1956', *LHSA-Ma Rep P* 16 IV/5/1/163 Film Nr 54, p. 255.
25. 'Situationsbericht, den 1.11.1956', *LHSA-Ma Rep P* 16 IV/5/1/163 Film Nr 54, p. 287.
26. *BStU MfS BV KD Magdeburg* 11770, pp. 7–36.
27. 'Informationsbericht, den 8.10.1956', *LHSA-Ma Rep P* 16 IV/5/1/72 Film Nr 26, p. 732.
28. 'Situationsbericht, den 1.11.1956', *LHSA-Ma Rep P* 16 IV/5/1/163 Film Nr 54, p. 287.
29. 'Situationsbericht, den 3.10.1956', *LHSA-Ma Rep P* 16 IV/5/1/163 Film Nr 54, pp. 234–7.
30. 'Protokoll Nr 17 der Bürositzung der Stadtleitung am 24.10.1956', *LHSA-Ma Rep P* 16 IV/5/1/72 Film Nr 26, pp. 795–8.
31. 'Sonderbericht zum 17. Juni 1961', *LHSA-Ma Rep M* 24 Film Nr 50, pp. 137–8.
32. 'Situationsbericht zur Vorbereitung der Volkswahlen, den 5.10.1954', *LHSA-Ma Rep P* 43 Film Nr 115, p. 328.
33. 'Sicherheitsmaßnahmen zum 17. Juni 1962', *LHSA-Ma Rep M* 24 Film Nr 1, pp. 193–4.
34. 'Lagebericht, Sicherungsmaßnahmen zum 17.6.1962', *LHSA-Ma Rep M* 24 Film Nr 52, p. 135.
35. 'Sicherungsmaßnahmen zum 17.6.1962', *BStU MfS BV Magdeburg KD Haldensleben* 687, p. 91.
36. 'Rapport Nr 135/64 für die Zeit vom 16.6.64, 05.00 Uhr bis 17.6.64, 05.00 Uhr. Vorkommnisse entlang der Staatsgrenze', *LHSA-Ma Rep M* 24 Film Nr 54, p. 128.
37. 'Rapport Nr 136/64 für die Zeit vom 17.6.64, 05.00 Uhr bis 18.6.64, 05.00 Uhr. Lage an der Staatsgrenze', *LHSA-Ma Rep M* 24 Film Nr 54, p. 131.
38. 'Rapport Nr 134/65 für die Zeit vom 15.6.65, 05.00 Uhr bis 16.6.65, 05.00 Uhr. Vorkommnis an der Staatsgrenze-West', *LHSA-Ma Rep M* 24 Film Nr 55, p. 308.
39. 'Rapport Nr 144/66 für die Zeit vom 17.6.66, 05.00 Uhr bis 18.6.66, 05.00 Uhr. Einschätzung der Lage an der Staatsgrenze', *LHSA-Ma Rep M* 24 Film Nr 56, p. 273.
40. 'Rapport Nr 142/67 für die Zeit vom 16.6.67, 05.00 Uhr bis 17.6.67, 05.00 Uhr. Information zur Lage an der Grenze', *LHSA-Ma Rep M* 24 Film Nr 57, p. 346.
41. 'Rapport Nr 139/61 Teil A für die Zeit vom 17.6.61, 05.00 Uhr bis 18.6.61, 05.00 Uhr', *LHSA-Ma Rep M* 24 Film Nr 50, p. 140.
42. 'Rapport Nr 139/61 Teil B für die Zeit vom 18.6.61, 05.00 Uhr bis 19.6.61, 05.00 Uhr', *LHSA-Ma Rep M* 24 Film Nr 50, p. 142.
43. 'Rapport Nr 136/64 für die Zeit vom 17.6.64, 05.00 Uhr bis 18.6.64, 05.00 Uhr', *LHSA-Ma Rep M* 24 Film Nr 54, p. 135.

44. 'Stimmung der Bevölkerung: Arbeiter, den 8.7.1960', *LHSA-Ma Rep P* 16 IV/5/1/1110 Film Nr 39, p. 54.
45. 'Informationsbericht. Ernst-Thälmann-Werk, den 1.9.1960', *LHSA-Ma Rep P* 43 956, pp. 4–5.
46. 'Stimmung der Bevölkerung, den 23.6.1961', *LHSA-Ma Rep P* 16 IV/5/1/120 Film Nr 42, p. 368.
47. 'An VfS Magdeburg Arbeitsgruppe Auswertung/Information: Betreff 17. Juni, den 18.6.1963', *MfS BV Mgb KD HDL* 595, p. 31.
48. 'Rapport Nr 140/68 für die Zeit vom 18.6.68, 03.00 Uhr bis 19.6.68, 03.00 Uhr', *LHSA-Ma Rep M* 24 Film Nr 58, p. 342.
49. 'Rapport Nr 136/65 für die Zeit vom 17.6.65, 05.00 Uhr bis 18.6.65, 05.00 Uhr', *LHSA-Ma Rep M* 24 Film Nr 55, p. 325.
50. 'Rapport Nr 143/67 für die Zeit vom 17.6.67, 05.00 Uhr bis 18.6.67, 05.00 Uhr', *LHSA-Ma Rep M* 24 Film Nr 57, p. 362.
51. 'Verhinderung feindlicher Handlung und Provokationen in der DDR anläßlich des 17. Juni 1975. 14.6.1975', *BStU MfS BV Magdeburg/BdI/Dok.* 2281, p. 1.
52. 'Maßnahmeplan der BV Magdeburg zur Aufklärung und Abwehr geplanter feindlicher Handlungen und Provokationen im Zusammenhang mit dem 17. Juni 1977 und der KSZE-Nachfolgekonferenz in Belgrad gemäß Befehl 20/77 des Genossen Minister', *BStU MfS BV Magdeburg/BdL/Dok.* 2556, pp. 1–14.
53. 'Kontrollelemente', *LHSA-Ma Rep M* 24 11976, p. 1.
54. 'Bericht an Gen. Kirnich, den 6.11.79', *LHSA-Ma Rep. P* 13, IV/D-2/5/348, p. 2.
55. 'Rapport Nr 144/70 für die Zeit vom 18.6.70, 03.00 Uhr bis 19.6.70, 03.00 Uhr', *LHSA-Ma Rep M* 24 Film Nr 60, p. 320.
56. 'Lageeinschätzung 13.6.74 – 27.6.74', *LHSA-Ma Rep M* 24 Film Nr 40, p. 151.
57. 'Rapport Nr 119/73 für die Zeit vom 18.6.73, 02.00 Uhr bis 19.6.73, 02.00 Uhr', *LHSA-Ma Rep M* 24 Film Nr 63, p. 749.
58. 'Rapport Nr 130/75 für die Zeit vom 27.6.75, 02.00 Uhr bis 28.6.75, 02.00 Uhr: Teil B', *LHSA-Ma Rep M* 24 Film Nr 64, p. 1026.
59. 'Rapport Nr 118/78 für die Zeit vom 17.6.78, 02.00 Uhr bis 18.6.78, 02.00 Uhr: Teil B', *LHSA-Ma Rep M* 24 11348, n.p.
60. 'Maßnahmeplan zur politisch-operativen Sicherung des 24. Pressefests der "Volksstimme Magdeburg" und zur Verhinderung feindlicher Aktivitäten im Zusammenahng mit dem 17. Juni 1978', *BStU MfS BV Magdeburg/BdL/Dok.* 2662, pp. 1–5.
61. 'Fernschreiben zu geplanten gegnerischen Aktivitäten an der Staatsgrenze anläßlich des Jahrestages des 17. Juni 1985', *BStU MfS BV Magdeburg/BdL/Dok.* 1576, pp. 3–4.
62. 'Hinweise auf die gegen die DDR gerichteten Aktivitäten im Zusammenhang mit dem sogenannten Tag der deutschen Einheit am 17. Juni 1989', *BStU MfS BV Magdeburg/BdL/Dok.* 97, pp. 7–9.
63. 'Rapport Nr 119/83 für die Zeit vom 17.6.83, 02.00 Uhr bis 18.6.83, 02.00 Uhr: Teil A', *LHSA-Ma Rep M* 24 14203, n.p.
64. 'Rapport Nr 135/84 für die Zeit vom 17.6.84, 00.00 Uhr bis 18.6.84, 24.00 Uh', *LHSA-Ma Rep M* 24 14200, n.p.
65. 'Rapport Nr 117/85 für die Zeit vom 17.6.85, 02.00 Uhr bis 18.6.85, 02.00 Uhr', *LHSA-Ma Rep M* 24 15099, n.p.

66. *BStU MfS BV Magdeburg Abt.* XX 2556, p. 2.
67. Ibid., p. 42.
68. Ibid, pp. 47–9.
69. Ibid, pp. 43–4.
70. Ibid, pp. 47–9.
71. Ibid, pp. 50–3.

8 Conclusion

1. 'Bericht über die Stimmung der Bevölkerung, 1.11.1956', *LHSA-Ma Rep P* 13 IV/2/5/46, p. 59.

Appendix B: Publishing Figures of the Novels Featuring Scenes of 17 June 1953

1. 'DEFA-Kinospielfilmproduktion Band 3, 1983–1985', BArch DR117, p. 175.
2. 'DEFA-Kinospielfilmproduktion Band 4, 1983–1985', BArch DR117, p. 181.

Bibliography

Archives

ARD Archive
Die Tagesschau 1954–1989

Der Bundesbeauftragte für die Unterlagen des Staatssicherheitsdienstes der ehemaligen DDR, Außenstelle Magdeburg

British Library
MF.538.H   Neues Deutschland

Bundesarchiv Berlin
DR 1   Ministerium für Kultur
DY 7   Kongreß Verlag
DY 30   Büro Hager
DY 32   Gesellschaft für Deutsch-Sowjetische Freundschaft
DY 34   FDGB
DY 78   Verlag Tribüne
DR 117   VEB DEFA Studio für Spielfilme

Deutsches Rundfunkarchiv Frankfurt am Main
Fernseh-Programmfahne, 17 June 1977–1989
Hörfunk-Programmfahne, 17 June 1977–1989

Landeshauptarchiv Sachsen-Anhalt Abteilung Magdeburg
Rep M 24   Bezirksbehörde der Deutschen Volkspolizei Magdeburg
Rep P 13   Bezirksleitung der SED Magdeburg
Rep P 16   Stadtleitung der SED Magdeburg
Rep P 30   Magdeburger Volksstimme
Rep P 43   Bezirksvorstand des FDGB Magdeburg
Rep P 45   Stadtvorstand des FDGB Magdeburg

Staatsbibliothek Berlin
Hörzu 1953–1989

Stadtarchiv Magdeburg

Rep 18/4 Ra 34   Sitzungen des Rates der Stadt Magdeburg
Rep 18/4 St 16   Stadtverordnetenversammlung Magdeburg
Rep 41   Rat der Stadt Magdeburg

Secondary Literature

Ahrberg, E., Hertle, H.-H., and Hollitzer, T. (2004). *Die Toten des Volksaufstandes vom 17. Juni 1953* (Münster: Lit Verlag).
Anon. (2011). 'Damals in der DDR. Lexikon: Literatur der DDR II'. Available from: http://www.mdr.de/damals/archiv/artikel75316.html [5 March 2014].
Asmus, H. (1975). *Geschichte der Stadt Magdeburg* (Berlin: Akademie Verlag).
Assmann, A. (2006). *Der lange Schatten der Vergangenheit: Erinnerungspolitik und Geschichtspolitik* (Munich: C.H. Beck).
Assmann, A., Assmann, J. (1994). 'Das Gestern im Heute. Medien und soziales Gedächtnis', in Klaus Merten (ed.). *Die Wirklichkeit der Medien* (Opladen: Westdeutscher Verlag), pp. 114–41.
Assmann, A., Frevert, U. (1999). *Geschichtsvergessenheit, Geschichtsversessenheit: Vom Umgang mit deutschen Vergangenheiten nach 1945* (Stuttgart: Deutsche Verlags-Anstalt).
Ausschuß für Deutsche Einheit. (1953). *Wer zog die Drähte? Der Juni-Putsch 1953 und seine Hintergründe* (Berlin Ost: Ausschuß für Deutsche Einheit).
Autorenkollektiv. (1960). *Lehrbuch für Geschichte der 10. Klasse* (Berlin: Volk und Wissen Verlag).
Autorenkollektiv. (1963). *Die Errichtung der Grundlagen des Sozialismus in der Industrie der DDR 1951–1955* (Berlin: Dietz Verlag).
Autorenkollektiv. (1963). *Grundriß der Geschichte der deutschen Arbeiterbewegung* (Berlin: Dietz Verlag).
Autorenkollektiv. (1966). *Geschichte der deutschen Arbeiterbewegung. Bd 7: Von 1949–1955* (Berlin: Dietz Verlag).
Autorenkollektiv. (1967). *Geschichte der deutschen Arbeiterbewegung: Chronik. Teil III: Von 1945–1963* (Berlin: Dietz Verlag).
Autorenkollektiv. (1968). *Unterrichtshilfen. Geschichte 10. Klasse* (Berlin: Volk und Wissen Verlag).
Autorenkollektiv. (1969). *Kurze Geschichte der DDR* (Berlin: Dietz Verlag).
Autorenkollektiv. (1971). *Unterrichtshilfen. Geschichte 10. Klasse: Teil I* (Berlin: Volk und Wissen Verlag).
Autorenkollektiv. (1974). *Unterrichtshilfen. Geschichte 10. Klasse: Teil I* (Berlin: Volk und Wissen Verlag).
Autorenkollektiv. (1978a). *Geschichte der SED. Abriß* (Berlin: Dietz Verlag).
Autorenkollektiv. (1978b). *Kleines Politisches Wörterbuch* (Berlin: Dietz Verlag).
Autorenkollektiv. (1980). *Unterrichtshilfen. Geschichte Klasse 11* (Berlin: Volk und Wissen Verlag).
Autorenkollektiv. (1989). *Unterrichtshilfen. Geschichte 10* (Berlin: Volk und Wissen Verlag).
Barck, S. (2002). 'Kultur im Wiederaufbau. Teil 2: Bildung und Kultur in der DDR'. Available from: http://www.bpb.de/publikationen/WV9LQV,4,0,Kultur_im_Wiederaufbau_(Teil_2).html [5 March 2014].

Barck, S., Langermann, M., Lokatis, S. (1997). *"Jedes Buch ein Abenteuer": Zensur-System und literarische Öffentlichkeiten in der DDR bis Ende der sechziger Jahre* (Berlin: Akademie Verlag).
Barck, S., Langermann, M., Lokatis, S. (2001). 'The GDR as a "Reading Nation": Utopia, Planning, Reality and Ideology', in Michael Geyer (ed.). *The Power of the Intellectuals in Contemporary Germany* (Chicago: Chicago University Press), pp. 88–112.
Baring, A. (1957). *Der 17. Juni 1953* (Bonn: Bundesministerium für Gesamtdeutsche Fragen).
Bastian, H. (1974). *Gewalt und Zärtlichkeit: Erster Roman* (Berlin: Verlag Neues Leben).
Bathrick, D. (1995). *The Powers of Speech: The Politics of Culture in the GDR* (Lincoln: University of Nebraska Press).
Beratergruppe Dom des Gebetes um gesellschaftliche Erneuerung im Magdeburger Dom. (1991). *Herbst '89 in Magdeburg* (Magdeburg: Impuls-Verlag).
Bessel, R. (2002). 'The People's Police and the People in Ulbricht's Germany', in P. Major and J. Osmond (eds.). *The Workers' and Peasants' State: Communism and Society in East Germany under Ulbricht, 1945–1971* (Manchester: Manchester University Press).
Bodnar, J. (1992). *Remaking America: Public Memory, Commemoration, and Patriotism in the Twentieth Century* (Princeton, NJ: Princeton University Press).
Brant, S. (1954). *Der Aufstand. Vorgeschichte, Geschichte und Deutung des 17. Juni 1953* (Stuttgart: Steingrüben Verlag).
Braun, M. (2007). 'Der 17. Juni 1953 in der Prosaliteratur in der DDR', in Carsten Gansel (ed.). *Gedächtnis und Literatur in den 'geschlossenen Gesellschaften' des Real-Sozialismus zwischen 1945 und 1989* (Göttingen: V & R unipress).
Brockmann, A. (2006). *Erinnerungsarbeit im Fernsehen: das Beispiel des 17. Juni 1953* (Cologne: Böhlau).
Bruhn, P. (2003). *17. Juni 1953: Bibliographie* (Berlin: Berliner Wissenschafts-Verlag).
Buchheim, C. (1990). 'Wirtschaftliche Hintergründe des Arbeiteraufstandes vom 17. Juni 1953 in der DDR', *Vierteljahreshefte für Zeitgeschichte* 38.3, 415–33.
Buchholz, I. (1985). *Was Magdeburger Straßennamen erzählen* (Magdeburg: Volksstimme Verlag).
Childs, D. (2001). *The Fall of the GDR* (Harlow: Longman).
Clarke, D., Wölfel, U. (eds.). (2011). *Remembering the German Democratic Republic* (Basingstoke: Palgrave).
Claudius, E. (1957). *Von der Liebe soll man nicht nur sprechen* (Berlin: Volk und Welt).
Confino, A. (2008). 'Memory and the History of Mentalities', in A. Erll, A. Nünning (eds.). *Cultural Memory Studies: An International and Interdisciplinary Handbook* (Berlin: Walter de Gruyter), pp. 77–85.
Dale, G. (2005). *Popular Protest in East Germany, 1945–1989* (London: Routledge).
Diedrich, T. (1992). *Der 17. Juni in der DDR. Bewaffnete Gewalt gegen das Volk* (Berlin: Dietz Verlag).
Diedrich, T. (2003). *Waffen gegen das Volk: Der 17. Juni 1953 in der DDR* (Munich: R. Oldenbourg).
Diedrich, T., Hertle, H.-H. (2003). *Alarmstufe "Hornisse": Die geheimen Chef-Berichte der Volkspolizei über den 17. Juni 1953* (Berlin: Metropol).

Doernberg, S. (1964). *Kurze Geschichte der DDR* (Berlin: Dietz Verlag).
Dorrill, S. (2000). *MI6: Fifty Years of Special Operations* (London: Fourth Estate Limited).
Eckstein, G. (1953). *Verratener Verräter* (Berlin Ost: Bundesvorstand des FDGB).
Eisenfeld, B. (2005). 'Der "17. Juni" – das doppelte Trauma: Machthaber und Opposition', in R. Engelmann, I.-S. Kowalczuk (eds.). *Volkserhebung gegen den SED Staat: eine Bestandsaufnahme zum 17. Juni 1953* (Berlin: Vandenhoeck & Ruprecht), pp. 349–77.
Eisenfeld, B., Kowalczuk, I.-S., Neubert, E. (2004). *Die verdrängte Revolution: Der Platz des 17. Juni 1953 in der deutschen Geschichte* (Bremen: Edition Temmen).
Emmerich, W. (2000). *Kleine Literaturgeschichte der DDR* (Leipzig: Aufbau Taschenbuch Verlag).
Feinstein, J. (2002). *The Triumph of the Ordinary: Depictions of Daily Life in the East German Cinema* (Chapel Hill, N.C.: University of North Carolina Press).
Friedenspost. (1953). *Berlin im Juni 1953. Ein Bild und Erlebnisbericht aus jenem Tagen, die ganz anders endeten, als manche erwartet hatten* (Berlin Ost: Verlag Kultur und Fortschritt).
Fuhrmann, H. (1997). *Warten auf 'Geschichte': Der Dramatiker Heiner Müller* (Würzburg: K&N).
Fulbrook, M. (1995). *Anatomy of a Dictatorship: Inside the GDR, 1949–1989* (Oxford: Oxford University Press).
Fulbrook, M. (1996). 'Methodologische Überlegungen zu einer Gesellschaftsgeschichte der DDR', in R. Bessel and R. Jessen (eds.). *Die Grenzen der Diktatur: Staat und Gesellschaft in der DDR* (Göttingen: Vandenhoeck & Ruprecht), pp. 274–97.
Fulbrook, M. (2005). *The People's State: East German Society from Hitler to Honecker* (New Haven: Yale University Press).
Fulbrook, M. (2009). *Power and Society in the GDR, 1961–1979* (Oxford: Berghahn).
Fulbrook, M. (2011a). *Dissonant Lives: Generations and Violence Through the German Dictatorships* (Oxford: Oxford University Press).
Fulbrook, M. (2011b). 'Histories and Memories: Verklärung or Erklärung', in D. Clarke, U. Wölfel (eds.). *Remembering the German Democratic Republic* (Basingstoke: Palgrave Macmillan), pp. 91–102.
Gauck, J. (2013). 'Gedenkstunde des Deutschen Bundestags zum 60. Jahrestag des Volksaufstands vom 17. Juni 1953 in der DDR'. Available from: http://www.bundespraesident.de/SharedDocs/Reden/DE/Joachim-Gauck/Reden/2013/06/130614-17-Juni-BT.html [11 March 2014].
Gieseke, J. (2000). *Die hauptamtlichen Mitarbeiter der Staatssicherheit* (Berlin: Links).
Görldt, A. (2002). *Rudolf Herrnstadt und Wilhelm Zaisser. Ihre Konflikte in der SED-Führung im Kontext innerparteilicher Machtsicherung und sowjetischer Deutschlandpolitik* (Frankfurt am Main: Peter Lang).
Grele, R. J. (1998). 'Movement Without Aim. Methodological and Theoretical Problems in Oral History', in R. Perks, A. Thomson (eds.). *The Oral History Reader* (London: Routledge), pp. 38–53.
Grünwald, K., Puhle, M. (1993). *Magdeburg 17. Juni 1953* (Magdeburg: Magdeburger Museen).

Gursky, A. (2003). 'Erna Dorn: "KZ Kommandeuse" und "Rädelsführerin" von Halle – Rekonstruktion einer Legende', in H.-J. Rupieper (ed.). *"...Und das Wichtigste ist doch die Einheit." Der 17. Juni 1953 in den Bezirken Halle und Magdeburg* (Münster: Lit Verlag), pp. 350–81.
Haertel, A. (2003). *Die Ereignisse um den 17. Juni 1953 im Bezirk Magdeburg* (Magdeburg: Schlaglichter).
Hagen, M. (1992). *DDR, Juni '53: die erste Volkserhebung im Stalinismus* (Stuttgart: F. Steiner).
Halbwachs, M. (1992). *On Collective Memory* (Chicago: University of Chicago Press).
Haupts, L. (1992). 'Die Blockparteien in der DDR und der 17. Juni 1953', *Vierteljahreshefte für Zeitgeschichte* 40.2, 383–412.
Heiduczek, W. (1977). *Tod am Meer: Roman* (Halle/Saale: Mitteldeutscher Verlag).
Hein, C. (1982). *Der fremde Freund* (Berlin: Aufbau Verlag).
Heise, J., Hofmann, J. (1988). *Fragen an die Geschichte der DDR* (Berlin: Verlag Junge Welt).
Heitzer, H. (1979). *Geschichtlicher Überblick* (Berlin: Dietz Verlag).
Hermann-Josef Rupieper (ed) (2003). *"...Und das Wichtigste ist doch die Einheit." Der 17. Juni 1953 in den Bezirken Halle und Magdeburg* (Münster: Lit Verlag).
Hermlin, S. (1954). 'Die Kommandeuse', *Neue deutsche Literatur* 2, 19–28.
Hermlin, S. (1983). 'Die Kommandeuse', in *Erzählungen* (Berlin: Buchclub 65), pp. 215–31.
Hirte, C. (2005). 'Zensoren und Verlagsstrategen', in S. Barck, S. Lokatis (eds.). *Fenster zur Welt. Eine Geschichte des DDR-Verlages Volk&Welt* (Berlin: Ch. Links Verlag), pp. 392–7.
Hofman, H., Praschl, G. (2003). *Der Aufstand. Juni 53 – Augenzeugen berichten* (Berlin: Das Neue Berlin).
Holzweißig, G. (2002). *Die schärfste Waffe der Partei: Eine Mediengeschichte der DDR* (Cologne: Böhlau).
Horn, W. (1960). *Der Kampf der SED um den Aufbau der Grundlagen des Sozialismus in der DDR* (Berlin: Dietz Verlag).
Horn, W. (1963) *Die Errichtung der Grundlagen des Sozialismus in der Industrie der DDR, 1951–1955* (Berlin: Dietz Verlag).
Hutchinson, P. (1992). *Stefan Heym: The Perpetual Dissident* (Cambridge: Cambridge University Press).
Jakobs, K.-H. (1961). *Beschreibung eines Sommers* (Berlin: Verlag Neues Leben).
Jarausch, K. H. (1999). 'Care and Coercion: The GDR as Welfare Dictatorship', in Konrad H. Jarausch (ed.). *Dictatorship as Experience: Towards a Socio-Cultural History of the GDR* (New York: Berghahn), pp. 47–69.
Jesse, E., Mitter, A. (1992). *Die Gestaltung der deutschen Einheit: Geschichte, Politik, Gesellschaft* (Bonn: Bouvier).
Jessen, R. (1995). 'Die Gesellschaft im Staatssozialismus. Probleme einer Sozialgeschichte der DDR', *Geschichte und Gesellschaft* 21.1, 96–110.
Joho, W. (1972). *Die Kastanie* (Berlin: Aufbau Verlag).
Kampling, H. (1981). *Der Mann aus der Siedlung* (Halle/Saale: Mitteldeutscher Verlag).

Kansteiner, W. (2002). 'Finding Meaning in Memory: A Methodological Critique of Collective Memory Studies', *History and Theory* 41.2, 179–97.
Kant, H. (1965). *Die Aula* (Berlin: Rütten und Loening).
Kant, H. (1972). *Das Impressum* (Berlin: Rütten und Loening).
Kleßmann, C. (2007). *Arbeiter im 'Arbeiterstaat' DDR* (Bonn: Dietz Verlag).
Klötzer, S., Lokatis, S. (1999). 'Criticism and Censorship: Negotiating Cabaret Performance and Book Production', in K. H. Jarausch (ed.). *Dictatorship as Experience: Towards a Socio-Cultural History of the GDR* (New York: Berghahn), pp. 241–64.
Knabe, H. (2003). *17. Juni 1953: Ein deutscher Aufstand* (München: Propyläen).
Knappe, J. (1966). *Mein namenloses Land* (Halle/Saale: Mitteldeutscher Verlag).
Kocka, J. (1994). 'Eine durchherrschte Gesellschaft', in H. Kaelble, J. Kocka, H. Zwahr (eds.). *Sozialgeschichte der DDR* (Stuttgart: Klett-Cotta), pp. 547–53.
Koop, V. (2003). *Der 17. Juni 1953: Legende und Wirklichkeit* (Berlin: Siedler).
Kowalczuk, I.-S. (2003). *17.6.53: Volksaufstand in der DDR* (Bremen: Edition Temmen).
Krämer, H. (1999). *Ein dreißigjähriger Krieg gegen ein Buch* (Tübingen: Stauffenburg).
Leo, A. (1999). 'Tabu und Tradition. Der 17. Juni und der 100-Tage-Streik in der Erinnerung der Hennigsdorfer Stahlarbeiter', *BIOS* 12.1, 58–72.
Lindenberger, T. (2003). *Volkspolizei: Herrschaftspraxis und öffentliche Ordnung im SED-Staat, 1952–1968* (Cologne: Böhlau).
Loth, W. (1997). *Stalin's Unwanted Child: The Soviet Union, the German Question and the Founding of the GDR* (Basingstoke: Macmillan).
Lübeck, W., Ruden, G. (eds.). (2000). *Knüppel, Kerzen, Diaolg: Die friedliche Revolution im Bezirk Magdeburg* (Halle/Saale: Mitteldeutscher Verlag).
Lüdtke, A., Becker, P. (1997). *Akten, Eingaben, Schaufenster. Die DDR und ihre Texte: Erkundungen zu Herrschaft und Alltag* (Berlin: Akademie Verlag).
Madarász, J. Z. (2003). *Conflict and Compromise in East Germany, 1971–1989: A Precarious Stability* (Basingstoke: Palgrave Macmillan).
Magdeburger Volksstimme. (1953a). 'Bürger von Magdeburg!', 18 June, 1.
Magdeburger Volksstimme. (1953b). 'Arbeiter antworten den Provokateuren: Arbeiter des Thälmannwerkes nahmen einen Rädelsführer fest', 19 June, 1.
Magdeburger Volksstimme. (1953c). 'Klassenbewußte Arbeiter schützten Karl-Liebknecht-Werk: Die brigade "Walter Ulbricht" verteidigte ihre Siegerauszeichnung, das Karl-Liebknecht-Banner', 21 June, 1.
Magdeburger Volksstimme. (1953d). 'Eisenbahner kämpften gegen faschistische Provokation: Im Reichsbahndirektionsbezirk Magdeburg bekamen die Banditen eine entschiedene Abfuhr', 24 June, 2.
Magdeburger Volksstimme. (1953e). 'Gerechte Strafe für den faschistischen Banditen Dartsch', 22 June, 2.
Magdeburger Volksstimme. (1953f). 'Unsere Kinder sollen ungestört lernen: Faschistische Rowdys müssen streng bestraft werden', 24 June, 3.
Magdeburger Volksstimme. (1953g). 'Strafgefangene leisten Provokateuren Widerstand', 20 June, 1.
Magdeburger Volksstimme. (1953h). 'Das waren die "Argumente" der Provokateure des', 17 Juni, 2.
Magdeburger Volksstimme. (1953i). 'Lebenslänglich Zuchthaus für Putsch und Mordversuch', 27 August, 2.

Magdeburger Volksstimme. (1953j). 'Das Leben und die Arbeit gehen normal weiter', 19 June, 1.
Magdeburger Volksstimme. (1953k). 'Neuerscheinungen des Dietz Verlages: "Der Tag X"', 7 August, 3.
Magdeburger Volksstimme. (1953l). 'Sie fielen als wahre Patrioten!', 20 June, 2.
Magdeburger Volksstimme. (1956). 'Was steckt hinter der Lüge des "Tags"?', 19 October, 1.
Magdeburger Volksstimme. (1959). 'Abfuhr für kalte Krieger', 18 June, 2.
Magdeburger Volksstimme. (1960). 'Rattenfängermelodie ohne Resonanz', 17 June, 2.
Mählert, U. (2003). *Der 17. Juni 1953. Ein Aufstand für Einheit, Recht und Freiheit* (Bonn: Dietz Verlag).
Merkel, A. (2013). 'Rede von Bundeskanzlerin Merkel bei der Gedenkveranstaltung zum 60. Jahrestag des Volksaufstandes vom 17. Juni 1953. Available from: http://www.bundesregierung.de/ContentArchiv/DE/Archiv17/Reden/2013/06/2013-06-17-merkel-17-juni.html [13 May 2014].
Millington, R. (2013). 'The Limits of Control: The "Public Discourse" about the Uprising of 17 June 1953 in Novels and Films in the German Democratic Republic', *German History* 31.1, 42–60.
Mitter, A., Wolle, S. (1993). *Untergang auf Raten* (Munich: Bertelsmann).
Mohr, H. (1978). 'Der 17. Juni als Thema der Literatur in der DDR', *Deutschland Archiv* 6, 591–616.
Mohr, H. (1983). 'Der Aufstand vom 17. Juni 1953 als Thema belletristicher Literatur aus dem letzten Jahrzehnt', *Deutschland Archiv* 16, 478–97.
Müller-Enbergs, H. (1991). *Der Fall Rudolf Herrnstadt: Tauwetterpolitik vor dem 17. Juni* (Berlin: LinksDruck).
Müller-Enbergs, H. (2008). *Inoffizielle Mitarbeiter des Ministeriums für Staatssicherheit, Teil 3: Statistiken* (Berlin, Ch. Links Verlag).
Müller-Enbergs, H., Wielgohs J., Hoffmann, D. (eds.). 'Wer war wer in der DDR'. Available from: http://www.bundesstiftung-aufarbeitung.de/wer-war-wer-in-der-ddr-%2363%3B-1424.html [4 March 2014].
Münchow, M. (2007). *Die friedliche Revolution 1989/90 in Magdeburg* (Kremkau: Block-Verlag).
Nationalrat der Nationale Front der DDR. (1953). *Der Tag X. Zusammenbruch der faschistischen Kriegsprovokation* (Berlin: Kongreß Verlag).
Neubert, E. (1997). *Geschichte der Opposition in der DDR* (Bonn: Bundeszentrale für politische Bildung).
Neues Deutschland. (1953a). 'Provokationen von Westberliner Kriegshetzern im demokratischen Sektor lins', 17 June, 1.
Neues Deutschland. (1953b). 'Was ist in Berlin geschehen?', 18 June, 1.
Neues Deutschland. (1953c). 'US-Spionage-Chef Dulles führte den faschistischen Putschversuch', 24 June, 1.
Neues Deutschland. (1953d). 'Berlin – "Wir Arbeiter müssen einen klaren Kopf behalten"', 18 June, 1.
Neues Deutschland. (1953e). 'Briefe und Telegramme an Ministerpräsident Otto Grotewohl', 20 June, 1.
Neues Deutschland. (1953f). 'Deutsche Schriftsteller an ihre Leser', 19 June, 6.
Neues Deutschland. (1953g). 'Der Zusammenbruch des faschistischen Abenteuers', 19 June, 1.

Neutsch, E. (1973). *Auf der Suche nach Gatt* (Halle/Saale: Mitteldeutscher Verlag).
Neutsch, E. (1978). *Der Friede im Osten. Zweites Buch: Frühling mit Gewalt* (Halle/Saale: Mitteldeutscher Verlag).
Niethammer, L. (2008). 'Where Were You on 17 June? A Niche in Memory', in L. Passerini (ed.). *Memory and Totalitarianism* (London: Transaction Publishers), pp. 45–71.
Niethammer, L., Wierling, D., von Leo, A. (1991). *Die volkseigene Erfahrung: Eine Archäologie des Lebens in der Industrieprovinz der DDR: 30 biographische Eröffnungen* (Berlin: Rowohlt).
Niven, B. (2002). *Facing the Nazi Past: United Germany and the Legacy of the Third Reich* (London: Routledge).
Ostermann, C. F. (2001). *Uprising in East Germany 1953: The Cold War, the German Question, and the First Major Upheaval Behind the Iron Curtain* (Budapest: Central European University Press).
Pernkopf, J. (1982). *Der 17. Juni in der Literatur der beiden deutschen Staaten* (Stuttgart: Akademischer Verlag Hans-Dieter Heinz).
Pritchard, G. (2000). *The Making of the GDR 1945–53: From Antifascism to Stalinism* (Manchester: Manchester University Press).
Reimann, B. (1969). *Die Frau am Pranger. Das Geständnis. Die Geschwister. Drei Erzählungen* (Berlin: Verlag Neues Leben).
Reinowski, W. (1956). *Die Versuchung* (Halle/Saale: Mitteldeutscher Verlag).
Riess, C. (1954). *Der 17. Juni* (Berlin: Ullstein).
Ross, C. (2002). *The East German Dictatorship: Problems and Perspectives in the Interpretation of the GDR* (New York: Arnold).
Roth, H. (2002). *Der 17. Juni 1953 in Sachsen* (Cologne: Böhlau).
Rubin, E. (2009). *Synthetic Socialism: Plastics and Dictatorship in the German Democratic Republic* (London: University of North Carolina Press).
Rupieper, H.-J. (2003). *"– und das Wichtigste ist doch die Einheit": Der 17. Juni 1953 in den Bezirken Halle und Magdeburg* (Münster: Lit-Verlag, 2003).
Rüther, G. (1997). *Literatur in der Diktatur: Schreiben im Nationalsozialismus und DDR-Sozialismus* (Paderborn: Verlag Schöningh).
Schmidt, S. J. (2008). 'Memory and Remembrance: A Constructivist Approach', in A. Erll, A. Nünning (eds.). *Cultural Memory Studies: An International and Interdisciplinary Handbook* (Berlin: Walter de Gruyter), pp. 191–203.
Scholz, R. (1981). *Mein lieber alter Lukowski* (Halle/Saale: Mitteldeutscher Verlag).
Schöneburg, K.-H. (1968). *Vom Werden unseres Staates: Eine Chronik. Band 2: 1949–1955* (Berlin: Staatsverlag der DDR).
Schröter, M. (2008). 'Verschweigen und Redeerwartung im politischen Skandal am Beispiel des CDU-Parteispendenskandals', in S. Pappert, M. Schröter, U. Fix (eds.). *Verschlüsseln, Verbergen, Verdecken in öffentlicher und institutioneller Kommunikation* (Berlin: Erich Schmidt), pp. 111–32.
Schulz, M. (2006). 'Die Staatssicherheit und der 17. Juni in Magdeburg', *MA Thesis*. (Landesprüfungsamt fur Lehrämter in Sachsen-Anhalt).
Schulz, M. (2008). 'Erinnerungskultur des Ministeriums für Staatssicherheit. Gedenken an den 17. Juni 1953 in der MfS-Untersuchungshaftanstalt Magdeburg-Neustadt', *Deutschland Archiv* 41, 434–40.
Seeger, B. (1981). *Der Harmonikaspieler* (Halle/Saale: Mitteldeutscher Verlag).
Seghers, A. (1968). *Das Vertrauen* (Berlin: Aufbau Verlag).

Selbmann, F. (1966). *Die Söhne der Wölfe* (Halle/Saale: Mitteldeutscher Verlag).
Sperber, J. (2003). '17 June 1953: Revising a German revolution', *German History* 22.4, 619–43.
Staatliche Zentralverwaltung für Statistik. (1989). *Statistisches Jahrbuch der Deutschen Demokratischen Republik 1989. 34. Jahrgang* (Berlin: Staatsverlag der DDR).
Steininger, R. (2003). *17. Juni 1953: Der Anfang vom langen Ende der DDR* (Munich: Olzog).
Teller, H. (1979). *Der kalte Krieg gegen die DDR* (Berlin: Akademie Verlag).
von Richthofen, E. (2009). *Bringing Culture to the Masses: Control, Compromise and Participation in the GDR* (New York: Berghahn).
von Wangenheim, I. (1957). *Am Morgen ist der Tag ein Kind* (Berlin: Verlag Tribüne).
Whiting, B. J. (1949). 'Recent Historical Novels', *Speculum* 24, 95–106.
Wichard, R. (1983). 'Der 17. Juni 1953 im Spiegel der DDR-Literatur', *Aus Politik und Zeitgeschichte* 20–21, 3–15.
Wills Jr, J. E. (1984). 'Taking Historical Novels Seriously', *The Public Historian* 6, 38–46.
Wolfrum, E. (1999). *Geschichtspolitik in der Bundesrepublik Deutschland: der Weg zur bundesrepublikanischen Erinnerung, 1948–1990* (Darmstadt: Wissenschaftliche Buchgesellschaft).
Wolfrum, E. (2005). 'Ein ungebetener Erinnerungsort? Der 17. Juni 1953 im nationalen Gedächtnis der Bundesrepublik Deutschland', in R. Engelmann, I.-S. Kowalczuk (eds.). *Volkserhebung gegen den SED-Staat: Eine Bestandsaufnahme zum 17. Juni 1953* (Göttingen: Vandenhoeck & Ruprecht), pp. 414–26.
Wolfrum, E. (2006). *Die geglückte Demokratie.Geschichte der Bundesrepublik Deutschland von ihren Anfängen bis zur Gegenwart* (Stuttgart: Klett-Cotta Verlag).
Wolle, S. (1996). '"Ist es so, dass morgen der 17. Juni ausbricht?" Der Volksaufstand in der DDR als Trauma, Hoffnung und Menetekel', *Kirchliche Zeitgeschichte* 9, 111–19.
Wolle, S. (2006a). 'Die SED im Krisenjahr 1956. Erster Teil: Götzendämmerung im Kreml', *Über Horch und Guck* 53, 7–13.
Wolle, S. (2006b), 'Die SED im Krisenjahr 1956, Zweiter Teil: Der verhinderte Aufstand', *Über Horch und Guck* 55, 41–6.
Young, J. E. (1993). *The Texture of Memory: Holocaust Memorials and Meaning* (New Haven: Yale University Press).
Zipser, R. (1995). *Fragebogen: Zensur. Zur Literatur vor und nach dem Ende der DDR* (Leipzig: Reclam).

Index

Adenauer, Konrad, 6, 29, 32, 41, 75
Am Morgen ist der Tag ein Kind (1957), 54, 63, 67–8
Auf der Suche nach Gatt (novel, 1973), 51, 52, 55, 56–9, 62–7, 68
Auf der Suche nach Gatt (TV film, 1976), 51, 55, 56–7

Baring, Arnulf, 80, 84, 88, 89
Benjamin, Hilde, 15
Beria, Lavrenti, 2, 172
Berlin Wall, 121–2
Beschreibung eines Sommers (1961), 51, 54, 185
Biermann, Wolf, 61, 122
Brandt, Heinz, 3
Brandt, Willy, 81, 83, 84, 85, 133
Brant, Stefan, *see* Harpprecht, Klaus

Carstens, Karl, 85
censorship
 of novels and films featuring uprising of 17 June 1953, 61–7
 process, 59–61
Claudius, Eduard, 49
collected awareness, 11
collective memory, 10–11

Dartsch, Alfred, 14–15
Das Impressum (1972), 55, 64–7, 173–4
Das Vertrauen (1968), 53–4
Daub, Philipp, 14
Day of German Unity, *see Tag der deutschen Einheit*
Der fremde Freund (1982), 51, 52, 54–5, 56
Der Friede im Osten (1978), 55, 64, 67, 68, 69–70
Der Mann aus der Siedlung (1981), 53, 57–9, 63, 68
Die Kastanie (1972), 49, 54, 55, 185

'Die Kommandeuse' (1954), 38, 49, 52, 54, 56–59
Die Söhne der Wölfe (1966), 49, 52, 55, 186
Die Versuchung (1956), 49, 51, 67, 68, 185
Dorn, Erna, 29, 46, 57, 84, 112
Dulles, Alan, 29

Eckhart, Gabriele, 60

FDGB, 13, 67, 128, 173
FDJ, 13, 44, 95, 104, 166

Gaidzik, Georg, 14, 15, 42–5
Gauck, Joachim, 18
Gerstenmaier, Eugen, 78
Geschichten jener Nacht (1967), 51, 55–6, 186
Gewalt und Zärtlichkeit (1974), 53, 54, 55, 68, 69
Gorbachev, Mikhail, 158
Grotewohl, Otto, 3, 4, 172

Hager, Kurt, 61
Händler, Gerhard, 14, 15, 42–5
Harpprecht, Klaus, 77–8
Heiduczek, Werner, 50
Hein, Christoph, 50
Hermlin, Stephan, 49, 50
Herrnstadt, Rudolf, 172–3
Hirte, Christlieb, 60
Hitler, Adolf, 5
Honecker, Erich, 36, 50, 55, 61, 65, 66, 145, 146, 153, 171

Jakobs, Karl-Heinz, 61
Jenninger, Philipp, 144
Jennrich, Ernst, 15, 30, 100
Joho, Wolfgang, 49, 50
Junge Union, 52, 141, 142

Kaiser, Jakob, 78
Kampfgruppen der Arbeiterklasse, 173
Kampling, Harry, 50, 53
Kant, Hermann, 50, 66
KFERF, 145–6, 149
Khrushchev, Nikita, 2, 132, 134, 172
Kiesinger, Kurt-Georg, 82
Kohl, Helmut, 86–7
KPD, 6
Krenz, Egon, 153
KUD, 75–6, 81, 85, 144
KVP, 69, 173

LDPD, 15
Lehmann, Lutz, 84
Löwenthal, Richard, 107–8
Lübke, Heinrich, 80–1
Lummer, Heinrich, 144

Magdeburg
  city, 11–12
  and strikes in 1952, 12
  and uprising of 17 June 1953,
    12–15
Malenkov, Georgi, 2, 172
Matern, Hermann, 171, 173
Mein lieber alter Lukowski (1981), 51,
  52, 185
Mein namenloses Land (1966), 51
Merkel, Angela, 18, 179
Mielke, Erich, 6–7, 128, 141, 150, 170
Molotov, Vyacheslav, 172

Narodnyi Trudovoy Soyuz, 133–4
NDPD, 16
Neutsch, Erik, 50, 66–7
Nolte, Ernst, 89

Oelßner, Fred, 3
official memory, 10
oral history, 17–18, 175–81

Paulsen, Herbert, 12

Reinowski, Werner, 49, 50
Renger, Annemarie, 85–6

Schiller, Karl, 82
Schlösser und Katen (1958), 50, 54, 186

Schmidt, Helmut, 86
Schmude, Juergen, 86
Schütz, Klaus, 82
SED
  and causes of uprising of 17 June
    1953, 1–5
  and trauma of uprising of 17 June
    1953, 6–7, 128–9, 135–6
Seeger, Bernhard, 50
Seghers, Anna, 49, 50
Selbmann, Fritz, 4, 49–50, 171, 186
Semenov, Vladimir, 3
Stalin, Joseph, 2, 69, 172
Stasi
  and commemoration of Hans
    Waldbach, *see* Waldbach, Hans
  and its expansion after uprising of
    17 June 1953, 173–4
  and investigation of KFERF, *see*
    KFERF
  and security measures taken on
    anniversaries of 17 June 1953,
    129–30, 139, 141–2, 143–4
Stauch, Herbert, 14–15

Tag der deutschen Einheit, 6, 41, 75,
  81–3, 86, 87
West German popular attitude
  toward, 82–3, 86–7, 88–9
5 Tage im Juni (1974), 73
Tiananmen Square massacre, 10
Tod am Meer (1977), 51, 52, 55, 62, 63

Ulbricht, Walter, 1, 3, 4, 19, 34, 36, 50,
  61, 66, 84, 101, 170–3, 174
uprising of 17 June 1953
  causes, 1–5
  collected awareness of, 11
  collected memories of, 11,
    98–109, 178
  collective memory of, 11
  communicated memories of, 8–10,
    97, 109–23, 155, 162, 165
  deaths, 1, 170
  and 'escape into the passive', 8,
    108–9, 176
  external collective memory of, 10,
    18, 75, 97, 161, 162, 163,
    164, 178

uprising of 17 June 1953 – *continued*
  failure, 1, 14
  and 'informed non-participants', 8, 108–9, 176
  and opposition groups in the GDR, 9
  post-1990 debate on nature of, 18–20
  protesters' demands, 1, 4–5, 12
  scale, 1
  as taboo amongst citizens of the GDR, 26, 39, 49, 56, 69–74, 92, 96, 97–8, 123–7, 181
  teaching of in schools in the GDR, 37–41, 86, 110–11

Volkspolizei
  and commemoration of Georg Gaidzik, *see* Gaidzik, Georg
  and commemoration of Gerhard Händler, *see* Händler, Gerhard
  and events of 1989 in Magdeburg, 152, 158–9
  and its expansion after uprising of 17 June 1953, 173
  and security measures taken on anniversaries of 17 June 1953, 130–1, 136–7, 138, 141, 142, 143, 148
  and security measures taken in Magdeburg in anticipation of 17 June 1953, 12
Von der Liebe soll man nicht nur sprechen (1957), 51, 54
von Hassel, Kai-Uwe, 85, 138
von Stauffenberg, Claus, 5
von Wangenheim, Inge, 49, 50, 186

Waldbach, Hans, 14, 42–5
Walden, Matthias, 79–80
Wessel, Horst, 33
Wohlrabe, Jürgen, 144
Wolf, Christa, 50

Zaisser, Wilhelm, 172–3

Printed in Great Britain
by Amazon